WATER SUPPLY AND SANITARY INSTALLATIONS

WATER SUPPLY AND SANITARY INSTALLATIONS

(Within Building)

Design, Construction and Maintenance

(SECOND EDITION)

A C Panchdhari

NEW AGE INTERNATIONAL (P) LIMITED, PUBLISHERS
LONDON • NEW DELHI • NAIROBI
Bangalore • Chennai • Cochin • Guwahati • Hyderabad • Kolkata • Lucknow • Mumbai
Visit us at www.newagepublishers.com

Published by New Age International (P) Ltd., Publishers
First Edition: 1993
Second Edition: 2000
Reprint: 2017

GLOBAL OFFICES

- **New Delhi** **NEW AGE INTERNATIONAL (P) LIMITED, PUBLISHERS**
  7/30 A, Daryaganj, New Delhi-110002, (INDIA)
  Tel.: (011) 23253771, 23253472, **Telefax:** 23267437, 43551305
  E-mail: contactus@newagepublishers.com • Visit us at www.newagepublishers.com
- **London** **NEW AGE INTERNATIONAL (UK) LTD.**
  27 Old Gloucester Street, London, WC1N 3AX, UK
  E-mail: info@newacademicscience.co.uk • Visit us at www.newacademicscience.co.uk
- **Nairobi** **NEW AGE GOLDEN (EAST AFRICA) LTD.**
  Ground Floor, Westlands Arcade, Chiromo Road (Next to Naivas Supermarket)
  Westlands, Nairobi, KENYA, **Tel.:** 00-254-713848772, 00-254-725700286
  E-mail: kenya@newagepublishers.com

BRANCHES

- **Bangalore** 37/10, 8th Cross (Near Hanuman Temple), Azad Nagar, Chamarajpet, Bangalore- 560 018
  Tel.: (080) 26756823, **Telefax:** 26756820, **E-mail: bangalore@newagepublishers.com**
- **Chennai** 26, Damodaran Street, T. Nagar, Chennai-600 017, **Tel.:** (044) 24353401
  Telefax: 24351463, **E-mail: chennai@newagepublishers.com**
- **Cochin** CC-39/1016, Carrier Station Road, Ernakulam South, Cochin-682 016
  Tel.: (0484) 2377303, **Telefax:** 4051304, **E-mail: cochin@newagepublishers.com**
- **Guwahati** Hemsen Complex, Mohd. Shah Road, Paltan Bazar, Near Starline Hotel
  Guwahati-781 008, **Tel.:** (0361) 2513881, **Telefax:** 2543669
  E-mail: guwahati@newagepublishers.com
- **Hyderabad** 105, 1st Floor, Madhiray Kaveri Tower, 3-2-19, Azam Jahi Road, Near Kumar Theater
  Nimboliadda Kachiguda, Hyderabad-500 027, **Tel.:** (040) 24652456, **Telefax:** 24652457
  E-mail: hyderabad@newagepublishers.com
- **Kolkata** RDB Chambers (Formerly Lotus Cinema) 106A, 1st Floor, S N Banerjee Road
  Kolkata-700 014, **Tel.:** (033) 22273773, **Telefax:** 22275247
  E-mail: kolkata@newagepublishers.com
- **Lucknow** 16-A, Jopling Road, Lucknow-226 001, **Tel.:** (0522) 2209578, 4045297, **Telefax:** 2204098
  E-mail: lucknow@newagepublishers.com
- **Mumbai** 142C, Victor House, Ground Floor, N.M. Joshi Marg, Lower Parel, Mumbai-400 013
  Tel.: (022) 24927869, **Telefax:** 24915415, **E-mail: mumbai@newagepublishers.com**
- **New Delhi** 22, Golden House, Daryaganj, New Delhi-110 002, **Tel.:** (011) 23262368, 23262370
  Telefax: 43551305, **E-mail: sales@newagepublishers.com**

ISBN: 978-81-224-1225-3

C-17-02-10143

Printed in India at Nisha Enterprises, New Delhi.
Typeset by Laser Print Craft, Delhi.

NEW AGE INTERNATIONAL (P) LIMITED, PUBLISHERS
7/30 A, Daryaganj, New Delhi-110002
Visit us at **www.newagepublishers.com**
(CIN: U74899DL1966PTC004618)

PREFACE TO THE SECOND EDITION

It is a pleasure to present the second edition of the book. In this edition, a few new topics have been included to make the coverage more comprehensive.

New Topics in Part I include Water Borne Bacteria and Man, Water Contamination, Corrosion, Plastics and Sprinkler Installation in a Building. In Parts II and III of the book new additions include Drainage and Sanitation of Basement, Day-to-Day Care of Bathrooms and WCS in Home and Leak Detection.

The book will prove useful for civil engineering students as well as for professionals dealing in architecture, building construction, design and maintenance of services.

I wish to thank all my friends and family members for their help and encouragement which made it possible for me to publish this book.

PREFACE TO THE FIRST EDITION

In a public building, a person asked for the direction to the public conveniences, the reply given was characteristic "Follow the stench and you will finally reach the sanitary installation."

The above incidence almost correctly depicts the state of affairs of sanitary installations and its maintenance in India.

Water not reaching upper floors is accepted as a normal feature. People are prepared to dig a pond to receive municipal supply.

There is general despondency about water supply and sanitary installations.

What is taught in the colleges of engineering is town water supply and sanitary installations. Most of the students have scant knowledge of intricacies of such installations within building. The job of design and installation is left to the plumber.

It is not that the information is not available. It is scattered over many pamphlets and books. An individual does not have access to many of the books and libraries.

Thus there is a need for a compilation where most of the information would be available.

An attempt has been made to compile this information. The idea has been to present all the related aspects of the subject i.e. design, construction and maintenance in a single book form.

A book of this nature has obviously to depend upon published books both Indian and foreign, articles and pamphlets. I have drawn freely from all these sources and I am grateful to all those authors who have been the guiding lights. But the book is not a compilation only. The information has been digested and put up in an intelligible form. I have supplemented the information with the experience I have gathered over 30 years of civil engineering practical field.

I want to thank all my friends who have encouraged me in this job.

I shall be glad to correct all mistakes which might have crept in inspite of best efforts.

A.C. Panchdhari

CONTENTS

INTRODUCTION

In human habitation many services are needed which serve the purpose of making a person comfortable in his house. These services include heating, ventilation, air-conditioning and sanitation, apart from the transportation and communication services.

Out of all these services, in climatic zone like that of India, heating and air conditioning are normally not required as the ambient temperatures are within the acceptable limits of human comfort. However with high density of population provision of safe and pure drinking water supply and disposal of garbage and other undesirable materials has become an important factor to live with. The provision of these services outside the premises is the responsibility of the local corporation, committee or a panchayat. Yet within the premises it is the responsibility of the owner to design, construct and maintain these services upto standards laid down. It is quite likely that the services provided by the Municipal Corporation may be upto the mark as required under the various regulations yet neglect by the owner of the services in his own premises may even lead to an epidemic.

Water supply and sanitation are the root causes of many of the diseases which afflict the man kind. Typhoid, Dysentry and Jaundice are some of the diseases which can be many times fatal.

Control of these water-borne diseases and diseases caused by sanitation is not difficult. However, what is required herein is the knowledge of principles which are very simple yet which require to be consistently followed in the design construction and the maintenance phase of water supply and sanitation.

There are many text books available on the subject of water supply and sanitary installations which deal with locating the supply, purifying the water at the source and conveying it by large diameter conduits to the place where it is supposed to be given to the individual premises. In Engineering Colleges this subject is given more importance. For the distribution of water and sanitation services within the building the knowledge is available in a scattered way and there is no compilation of these provisions of the design construction and maintenance of these services within the premises.

An attempt has been made to collect all knowledge together and present it. This compilation is not expected to be a design hand book but it is more or less in a form to whett the curiosity of the Engineers and Architects and even the lay man in design construction and maintenance of services. It is hoped that this compilation may be found to be useful.

PART I—WATER SUPPLY INSTALLATIONS

1. WATER WITHIN REACH

Historically human settlements have always been around available water supply points like river, spring etc. Most of the civilisations have been knit around rivers and thus the civilisations were known as River Valley Civilisations like Indus Valley Civilisation etc.

Drinking water is a precious commodity. A man can survive without food for months together but without water to quench his thirst, his survival beyond 40 hours would be a miracle. The water utilised for drinking can either be a boon by way of potable water or a bane, as unfit for human consumption water supply which can almost kill a person by serious water-borne diseases like typhoid, cholera etc. Even in the best of the civilisation from time to time contamination of the water supply source has been happening either as a man made feature by which a man has been supplying the water contaminated due to some to his habits like washing clothes, animals etc, at the same place where drinking water supply is taken or by discharge of dangerous chemicals in the water streams supply is taken or discharge of dangerous chemicals in the water streams meant for human consumption.

A potable water supply, which is needed for existence of the population, has to be in the right quantity and of right quality.

As of today water is a very precious commodity both in terms of its availability as well as cost. The sources of water supply of a particular localities are inflexible like a lake, a stream and the energy cost spent in treating water to make it fit for human consumption and pumping it from the source like lake or river to the overhead tanks can be very high. When water resources near the city get exhausted, then new sources of water have to be located which in most of the cases are very far off. For example, water for Bombay is brought over 100 km by pumping. Cost of such pumping is high enough.

If such a costly water is wasted either through sheer carelessness or through leaky pipe lines, the community pays for such avoidable wastage.

2. WATER AND DISEASES

One of the basic objectives of providing a piped water supply is to make available to the consumers pure and wholesome drinking water. But what is pure and wholesome.

Water to be termed as pure and wholesome and fit for drinking purpose should be:

1. Colourless and clear.
2. Free from all suspended, soluble and colloidal impurities of both organic and inorganic nature.
3. Free from sediments.
4. Free from taste and odour.
5. Free from pathogenic organisms.
6. Free from radio-active substances like radium, strontium etc.

7. Free from phenolic compounds, chlorides, fluorides and iodine beyond standards laid down.
8. Free from hardness (should not contain impurities like calcium or magnesium bicarbonates and sulphates which make the water hard and unsuitable from domestic and industrial use).
9. Free from corrosive substances.
10. Free from iron, manganese, lead, arsenic and other poisonous materials.

3. WATER BORNE BACTERIA AND MAN

Diseases in man can be caused by presence of pathogenic bacteria and also other organism such as virus, protozoa and worms.

Bacterial Diseases

Cholera—The cause is bacterium Vibro Cholerae and its variant El tor vibrio. Infection is contracted by ingestion of water contaminated by infected human faecal material.

Typhoid—The cause is bacterium Salmonella Typhi. Infection is contracted by ingestion of material contaminated by human faeces or urine.

Para-typhoid—These are caused by Salmonella paratyphi A, B or C.

Bacillary Dysentry—This is caused by bacteria of the genus Shigella, sh dysenteriae 1, Sh, flexneri, Sh. boydii, Sh Sonnei.

Travellers diarrhoea—This may be some form of pathogenic Escherichia Coli or rarely shigella. Water may be some times a vehicle.

Leptospirosis—This may vary from mild fever to severe jaundice and are caused by Leptospira. They infect rats, dogs, pigs and other vertebrates and are shed in the urine of these animals. They are often present in the ponds and slow moving streams where animals go in and people who bathe in, fish in, or sail on these waters being infected via mouth, nose conjunctiva through cuts in the skins. Workers in rat infested sewers are at greater risk. Normal water treatment eliminates these risks.

Legionnaires disease—This is caused by genus Legionella, the bacterium L-preumo phila is most dangerous. The infection is through inhalation of air borne water droplets. These pathogens cause a rare form of pneumonia.

Legionella organisms can survive water-treatment process inlcuding chlorination. They colonise the pipe surfaces.

Infection occurs due to inhalation of air-borne water droplets from cooling towers, whirl pools, jacuzzis etc. where recirculated warm water is sprayed.

Preventive measures including cleaning of pipes, disinfection with chlorine and controlling microbial growth by bio-cides.

Protozoa Diseases

Amaobiasis and amoebic dysentry.

Infection takes places by ingestion of cysts usually from carriers who might be handling food. Flies also carry them.

It flourishes where sanitation is poor. This can lead to lever abscess.

Crypto Sporidiosis

This results in self-limiting gastro-enteritis with diarrhoea and flu-like symptoms.

This is due to farm practices. Practice of allowing grazing of cattle near reservoirs or over an underground reservoir has to be stopped.

Giardiasis

This is a diarrhoeal disease caused by parasite Giardia Lamblia. This is caused by ingestion. This is due to faecal contamination. Normal chlorination eliminates bulk of them.

Virus

Poliomyelitis—This may be found in effluent from sewage disposal units. It is common where hygiene is poor.

Infectious Hepatitis—This disease does not require much explanation.

Worm Diseases

The cause is a group of trematode worms of the genus Schistosoma, S, haematobium, S, mansoni, S-japonicum. This is transmitted through urine and faecal matter.

In public water supplies filtration plus chlorination is effective if carefully done.

Swimmers Itch

The cause is a group of schistosomes of birds.

In addition to the above following aquatic plants cause discolouration, mal odour, and pollution:

1. Algae;
2. Water weeds;
3. Mosses;
4. Ferns and horsetails.

Virus such as infectious hepatitis carried through water

Various fungi such as algae, rusts, mushroom cause untolerable taste and odour due to their decomposition. Water contamination may also arise due to mixing of excreta or sewage with water meant for drinking.

Escherichia coli (E-Coli) are organisms which are contained in the intestinal tract of warm-blooded animals and human beings and are rarely found outside the animal body except through excreta. Presence of E-coli in drinking water supply is, therefore, indication of contamination of water supply through faecal discharge.

In the bacterial examination of water earlier the amount of coliform organism present was being decided by coliform index. This method has been superseded by Most Probable Number (MPN). This is bacterial density of a source based on sampling methods and use of probability.

In addition to the bacterial contamination which is harmful to human being as discussed above, some of the bacteria are troublesome from the water supply point of view. These bacteria and their by-products cause choking of pipe lines, and may lead to orrosion and pitting.

These bacteria can be described in the following terms which can be easily understood.

Iron Bacteria

These bacterias deposit iron on pipes and fittings by extracting it from water. The growth of these bacterias cause slimy reddish brown deposits causing colouration and turbidity. Water with such bacterias is unfit for food preparation, manufacture of paper, airconditioning and other industrial applications.

Sulphur Bacteria

They can oxidise sulphur in elemental form or reduce sulphur compounds. The acid produced during metabolic process destroys concrete. These are mainly responsible for bacterial corrosion of iron and steel pipe. Such corrosion is high in marshy and water-logged soil.

Gelatin Liquifying Bacteria

They render water useless for the photographic film manufacture, edible gelatin and glue manufacture.

All slim algae, moss are undesirable. They hold impurities and as such are undesirable in food processing plants, paper mills etc.

All premises intended for human habitation or use should have pure and whole some water as per Bureau of Indian Standards. These standards are as follows:

4. QUALITY STANDARDS

Sl. No.	*Characteristics*	**Acceptable*	***Cause for Rejection*
1.	Turbidity (units on J.T.U. Scale)	5	10
2.	Colour (units on Platinum cobalt scale)	5.0	25
3.	Taste and odour	unobjectionable	unobjectionable
4.	pH	6.5 to 8.5	6.5 to 8.5
5.	Total dissolved solids (mg/l)	500	2000
6.	Total hardness (mg/l) (as $CaCO_3$)	300	600
7.	Chlorides (as Cl) (mg/l)	250	1000
8.	Sulphates (as SO_4) (mg/l)	200	400
9.	Fluorides (as F) (mg/l)	1.0	1.5
10.	Nitrates (as NO_3) (mg/l)	45	100

11.	Calcium (as Ca) (mg/I)	75	200
12.	Magnesium (as Mg) (mg/I)	30	150
		If there are 240 mg/I of sulphates, Mg content can be increased to a maximum of 125 mg/I with the reduction of sulphates at the rate of 1 u per every 2.5 units of sulphate.	
13.	Iron (as Fe)	0.3	1.0 (mg/I)
14.	Manganese (as Mn) (mg/I)	0.1	0.3
15.	Copper (as Cu) (mg/I)	0.05	1.5
16.	Zinc (as Zn) (mg/I)	5.0	15.0
17.	Phenolic compounds (as Phenol) (mg/I)	0.001	0.002
18.	Alnionic detergents (mg/I) (as MBAS)	0.2	1.0
19.	Mineral Oil (mg/I)	0.01	0.03
20.	**Toxic Materials**		
21.	Arsenic (as As) (mg/I)	0.05	0.05
22.	Cadmium (as Cd) (mg/I)	0.01	0.01
23.	Chromium (as hexavalent Cr) (mg/I)	0.05	0.05
24.	Cyanides (as CN) (mg/I)	0.05	0.05
25.	Lead (as Pb) (mg/I)	0.1	0.1
26.	Selenium (as Se) (mg/I)	0.01	0.01
27.	Mercury (as Hg) (mg/I)	0.001	0.001
28.	Polynuclear aromatic hydrocarbons (PAH)	Nil	Nil
29.	Pesticide (mg/I)	—	0.001
30.	Boron (mg/I)	1	5
31.	Aluminium as Al in mg/I	0.03	0.2
32.	Residual Chlorine mg/I	0.2	—(at Consumer end)
Radio Activity			
33.	Gross Alpha activity	Nil	0.1 Bg/I max
34.	Gross beta activity PCi=pico curie	Nil	1

Notes: 1. The figures indicated under the column 'acceptable' are the limits upto which the water is generally acceptable to the consumers.

2. Figures in excess of those mentioned under 'acceptable' while the water not acceptable, but still may be tolerated in the absence of alternative and better source but upto the limits indicated under the column "cause for rejection". above which the supply will have to be rejected.

3. It is possible that some mine or spring waters may exceed these radioactivity limits and in such cases it is necessary to analyse the individual radionuclides in order to assess the acceptability or otherwise for public consumption.

The wholesome water supply provided for drinking purposes should not be liable to cross connection with any less satisfactory water. Therefore these should be no cross connection whatsoever between an impure and pure water supply, so that the possibility of any impurity coming into the drinking water can be obviated. Cross connection with a non return valve between a potable and non-potable water supply is not safe as the non return valve may not function effectively.

5. WATER CONTAMINATION

It is a common knowledge that some diseases are water borne and it is the endeavour of every person to drink as safe a drinking water as possible. As of today taste smell and appearance like colour turbidity are considered useful criteria for judging water quality and very few biological contaminants are considered in judging water quality.

In earlier times, the sources of water supply like a river, tank or even ground water were free from the contamination but with the improvements (?) in agriculture millions of tonnes of chemicals are being dumped on soil which finally finds its way to the water sources.

Pesticides of poisonous nature also contaminate the water. In addition the new industries dump chemical wastes. The thermal power stations which produces fly-ash also contribute to the contamination by the leachates from fly-ash ponds. Low levels of chemicals are much more likely to cause chronic effects on health.

Chemicals like nitrates, poly-cyclic aromatic hydro carbons aluminium poly acrylamide are suspects.

Nitrates may lead to formation of carcinogenic nitrosamines. The coal tar may get released from pipe walls and can be a cause of carcinogic problems.

Aluminium may give rise to Alzheimer disease etc. The data is conflicting but it can be a cause of concern.

Inappropriate disposal of toxic and other waste of industries can cause lot of damage.

Serious out-breaks of water-borne diseases like Typhoid, cryptosporidiosis, Rotavirus giardiasis have occurred in developed countries even though there was absence of faecal matter and with 0.8 mg/litre of free chlorine. Some micro-organisms get protected from the action of chlorine by organic material, slime, or even association with free living amoebae. Many times these contamination occur on account of inadequate treatment of water. The integrity of the distribution network may be doubtful with possible ingress of untreated ground water etc. through cracks in service reservoirs fractured mains, faulty fittings, bursting of water mains, corrosion holes. The problems are much more when water supply is of intermittent nature, thus the pressure of water being low, ingress of water may take place. The problem is more when mains get emptied of water due to level difference thus even a suction force may get created causing very high ingress of water.

A wide variety of bacteria are able to grow in drinking water, for example, Pseudomonas spp., Aeromonas spp. bacillus ssp, Acineto bacter ssp, alkaligenes spp, coliforms, micro cocci. The bio-film which is present in all piping including plastic pipes protects these bacterias. Temperature, available organic materials from fittings, degree of stagnation are all important factors. Bio-films will accumulate in the presence of 0.8 mg./litre of free chlorine and considerable accumulation can occur at concentration of less than 0.2 mg. litre. Bio-films protect micro-organisms from the effects of disinfectants and may produce turbid water and cause bad tastes and odours and corrosion.

Virus like Rotavirus, Norwalk agent small round viruses, Hepatitis A, Hepatitis Non A—No B, etc. can survive even ultra-violet rays when there are suspended matters.

Contamination of ground water can occur due to septic tanks, land fills incorrectly done and sludge disposal.

Therefore the water supply system cannot be neglected at all and the persons in-charge have to guard against all contamination.

6. BASIC PRINCIPLES OF DESIGN OF WATER SUPPLY SYSTEM

Plumbing fixtures and appurtances should be supplied with water in sufficient volume and at pressures adequate to function satisfactorily and without undue noise under all circumstances.

The design of pipe network should be so made that there is no contact between the lines feeding to the cistern or any such other appliance with those feeding water for human consumption.

Pipe network should be such that it should be completely watertight and also remain undamaged either by traffic loads, vibrations or by the temperature change and strains of the building.

The design of the pipe network in the premises should be such that optimum discharge of water is obtained consistent with economy. The system should be free from water hammer, corrosion and should also look aesthetic.

The pipe network should be so laid and fixed so that it does not pass by the side of any sewerage line or refuse drain nor it passes through any field of foul ground where dirt or city refuse drain not it passes through any field of foul ground where dirt or city refuse have been deposited and manure dumps.

The pipe network should be laid and fixed so that it shall be accessible at any time for attending to damages, leakages, etc.

The pipe net work should be of adequate size to give the desired rate of flow.

The pipe network should be divided into sections to facilitate repairs. These sections should be separated by valves in order that a section can be isolated for repairs keeping the rest of the distribution network functioning.

From the point of view of economy of running the system the pipe line should be so designed that the frictional losses are within the limits and the velocity of the flow of water is also within the limits. The methods of jointing should be such so as to avoid water losses.

Changes in diameter and in direction should be gradual rather than abrupt to avoid undue loss of discharge head. Whenever, the pipes are bent it should be so made that these are not likely to materially diminish or alter cross section.

The piping should be so laid that air locks do not occur and it should be possible to flush out the network from time to time.

The pipes to carry satisfactory and unsatisfactory water should be laid separately. Wherever a supply of less satisfactory water and satisfactory water has to be mixed, it shall be done only by discharging both the flows into a cistern and by a pipe discharging into the air gap above the top level of the cistern at the height equal to twice its nominal bore and in no case less than 15 cm. It is necessary to maintain a definite air gap in all plumbing used in the water closet.

In the building if a provision is required to be made for storage of water on account of (a) interruption of supply (b) to maintain a reserve supply (c) to regulate the discharge in the mains (d) to maintain a reserve for fire fighting arrangements, a tank for storage of water should be provided which should be watertight and also should be of sufficient thickness and capacity. Thus storage reserve should be dust proof and mosquito-proof. Each storage tanks should be easily accessible and placed in such a position as to facilitate thorough inspection and cleaning. Stagnation of water within the tank is to be avoided. The tank should be so arranged as to have periodical cleaning done without seriously interfering with the supply of water. It is to be understood that water when it is stagnant is likely to become a good breeding ground for various organisms which are very dangerous for the human beings. Therefore water tanks are required to be periodically cleaned and after cleaning properly disinfected.

In the case of underground tanks the contamination of stored water on account of above ground flow and due to seepage of underground water should be avoided. Whenever underground tanks are required for fire fighting purposes, the same should be approachable easily by fire tenders. The water which is required for fire fighting is so provided that every day it gets a renewal through an inflow of fresh water supply.

Lead piping should not be utilised anywhere in the domestic water supply system.

Polythene and PVC pipes should not be installed near hot water pipes or near any source of heat.

The dead ends in the pipe lines should be avoided to the extent possible. The mains should be arranged in a grid formation or a network fashion. Where dead ends are unavoidable, a hydrant should be provided as a washout as the deposition of solids is at a higher rate in the case of dead ends where water stagnates requiring cleaning of pipe lines at frequent intervals.

The wash hydrant should be connected to an effectively trapped chamber to avoid contamination. It should not discharge directly into a sewer line or a manhole or chamber on sewer line.

Air valves should be provided at all summits and wash out at low points. The pipe line may follow the general contours of the land. It should be so laid that it generally rises to air valves and falls to a water wash out. Care should be taken to maintain positive pressure at every point in the pipe line under normal working conditions.

The mains should be laid at least 90 cms below surface under road and at least 75 cms below surface under a foot path to protect it from various traffic loads coming on it. Otherwise, there are chances of pipes settling under load and breaking.

Safety demands that water pipes should be separated from electric, telephone and other such cables.

No piping should be so laid as to pass into or through any sew line or manhole pit, as pit or any material of such nature that it is likely to cause undue deterioration of pipe.

Where laying of any pipe through corrosive soil or environment is inevitable, the piping should be properly protected from contact with such conditions by being carried through cast iron tubes or some other suitable means.

Changes in diameter of pipe or changes in direction pipe should be gradual and not abrupt. Abrupt changes involve avoidable loss of head of water.

No boiler for generating steam or closed boiler of any description or any such machinery should be directly connected with supply pipe. Every such boiler or machinery should be supplied from a feed tank only.

The design of pipe work should be such that there is no possibility of back flow from any cistern or appliance whether by siphonage or otherwise. Non return valve should not be relied upon to prevent such back flow.

Where pipe network has to be laid in a recent fill, proper precautions have to be taken to provide continuous and even support.

7. COLLECTION OF DATA

Design of a proper water supply system should mean that water is available at all times to all consumers in required quantity and pressure.

Availability of water to the consumer all round the clock could be directly through mains or it could be through storage of water through underground tanks. Wherever the supply is of intermittent nature and water from mains is collected in underground tank, pressure of water is obtained through various pumping systems and overhead tanks. Quality of water is assured through various disinfection measures. Quantity of water is based on national calculations of number of persons using the system and their average requirements.

Requirement

Water distribution system is not built for only immediate requirement. It should be adequate for the immediate future up to 10 years minimum. For residential building the requirement of water should be based on the actual number of users which should include floating population. Where this information is not available the number of occupants for each residential unit may be based on the family unit of five. This is a rough and ready assumption. However, where families are generally large as in the case of joint families or where overcrowding of houses is a normal feature such as in metropolitan cities proper assessment of extent of average number of persons staying in a unit should be made.

The number of probable occupants is to be calculated on rational basis. In calculations of number of occupants, the gross floor area of the building is calculated and number of occupants is obtained by dividing gross floor area by average area per occupant. The average area per occupant as per accepted standards is as follows:

Occupancy	*Occupant per Floor area in m^2*
1. Residential	12.5
2. Educational	4.0
3. Institutional	15.0
4. Occupant load in dormitory, orphans homes etc.	7.5
5. Assembly	
(a) With fixed or loose seats	0.6
(b) Without seating facilities including dining rooms	1.5
The gross floor area should include in addition to the main assembly space any occupied connecting room or space in the same storey or storey above or below where entrance is common to such rooms and spaces and they are available for the use of the occupants of the assembly place. No deduction should be made in the gross area for corridors closets and other subdivisions, the area should include all space serving the particular assembly occupancy.	
6. Mercantile	
(a) Street floor and sales basement	3
(b) Upper sale floors	6
Business Industrial	10
Storage	30
Hazardous	10
In the case of mezzanine floors the occupant load should be added to the floor below. In addition to the occupant load calculated as above, floating population should be catered for.	

According to Bombay Municipal Corporation Byelaws (which is typical of crowded metropolitan occupancy in residential quarters) the number of occupants is taken as follows:

Sl. No.	*Carpet area of tenement*	*Occupants*
1.	Upto 50 sq mt.	7
2.	51 - 75 sq mt.	8
3.	76 - 100 sq mt.	9
4.	100 sq mt. and above	10
5.	Servants quarters which are not self-contained units with nahani trap, kitchen (Room)	2
6.	Shops where water for trade is not needed	2
7.	Garage	Nil

Source

The source of water supply should be clearly known both in quality and quantity. The source of water supply could be a river, pond, tube well, open well or municipal or town water mains.

In case of river, pond, open well and tube well supplies, it is necessary to know the optimum rate of recuperation of water in the dry period of the year and quality of water and its variation through the year.

In case where water supply is being obtained from water mains laid by local body, necessary permission from local body to tap water from their source should be obtained. When water is to be obtained from water pressure mains, the diameter of pressure main, distance of the water main from the building, the water pressure in the main during day time and during the night time should be ascertained. In many cases the pressure of water in the main may be less during the day time due to various tappings and loss due to friction etc.

All this information regarding pressure of water, frequency and timing of availability of water have got substantial impact on the designed capacity of the underground and overhead reservoirs. General performance of water supply system is also affected by wide variations in quantity and pressure in the mains.

Information collected should be authentic and it should not be a guess work. However intelligent such a guess is yet the field data may differ very much. In order to collect data in a systematic fashion following check list would be useful.

8. CHECK LIST

Water Supply Scheme

1. (a) Area served by the scheme.

(b) Present population to be catered for.
(c) Probable population after 20 years.
(d) Per capita water supply required.

2. (a) Contoured Site Plan of the area for which water supply is required showing layout of the buildings, roads, formation level etc.
(b) Future requirements of water for the additional areas.

3. Existing filtered water supply in the area or in the vicinity.
If so the following details be furnished:
(a) Key Plan
(b) Size of the main
(c) Pressure available in the main (time during which high pressure is available).

4. In case supply is taken from storage reservoir, the following details are to be furnished:
(a) Site for reservoir
(b) Capacity of the reservoir
(c) Whether it is capable of meeting the extra demand in the worst summer
(d) Reduced level of the reservoir floor and depth of water
(e) Longitudinal sections of the proposed alignment of water mains with nature of soil and sub-soil.

5. (a) If there is no water supply in the area, proposals for water supply:
(i) Open well or tubewells
(ii) From any existing perennial sources of water supply
(iii) Dry weather and monsoon flow and low water level requirement for purification of water.

6. In case storage or service reservoirs are required, possible location of reservoir to be indicated.

7. Information about the quality of water available.

8. Whether electric supply is dependable.

9. WATER REQUIREMENT FOR VARIOUS TYPES OF BUILDINGS

Water requirement of buildings can be divided into four broad types as given below:

(1) Residential
(2) Industrial buildings
(3) Office buildings
(4) Buildings with floating population

Man does not require more than 8 litres of water in liquid form for body needs. Rest of the requirement of water is for bathing, washing, cleaning, scavenging, horticulture etc. Statistically speaking, higher income groups have more consumption of water than low income group. This can be explained by the habits, availability of water and affordability of higher expenditure on cost of water of higher income groups.

Consumption of water is dependent on very many factors such as customs of user community, environment etc. Hence very great accuracy in estimation of water consumption is not feasible. Water supply systems are designed as per standards laid down for various types of buildings. There are averages based on statistical data and slight variation on lower side in actual availability should not worry the designer much.

In India, Bureau of Standards has laid down the following recommendations:

For residential buildings a minimum water supply of 200 litres per head per day is to be assured for a full flushing system. Out of the 200 litres per head per day 45 litres per head per day is meant for flushing requirement and remaining quantity for other domestic purposes.

Where buildings are meant for low income group the water supply may be reduced to 135 litres per head per day. There is no other explanation for the reduced requirement but the non-availability of adequate number of water points and community type latrines and the payment capacity of low income group being less. As per bureau of Indian Standards, for buildings other than residence requirement of water may be taken as follows:

	Type		*Consumption per head per day (in litres)*
1.	Factories with bath rooms		45
2.	Factories without bathrooms		30
3.	Hospitals including laundry per bed.		
	(a) Number of beds not exceeding 100		340
	(b) Number of beds exceeding 100		450
4.	Nurses home and Medical quarters		135
5.	Hostels		135
6.	Hostel per bed		180
7.	Offices		45
8.	Restaurants per seat		70
9.	Cinemas, Concert halls, Theatre per seat		15
10.	Day school		45
11.	Boarding School		135
	Railways	*With bath*	*Without bath*
1.	Traffic terminal stations Intermediate station excluding Mail and Express stop.	45	23
2.	Junctions, Mail & Express stop	70	45
3.	Terminal	45	45
4.	Airports	70	70

In working out the requirement of water the number of persons should be the average number of passengers expected to be handled daily and also station staff and vendors. The seasonal peak requirements have also to be considered.

In case of water supply for premises requirements for fire fighting should be provided for: according to byelaws applicable.

(For details refer chapter—Water for the fire fighting)

Water may also be required for air conditioning and air cooling purposes. Requirements for such use may be estimated as follows:

1. Desert coolers per 15 sq mt of area cooled	300 to 400 litres per day
2. Airconditioning	
(a) Induced or forced draft cooling tower	65 litres/tonne of Air Conditioning/day
(b) Natural cooling tower	90 litres/tonne of Air Conditioning/day
(c) Cooling pond	185 litres/tonne of Air Conditioning/day

It may also be estimated at 70 litres/hour/100 sq m. of area conditioned.

Water for

Fountains	3 to 4 litres/minute
Horticulture	2 to 3 litres/sq m/day
Kitchen garden	1.5 to 2 litres/sq m/day

Animals also require sufficient amount of water:

Cow or buffalo	40 to 60 litres/day/head
Horse	40 to 50 litres/day/head
Dogs	8 to 12 litres/day/head
Sheep/goats	5 to 10 litres/day/head

Losses in pipelines is a necessary evil. Losses in pipelines may occur due to corrosion holes, weak joints etc. A good system may have losses upto 20%. Where water is unmetered the losses wastages are high as people do not bother about wastage of water.

Some field studies have been carried to find out the actual demands of water under Indian conditions.

The sanitary installations and water supply installations have to be designed for peak hydraulic load in the buildings. The thumb rule of 3 times average peak hydraulic load is based on the conditions in the western countries, where continuous water supply from the corporation is taken for granted. Under Indian conditions intermittent water supply is almost universal. With intermittent water supply the simultaneous withdrawl rate becomes high and thumb rule of 3 times average withdrawl rate may not be applicable. Thus in actual practice with intermittent water supply the rate of flow may be much more than 3 times average and there would be higher frictional losses with the result persons drawing water from upper storeys may not get water. It would be of interest to note what exactly has been the pattern of use matter the Indian conditions. It has been observed that the intermittent water supply is giving rise to high consumption as an average of 100 litres of water which is stored in house-hold is spilled when fresh water supply starts. Even for continuous water supply requirement is 150 litres/head/day.

Residential Buildings

In Delhi a survey was carried out in Government Colonies in the 3 roomed and 4 roomed houses which typically represents the middle income group habitat with one WC one bath room, kitchen being provided. It was observed that under the Indian conditions the use of water closets was highest in the morning hours from 5 A.M. to 7 A.M. and at the highest the average use was 4 times an hourly average. Between 8 to 9 A.M. and 5 P.M. to 6 P.M. there is a drop to two times per hour. Similar is the position in the other systems like Bath, Sink and Wash basins. Use of fitments however depends on the habits of the people. Use frequency and discharge rates of sanitary appliances in residential buildings as seen are given in the below:

S.No.	*Appliances*	*Interval between Discharges in Seconds*	*Rate of Discharge lit/min*
	[Type III Residence] (About 70 sq m. plinth)		
1.	WC with 10.0 litre cistrn.	900.00 (15 min)	112
2.	H. Level cistern	196.6 (3.276 min)	9
3.	Sink	398.0 (6.63 min)	9
4.	Bath	1011.5 (16.85 min)	9
	[Type IV Residence] (About 90 sq m. plinth area)		
1.	WC with 10.0 litre cistern	900.0 (15 min)	112
2.	H. Level cistern	180.0 (3 min)	9
3.	Sink	704.0 (11.73 min)	9
4.	Bath	1,376.0 (22.93 min)	9

In the case of office buildings, the load consists of discharges from WCs, Wash basins and urinals and these appliances are usually located in ranges. Survey carried in the multistoreyed offices built in Delhi, peak use of WC observed was from 12 noon to 1 P.M. prior to lunch break. On the other hand, in the wash basins, the use is almost constant. The use frequency and discharge load are as follows:

S.No.	Appliances	Interval between Discharges in seconds	Rate of Discharge lit/min
1.	WC with 12.5 litre high level cistern	831.4 (13.85 min)	110
2.	Wash Basin	Depends on use	12
3.	Urinal with 4.5 litre cistern	100 (1.6 min)	27

10. DESIGN OF WATER SUPPLY NETWORK INSIDE THE BUILDING

Water when brought into the building premise from the mains or from the overhead tanks may be, either routed through the underground tank and overhead reservoir through pumping or it may be fed directly to the various outlets of water from mains.

Upfeed System of Water Supply

The system of water supply in which water is fed directly either from municipal main or through hydro-pneumatic system is called "upfeed system". In this system, the water is allowed to be drawn by individual consumers from rising mains and the amount of water which goes into overhead tank is the residual water after draw off by the various occupants at different floors. In case of hydro-pneumatic system there are no overhead water tanks at all and the water is pumped directly whenever a tap gets opened.

The 'Upfeed' system of water supply requires high pressure to be maintained in the pipe lines all the 24 hours. The high pressure in the pipe lines gives rise to high water loss due to pipe leakages. The pressure in water mains ranges from 35 metres of water head to about 60 metres of water head. (The pressure to be maintained in the pipe lines depends on the height of the buildings.) If water pressure exceeds 60 metres the pipe network may be overtaxed by the pressures created by water hammer. The upfeed system supplies water which is uncontaminated otherwise due to overhead tank which is unmaintained the water gets contaminated. The 'Upfeed' system avoids such contamination as the water for drinking and culminary purposes is drawn off before it reaches tank.

This system is not much of use under Indian conditions on acount of various factors enumerated below:

1. Most of the municipal water supply is intermittent. In case of intermittent water supply, if an unfeed system is adopted, there is every likelyhood of back siphonage occurring through sinks and wash basins wherein the

tap may be accidentally submerged in impure water. Such impure water if drawn in to the pipe system by back siphonage will contaminate the fresh supply of water.

2. Most of the mains have low water pressure on account of many more outlet connections given beyond what was designed in the original concept (having been given on account of pressure of increasing population). On account of constraint of funds, there is a time lag between the demand and construction of additional lines.
3. The high outlet pressure at tap, gives rise to wastage of water under Indian system of washing clothes and utensils.

Therefore in India, by and large upfeed system is not used. The system which is normally used is downfeed system where water from main is taken to the overhead tanks from where it is distributed. The provision of overhead tank ensures water supply over a longer duration than the supply of hours of municipal corporation. In this system the overhead tank is required to be kept compulsorily clean and hygenic. Otherwise even though the municipal water supply is wholesome and hygenic, the water supply to the consumer would be contaminated.

System of Downfeed Water Supply

Where the water pressure in the municipal mains is high enough to reach the terrace level, the mains discharge, water into the overhead tanks which are normally situated at the highest position. Capacity of overhead tanks is governed by the mass diagrams drawn for incoming water and outgoing water. Where electrical or diesel pumps are used the availability of power, water in the underground tank and pumping hours should be taken into account. (This has been covered in detail in the chapter on overhead reservoir.)

Most of the municipal authorities do not permits privately owned on the line booster pumps except with a permission and where water pressure in the mains is not sufficient to reach the terrace in required quanty, underground reservoirs will have to be built to collect water from municipal mains and pumping done to fill the overhead reservoir.

Aim of Designing Water Supply Network within the Building

1. The rate of flow of water of all outlets shall be more or less equal.
2. The installation should prevent wastage of water.
3. Water supply to an outlet should not be severely affected by operation of other outlets.
4. The rate of flow of water should be convenient and satisfying to the user. Rates of flow recommended as satisfactory for cold water:

(a)	W.C. Flushing cistern	0.11 lit/sec.
(b)	Basin	0.15 lit/sec.
(c)	Tap	0.13 lit/sec.
(d)	Shower Umbrella type	0.11 lit/sec.

(e) Sink tap 12 mm 0.19 lit/sec.
18 mm 0.30 lit/sec.
25 mm 0.40 lit/sec.
(f) Bath tub 18 mm 0.30 lit/sec.
25 mm 0.60 lit/sec.

These figures are for guidance and variation even on lower side can be allowed to some extent. These figures would give an idea of user's comfort. Thus a 20 litre bucket may get filled in 20/0.19 sec. i.e. 1.76 minutes, a comfortable time to wait. If there is only one tap outlet for a family of 4.5 member demanding 600 litres of water per day this would mean:

$$\text{Water filling time of } \frac{600}{0.19 \times 60} = 53 \text{ minutes, say one hour,}$$

which is also fair enough

Where there is only one tap, it may be in continuous use; but where there are many outlets in one system it would be unrealistic and uneconomic in pipe size and cost to assume that all outlets will be in use simultaneously. It is therefore usual to make an assumption of the frequency of the use of outlets to estimate required pipe sizes to give a reasonable rate of flow from outlets that is assumed will be in use simultaneously at peak use times. If the actual simultaneous use is less than what has been presumed, then the rate of flow will be higher and if the actual simultaneous use at peak hours is more than the estimate, then there will be a reduced rate of flow from outlet. However, there would be some flow and it cannot be a disaster. This type of occasional failure of water network to yield desired quantity has to be accepted in the interest of economy.

The rate of flow of water through pipes is dependent on the diameter of pipe, the length (including equivalent length of specials) and the hydraulic head.

In the design of pipe work for building, water pressure is generally expressed as static or hydraulic head. The static head is the vertical distance in metres between the tank water level and the outlet or tap. This head represents the energy available to provide a flow of water against the frictional resistance of pipe work.

The method of calculation is simple enough. The pipe runs are expressed in metres and suitable provision is made for all specials. The head is known. There are monograms and charts available (based on Hazen-William formula) which would give frictional loss per metre of pipe for a given discharge of water. From this, pipe size required for a given rate of flow in pipework and at outlets can be calculated.

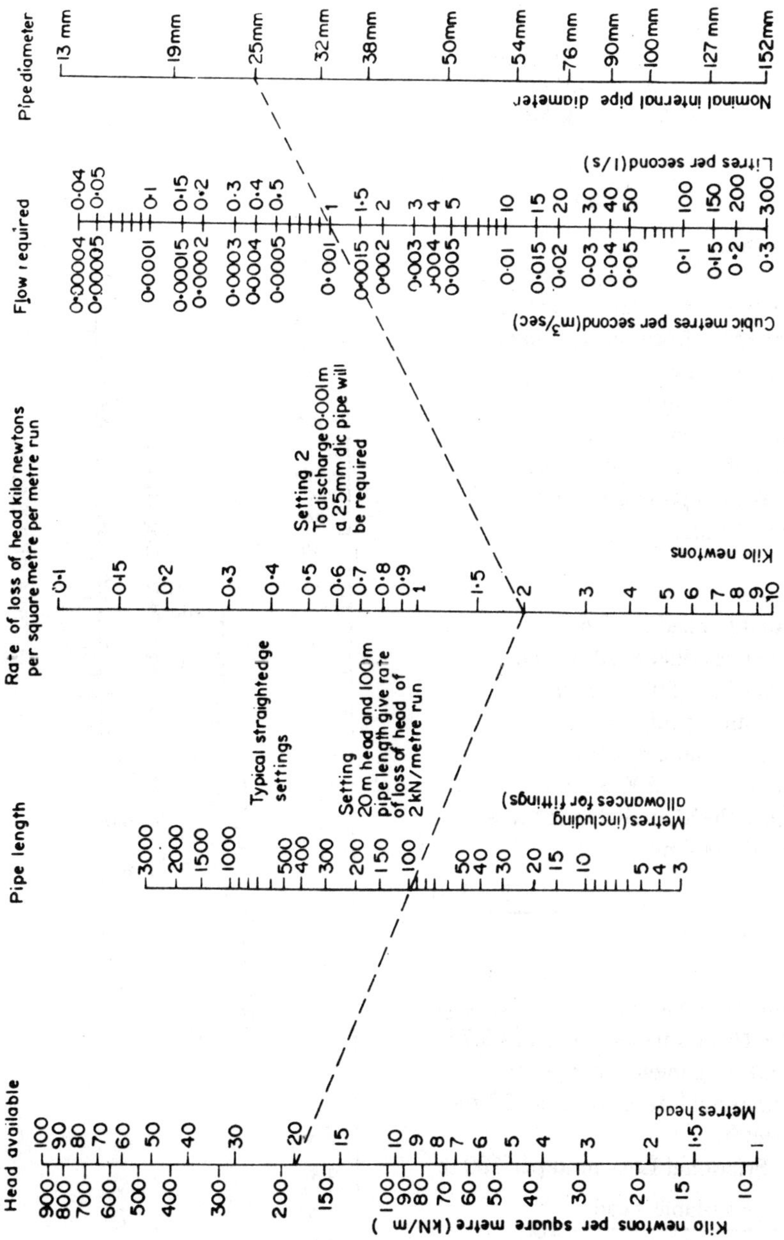

Fig. 1. Nomogram for water supply pipe sizing

Example 1.

Procedure

Q = 0.31/sec

Pipe dia = 30 mm

Frictional loss from nomogram

= 30 m/1000 m

Total friction loss in 300 m length

$$= \frac{30 \text{ m}}{1000 \text{ m}} \times 300 \text{ m}$$

Example 2.

Find suitable diameter pipe to carry 151/s from service line to overhead tank.

Total length of service main = 200 m

Residual pressure available at the take off point on supply line is 15 m.

Procedure

Available head = 15 m.

Deduct residual head = 2 m.

Deduct 25% for losses in bends and special = 3.25.

Friction head available for loss in pipe of 200 m. = 15–2–3.25 = 9.75

Friction head available for loss in pipe of 1000 m

$$= \frac{9.75 \times 100}{200}$$

= 48.75 m.

From the nomogram for a discharge of 15 l/s and friction loss of 48.75 m/100 m diameter of nearest commercial size of pipe is 120 mm diameter.

A = Frictional Loss in m per 100 m

$$= \frac{\text{Available head}}{\text{Length of pipe}} \times 100$$

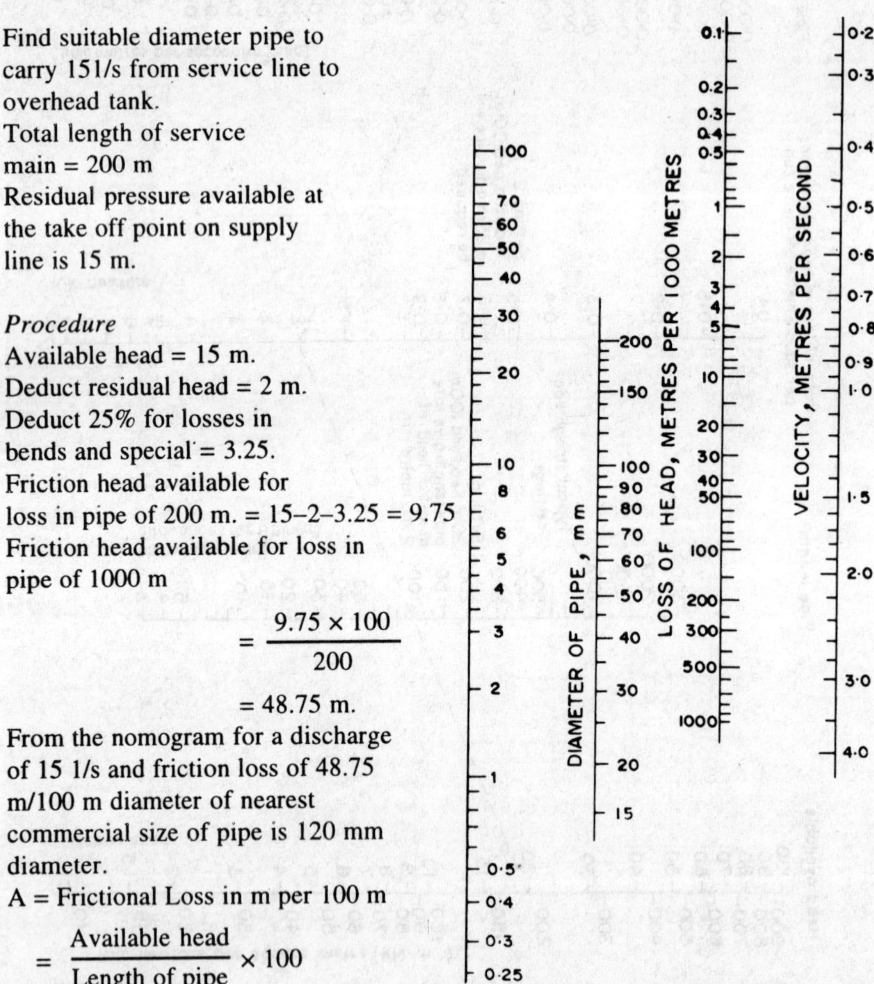

Fig. 2 Nomogram for Hazen and Williams Equation (C = 100

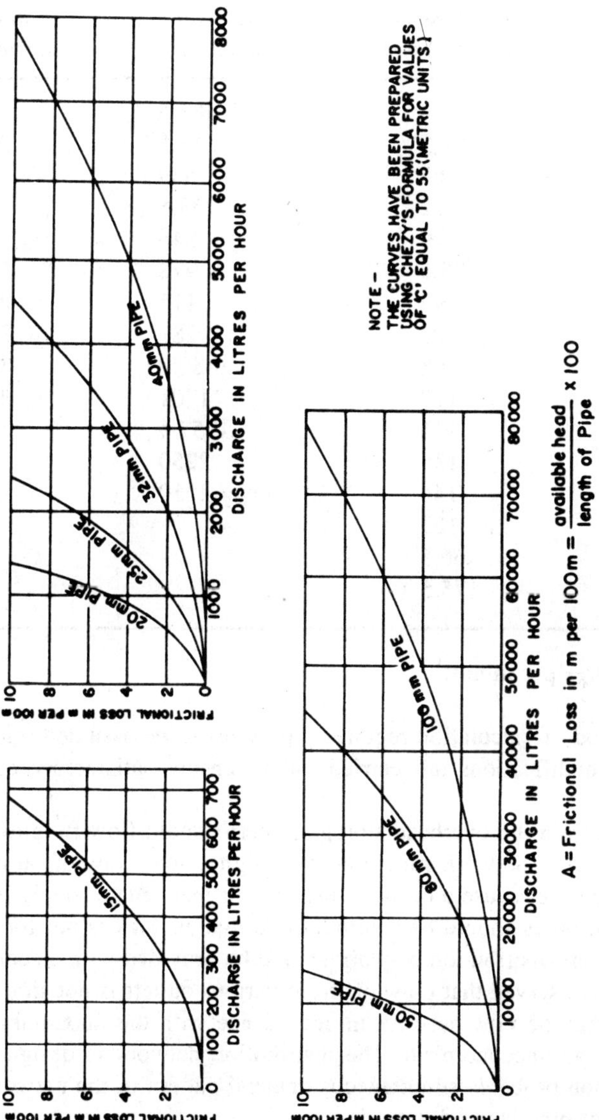

Fig. 3. Discharge curves

TABLE 1

Probable Simultaneous Demand from a Number of Draw off Points

Demand if all taps were opened l.p.m.	*Probable simultaneous demand l.p.m.*	*Demand if all taps were opened l.p.m.*	*Probable simultaneous demand l.p.m.*
54	54	481.5	189
63	58.5	553.5	202.5
72	65	639	216
81	72	733.5	234
90	79	846	252
103.2	85.5	972	274.5
117	92	1116	292.5
135	101	1287	319.5
157.5	108	1480.0	346.5
180	117	1701	382.5
207	126	1957.5	432
238.5	135	2250	468
274.5	144	Over 2250	20%
319.5	153		
364.5	166.5		
.423	175.5		

l.p.m. = litres per minute

This method of calculation requires pipe sizes to be assumed initially and later suitable modifications are carried out to ensure satisfactory outflow at every tap.

The water from the overhead storage system should flow by gravity to all draw off points. The network should be so designed that draw off at a point in the premises does not cause a negative pressure or inadequate supply in another part. The fall of pipes should be continuous so that air lock is not formed. The lowest point in the distribution network should be provided with a scour outlet.

It has been observed that draw off from various outlets is not simultaneous. Therefore, to provide pipe network in accordance with the maximum possible demand would be uneconomical. The distribution network is designed taking into consideration probable simultaneous demand pattern of the network served by the section of pipe being designed.

There are many formulae and approaches to the simultaneous demand problem. However, these have been designed for a 24 hour water supply. Where water supply timings are limited the simultaneous demand would be higher.

One rough and ready thumb rule is that to find out demand in gallons per minute, when all taps are kept open and to take a square-root and multiply by four. This would give simultaneous demand.

Another method of finding out simultaneous demand is to assume certain loading unit per type of fixture and total the fixture units served and find out from graph which has been arrived at after extensive experimentation of the simultaneous demand which is likely to result from a normal occupancy.

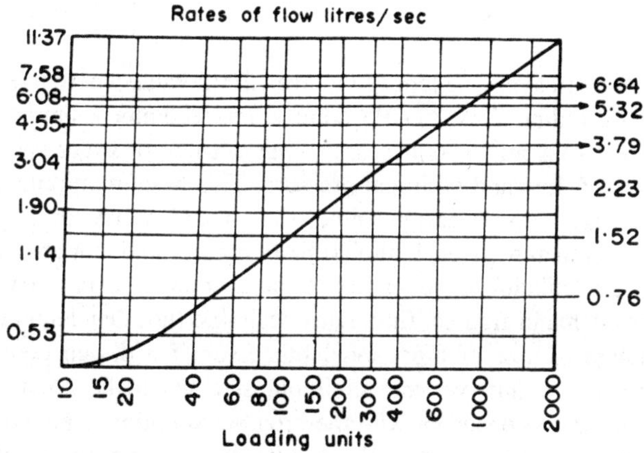

Fig. 4. Loading units and design flow rates.

Loading Units for Various Types of Outlet Fixtures

		Loading units
(1)	*Dwelling and flats*	
	W.C. flushing cistern	2
	Wash basin	1.5
	Bath (Tub)	10
	Sink	3-5
(2)	*Offices*	
	W.C. flushing cistern	2
	Wash basin	1-2
	Wash basin (use in rapid succession)	6
(3)	*Schools and industrial buildings.*	
	Wash basin	3
	Shower	3
	Public bath	22
	W.C. Flushing cistern	2

Having considered the loading units for all fixtures served by the pipeline in question, rate of flow of water need can be directly read from Fig. 4.

Apart from rate of flow water should also flow with proper pressure. In the case of a shower bath if the water comes out with very high pressure, it will sting the body and if the supply is at very low pressure, there is no charm of a shower bath. Similarly in a wash basin tap, if water gushes out at a high speed due to high pressure, then it will splash.

Recommended residual pressures at the outlets are:

	kg/cm²
1. Wash basin	0.564
2. Tap	0.35
3. Bath tub	0.35
4. Shower	0.845
5. Ball cock for closet	1.056

These pressures may be reduced to even 2/3rd value where it is inescapable. The National Building Code 83 (BIS publication) recommends minimum residual pressure of 0.19 kg/cm². It is necessary that outflow of water should be at the optimum rate of flow and otpimum pressure. This basic requirement is fulfilled by proper design. Proper design of network would ensure desired outflow in the most economical manner. It should be borne in mind that absolute accuracy in the design calculation is not called for on account of many assumptions like simultaneous demand figures, flow rates desirable (not mandatory) etc. and the restricted range of size of pipes available. Even if a design demands correct size of pipe as 7.5 mm yet the minimum size would be 15 mm. Therefore reasonable accuracy consistent with the broad assumption is aimed at.

The initial calculation of piping system may be carried out by presuming the following figures of equivalent length of pipe to account for extra frictional losses caused by fittings.

Pipe fittings	Equivalent length of pipe in pipe diameters
90° elbow	30
Tee	40
Gate valve	20
Globe valves, bibtaps	300

The velocity of flow of water should be a self cleansing one and not too high. Velocity should not be less than one metre per second and not more than 3 metres per second. Very high velocity of water gives rise to noise problems especially hissing noise and also water hammer.

Actual steps in the sizing of piping system are:

(a) Draw the Network (1) Main riser
(2) Down take pipes
(3) Branches

to scale indicating various fittings, valves, fixtures.

(b) Compute the load units of fixtures in each line.

(c) Determine total demand and expected simultaneous demand.

(d) Determine final pipe length in each line section taking into consideration various fittings like bends, tees and valves. (For the first time a rough approximation of adding 25 per cent of length for branches may be fair.)

(e) Considering the required exit pressure at the farthest point of each sub-section, work backwards by adding friction loss to the required head in riser.

(f) Work out all the sub-section of network and check up whether sizes of pipes assumed are correct. If the pressure available in the main is higher than the loss due to friction plus exit pressure then reduce the size of pipe and if the pressure available in the main is less than the exit pressure plus friction loss then increase the size of the pipe. This process of calculation of piping is to be repeated till almost equitable supply in all fixture is obtained.

(g) Nowhere the velocity of flow of water should be more than 3 metres/second or less than 1 metre/second.

(h) In the case of topmost storey, the pressure available at the outlet tap may be specially checked as the head available is very low and considerable part of which may be expended by the pipe network on terrace itself from tank to the shaft or down take point. To avoid problems it may be advisable to lay separate network of pipe for the topmost storey.

(i) Where the pipe network still has very high head of water (this would happen to lower storey fittings) the pressure may be reduced by use of diaphragms or by globe valve.

11. DESIGN OF A WATER SUPPLY PIPING IN A BUILDING—A WORKED OUT EXAMPLE

Normally the down feed system of piping is used in India where in the pipe network is fed from overhead tank.

Pipe Sizing

The object of any method of pipe sizing is to ensure that the available head of water or pressure is used in the most economical manner to give the desired outflow at the draw off point. An absolute accuracy in the calculation for pipe sizing is generally not called for, due to necessarily restricted range of commercial pipe sizes available. A best possible combination of commercial sizes is used to fulfill the requirements of practical design.

When flow of water starts the head of water available gets destroyed due to:

(a) Frictional resistance to flow through pipes.

(b) Resistance to flow offered by fittings, valves, taps etc.

Resistance to flow offered by fittings is quite considerable. The resistance to flow is normally expressed in terms of length of pipe that offers equivelent resistance as by this way calculations become easier. This method simplifies calculations as these lengths can be added to the measured length of pipe run giving effective pipe length.

The calculation for pipe sizing is basically a method of iteration. Initial phase of calculation can be very approximate where in the contribution by the equivalent length of piping to account for fittings, valves etc. can be expressed as an addition to the measured length. This is normally taken at 25 to 100% of measured length. Once the pipe sizes are approximately calculated in the second interation slightly detailed calculation can be made to correctly calculate the equivalent pipe length.

While designing pipe network, it should be kept in mind that water will flow in a path of least resistance. Water pipe for cultinary purposes (Kitchen, drinking, bathing etc.) is separated from the water piping for flushing purpose as in most of the cases ever overhead tanks for these uses are separate.

In the piping there are vertical runs of piping and horizontal runs. It should be kept in mind that the water flow in vertical pipe if it has to be deflected in the horizontal direction has to have a deflecting force to make it change its direction. In continuous and horizontal piping branch then water will find a line of least resistance in vertical run and thus water may not flow in horizontal pipe unless the flow in lower vertical pipe stops. For example, if first and second floor in a high rise building are both drawing water and the pipe is from overhead tank to second floor and then to first floor, then water will flow to the first floor readily on account of lower elevation and unless the first floor is stopped water would not flow to second floor, a phenomenon which is a routine experience where, in a building lower level resident opens tap the upper resident do not get water.

This is normally taken care of by reducing the diameter of vertical down take pipe at branch off point, thus the resistance to flow is more in vertical piping and water flows to the horizontal run.

Flow Rates of Fittings

The actual rate of flow from various draw off points depend upon the head of water available, the size of pipe installed and the layout of the system.

Table 2 gives the recommended flow rates that should be provided at various types of fitments.

TABLE 2

Recommended Rates of Flow for Various Fittings and Appliances (Rage of flow in litres per minute)

	Fitting or Appliance	*Cold Water*	*Hot Water*
1.	Flushing cisterns	4.5	
2.	Lavatory basins	9.0	7.0
3.	Bath (Private)	18.0	22.5
4.	Bath (Public)	27.0	36.0
5.	Shower or spray fittings	7.0	7.0
6.	Sinks	13.5	18.0
7.	Sluicing sinks	27.0	36.0

The Principles of Pipe Sizing

Having considered the storage, flow rates, and simultaneous demand that must be provided for, we must now consider the factor affecting the design of the piping. The object of any method of pipe sizing is to ensure that the available head or pressure is used in the most economical manner to give the desired outflow at the draw-off points. In a practical layout absoulte accuracy is in general unattainable due to the necessarily restricted range of commercial pipe sizes available, but providing the nearest available size is used the layout fulfils the requirements of a practical design.

The head of water available is absorded in supplying the draw off in two ways:

(a) In overcoming the resistance of the pipes themselves.

(b) In overcoming the resistance of fittings, valves, drawing off taps, etc.

The resistances of 'fittings in most domestic cold water layout are quite considerable. In any but the smallest systems they are of sufficient importance to require tabulation of their total resistance to be made. Theoretically all resistances are losses of head, but for convenience of application to design problem they are usually stated in terms of a length of pipe that is of equivalent resistance.

This method of testing resistances simplifies the subsequent pipe sizing as these lengths can be added to the measured pipe run, thus giving the effective resistance length.

The resistance length of all fittings is usually based upon the resistance of an elbow, the resistance of elbow being taken as unity. The resistance of elbows of various diameters in terms of the length of pipe of equivalent resistance is given in Table 3.

TABLE 3

Metre Length of Pipe having the Same Resistance as One Elbow

Diameter of pipe in mms.	*Length of pipe in metres*
15	0.45
20	0.75
25	0.90
32	1.20
40	1.35
50	1.80
80 m	2.70
100	3.60

It will be observed that a 25 mm elbow creates a resistance equal to 0.9 m of pipe, other diameters being prorata.

The resistance of other pipe fittings based on the resistance of elbows is given in Table 4.

TABLE 4

Relative Resistance of Various Specials or piping
(an elbow resistance = 1.0)

Right-angle bend, redius equals diameter of pipe (short radius bend)	0.3
Right-angle bend, radius equals three diameters of pipe (long-sweep) bend	0.14
Gate valve, fully open	0.00
Gate valve, half open	2.00
Gate valve, one-quarter open	15.00
Gate valve, one-eighth open	100.00
Tee, straight	0.05
Tee, reducing one size	0.75
Tee, reducing two size	1.00
Tee, branch outlet	2.00
Cylinder or calorifier	3.00
Single outlet from cylinder of cistern	1.50
Angle radiator valve	1.50
Globe valve	2.50
Draw-off tap or stop valve	1.50
Return bend	1.50

Normally, the contribution due to the number of fittings can have the measured length of the pipe increased by about 60 per cent 100 per cent i.e. effective frictional length of the pipe under consideration may be upto double the actual measured length.

Design of Line : -A-B-d-1-2-3

Length = 6.10 + 1.50 + 2.10 + 3.00 + 1.50 + 3.00 = 17.2 m.

No. of outlet points = 3

Demand = 3 × 13.5 = 40.5 litres.

Allowing 60 per cent more for equivalent frictional length due to bends valves etc.

Total equivalent length = 17.2 × 1.6 = 27.5 m.

Loss due to friction = 27.50 – 17.20 = 10.30 m.

Head available for the above flow, allowing a residual pressure of 1.20 m at the exit = 2.10 + 1.50 – 1.20 = 2.40 m.

$$\text{Allowable gradient in pipe} = \frac{2.4}{27.5} = 0.0873$$

Example Calculations

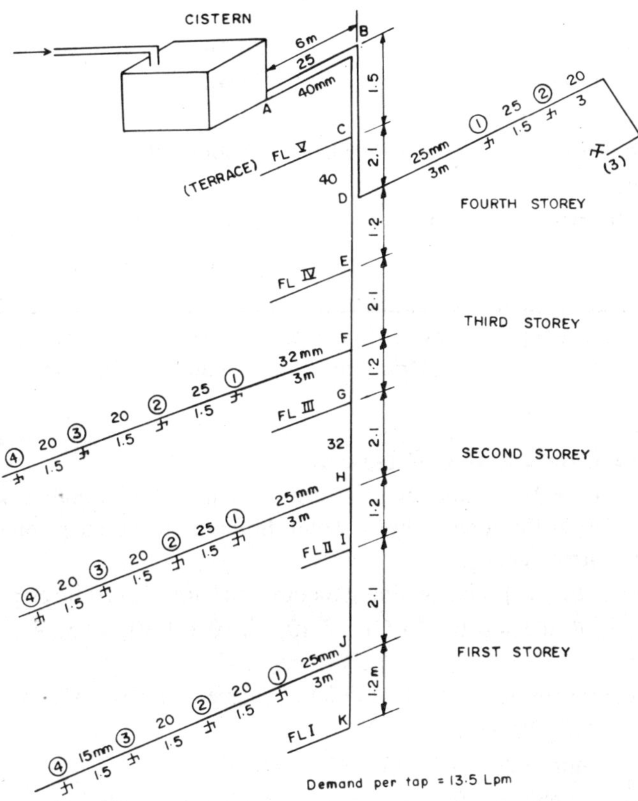

Fig. 5. Water supply scheme for drinking purposes.

The vertical down take pipe is to be designed for the probable simultaneous discharge. However since the discharge is small, the same is considered as the probable simultaneous discharge from the graph, provide 25 mm vertical pipe. 25 mm pipe is also required to supply a discharge of even 27 litres per minute. Hence 25 mm pipe is provided upto point 2. However diameter is changed to 20 mm in portion 2-3 as it accommodates the discharge at the gradient indicated. Frictional loss in bends actually takes place at 60 per cent. To check up this point the number of elbows/tees/valves actually present in the layout is converted into equivalent pipe length from Table–3 and Table–4.

S. No.	No. of elements present	Equivalent elbow length	Provided	Frictional length of pipe in metres
1.	Elbow-5	5	25 mm	4.5
2.	Elbow-1	1	20 mm	0.675
3.	Tees straight-2	2 × 0.5 = 1	25 mm	0.90
4.	Tee reducing one size-1	1 × 0.75 = 0.75	25 mm - 20 mm	0.675
5.	Gate valve (Half open)	2 × 2 = 4	25 mm	3.60
			Total :	10. 35 m

Note : 25 mm elbow creates resistance equal to 0.90 m of pipe, other diameters being pro-rata. This frictional loss calculated tallies with the assumed valve.

Design of Line = A-B-E-F-1-2-3-4

The line ABF should be designed to carry the probable simultaneous discharge for all the three storeys. Total discharge to be considered is 3 × 4 × 13.5 = 162 litres per min.

From Table–1, probable simultaneous discharge = 110 litres per min.

Length of line = 6.10 + 1.50 + 3.40 + 2.10 + 1.50 + 1.50 + 3.00 + 1.50 = 20.6 m

Let equivalent frictional loss due to bends etc. be 60 per cent.

20.6 × 0.6 = 12.36 m.

Total length = 20.6 + 12.36 = 32.96 say 33 m.

Head available for flow assuming a residual head of 3.35 at exit = 1.50 + 2.10 + 1.20 + 2.10 – 3.35 = 3.55

$$\text{Gradient available for flow} = \frac{3.55}{33.0} = 0.11$$

From graph provide 40 mm down take pipe.

Discharge in branch line 1-2-3-4 = 4 x 13.5 = 54 litres/min.

Provide Line F-1 = 32 mm
Line 1-2 = 25 mm
Line 2-3 = 20 mm
Line 3-4 = 20 mm

Check for Equivalent Frictional Losses

S. No.	*Description*	*Nos. of Elbows*	*EQ Length pipe*	*Dia of*	*Equivalent Length metres*
1.	Tees reducing One size.	1	0.75 × 1 = 0.75	40 mm	0.75 × 1.50 × 0.90 = 1.00
2.	Tees reducing.	1	0.75 × 1 = 0.75	32 mm	0.75 × 1.25 × 0.90 = 0.85
		1	0.50 × 1 = 0.5	32 mm	0.50 × 1.25 × 0.90 = 0.55
3.	Gate valve (3/4 open)	1	0.25 × 1 = 0.25	40 mm	0.25 × 1.50 × 0.90 = 0.3
4.	Gate valve (1/2 open)	1	2 × 1 = 2	32 mm	2 × 1.25 × 0.90 = 2.25
		1	2 × 1 = 2	25 mm	2 × 1 × 0.90 = 1.80
		2	2 × 2 = 4	20 mm	4 × 0.75 × 0.90 = 2.70
5.	Elbows	1	1 × 1 = 1	40 mm	1 × 1.50 × 0.90 = 1.35
		1	1 × 1 = 1	32 mm	1 × 1.25 × 0.90 = 1.15
		1	1 × 1 = 1	25 mm	1 × 1 × 0.90 = 0.90
					Total : 12.9

The assumed value tallies with the calculated value. Hence O.K.

Design of Line F-H-1-2-3-4

Total discharge to be considered for design of line FH = 2 × 4 × 13.5 = 108 per min

Corresponding probable discharge from Table 1 = 88.5 litres per mm say 90.00 litres per min.

Head available at point F.

(Assuming 3.35 m as exit pressure)

= 3.35 + (1.50 + 1.50 + 1.50 + 3.00) x 0.11 = 4.18 m

Head available for flow in line F-H-1-2-3-4 = 1.2 + 2.1 + 3.0 + 1.5 + 1.5 + 1.5 = 10.8 m

At 60 per cent for frictional loss in bends, equivalent pipe length

$$= 10.8 \times 0.60 = \frac{6.48 \text{ m}}{17.28 \text{ m}}$$

Total Length = (6.48 + 10.8 = 17.28) m

$$\text{Gradient available for flow} = \frac{6.48 \text{ m}}{17.28 \text{ m}} = 0.24$$

From graph

Provide line F-H = 32 mm to carry 90 litres per min

line H-1 = 25 mm " 54 " " "

line 1-2 = 25 mm " 40 " " "

line 2-3 = 20 mm " 27 " " "
line 2-3 = 20 mm " 13.4 " " "

As given earlier, the check for frictional loss in pipe can be made. In the present case, it is assumed to be O.K. in this respect.

Design of Line H-J-1-2-3-4

Total discharge to be carried by H-J = 1 × 4 × 13.5 = 54 litres per min

Simultaneous discharge from Table-1 = 54 litres per min.

Head available at H: 3.35 + (1.50 + 1.50 + 1.50 + 3.00) × 0.24 = 5.15 m

Head available for flow with exit pressure of 3.35 m

= 5.15 + 1.20 + 2.10 – 3.35 = 5.10 m

Length of flow = 2.10 + 1.20 + 3.00 + 1.50 + 1.50 + 1.50 = 10.8 m

Frictional length = 0.60 × 10.8 = 6.48 m

Equivalent pipe length = 10.80 + 6.48 = 17.28 m

$$\text{Gradient available} = \frac{5.10}{17.28 \text{ m}} \; 0.29$$

From graph provide vertical down take pipe

Line H-J = 25 mm
Line J-1 = 25 mm
Line 1-2 = 20 mm
Line 2-3 = 20 mm
Line 3-4 = 15 mm

As earlier, the friction loss in bends etc. can again be checked and is assumed to be O.K. in the present example.

12. PRINCIPLES OF DESIGN OF WATER DISTRIBUTION SYSTEM FOR A GROUP OF BUILDINGS IN A COLONY

The aim of the water mains is to convey wholesome water to the ultimate consumer at adequate residual pressure and in required quantity.

A geometrical configuration of pipes, reservoir boosters, valves, specials is used for efficient operation and maintenance of water supply with due respect to overall economy. This can be called the functional aspect of distribution system.

In hydraulic terms there should be adequate amount of water at optimal pressure at the maximum demand (which is a probabilistic guess).

A distribution system will have many types of consumers, some having heavy demand of water, some not requiring it in large quantities, some areas are predominantly residential and some non residential, thus requiring water at different times. The difference in ground contours of the buildings will also be an important factor. Correct zoning of areas to be served is a must. If designer of the water supply network caters primarily for high elevation areas, then in low elevation area in the same network then there would be very high pressure in pipe lines and if he caters for low elevation areas predominantly, the high elevation areas will get very scanty amount of water.

The water supply network zoning depends upon:

1. Topography.
2. Density of population.
3. Type of locality.
4. The wastage, leak detection and prevention.

Normally in average elevation difference of 15 to 25 m should call for a separate zone. The zones may be inter-connected to provide emergeny supplies yet the valves between zones should be kept normally closed and not kept partially opened.

The layout of piping should be such that the differences in pressure between the different areas of the same zone of same system does not exceed 3 to 5 m of water head.

Distribution system for a direct supply to buildings without an underground tank should be designed so as to have a residual pressure at ferrule point not less than:

For construction of buildings of normal 2.8 to 3.5 metre floor height

1. Single storey – 7 m of water head
2. Two storey – 14 m of water head
3. Three storey – 17 m of water head

The distribution system should not have residual pressure exceeding 22 m. of water head.

Where multistoreyed construction is to be served then units should have an underground tank where mains should discharge. Very high pressure in mains require high intense surveillance for leakage.

The distribution system may be

1. Gravity system. (Gravity tied from source)
2. Distributing reservoir system.
3. Direct pressure system.

The aim of all these systems is to obtain adequate pressure at various points in the distribution system. The choice of the system will depend upon the topography of the area of distribution and its elevation with reference to the source of the supply.

The gravity system is most reliable. This is useful in hilly areas where the elevation of source of supply with reference to the area of distribution is such that adequate pressure is obtained in the network directly.

In the distributing reservoir system the water from source is pumped into an elevated reservoir wherefrom water flows by gravity.

The direct pressure system is where mains pressure is high enough for ensuring supply of water at all floors of building without any tank system. This can be a hydro-pneumatic system also.

There are four systems of laying water mains:

1. Dead end or tree system.
2. Grid iron or reticulation system.
3. Ring or circular system.

4. Radial system.

Each method has its own merit according to the type and size of the area to be served. Water main are normally laid along existing and proposed roads and thus the road layout becomes an important factor in determining the system of water supply mains.

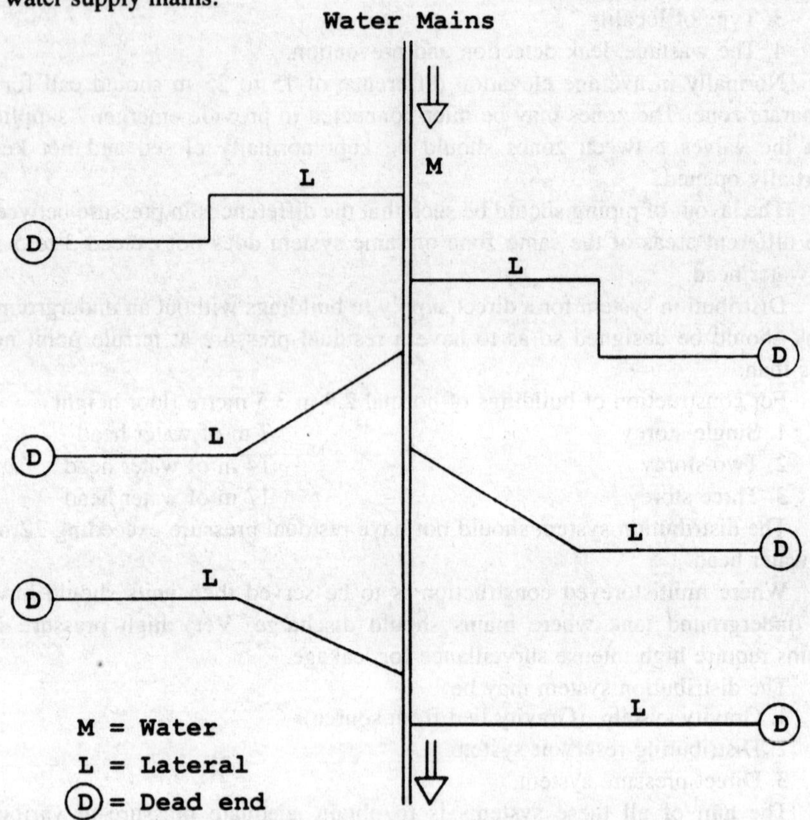

Fig. 6 Dead End System.

Dead End or Tree System

This system is applicable to the areas having uniformly distributed population. In the centre of the area one trunk supply line is run. To this main are connected a number of sub mains. Branches serving the houses are connected to the sub mains. In this way the entire distribution area is covered by a system like a tree which has a main trunk (main line) from where branches (submains) and finally leaves (House connection) take off.

In this arrangement a large number of dead ends are created. Various branches have no interconnection. Dead ends lead to stagnation of water and accumulation of sediments. Thus the tree system although it is simple and cheap, it is not very desirable from maintenance angle. Scouring of dead ends from time to time would lead to unnecessary wastage of water. Stagnation of water would lend water an undesired odour. Presence of iron bacteria is also found more in such dead ends.

Grid Iron or Reticulation System

By connecting the dead ends in the tree system, the water can be made to circulate through entire system.

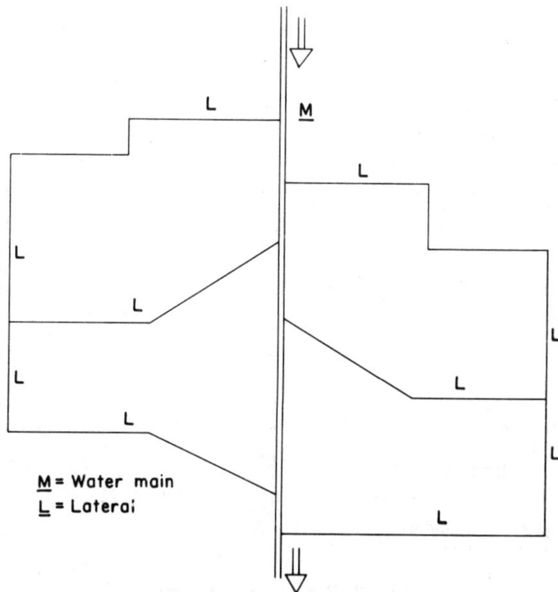

Fig. 7. Grid Iron System.

The system partially overcome the disadvantages of tree system yet it suffers from the following disadvantages:

(a) Necessity of large number of valves.

(b) Longer pipe lines and bigger diameter of pipes required to be used.

(c) Intricate calculations needed.

(d) High cost of construction.

The system is not suitable for growing cities or towns with isolated development.

Circular or Ring Main System

In this system a ring is formed by laying feeder mains around the distributing area instead of through the area. The branches are connected crosswise to the main.

Satisfactory, pressure and quick supply results from this arrangement.

Radial System (Fig. 9)

In this system the reservoir is at the centre of area and distribution pipes run radially to the periphery.

The system is suited to the colony with radial roads.

The design of a water supply distribution system involves the following steps:

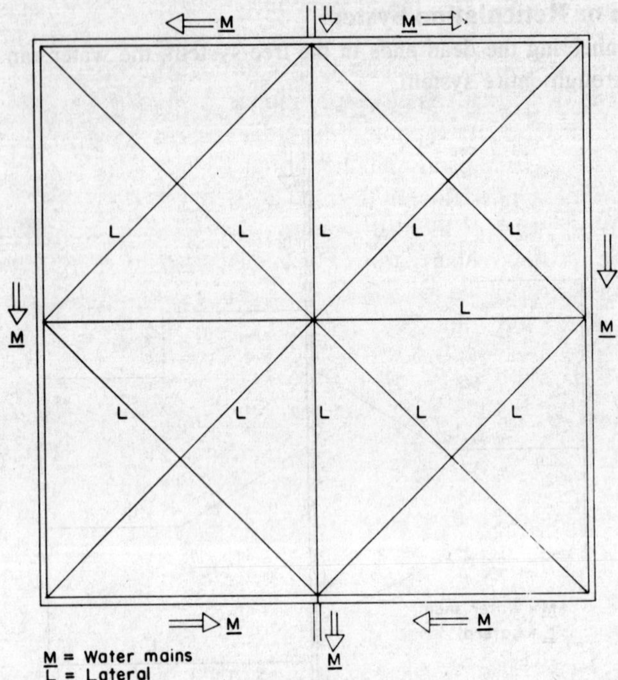

Fig. 8. Ring Main System.

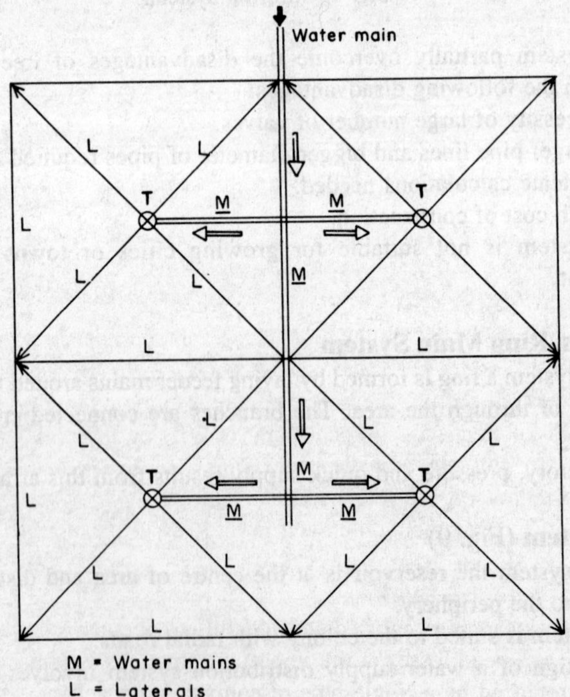

Fig. 9. Radial System

1. Surveying the area for deciding the alignment of the mains.
2. Making a-detailed contour survey (at 1 metre elevation difference).
3. Marking density of population for different sections.
4. Making a tentative network of piping.
5. Making first assumption of pipe diameter by assuming a velocity of 1 to 1.5 m/s and using suitable formula.
6. Assuming peak flow in the pipe lines.
   The capacity of the distribution network should be sufficient to meet the maximum hourly flow. For this purpose the average hourly flow is multiplied by the following peaking factor.
   Population upto 50000 – 3
   Population 50000 – 200000 – 2.5
   Population above 200000 – 2
7. For assessing requirements of fire demand, the local byelaw and local fire officers should be invariably consulted. Where there is no byelaw, the fire demand should be assessed on the importance of area, fire fighting facilities available, percentage of fire resisting building. A provision in Kilo-litres per day at $100\sqrt{P}$.......where P is the population in thousands may be adopted for population exceeding 50000. Where fire service is provided no pipe less than 150 mm diameter is to be used in the mains network. However 100 mm dia pipe upto 180 metre length may be used between connection at each end to larger main.
8. In the dead end or tree system 50 or 75 mm dia main may be used near dead ends for a length less than 100 metres and 100 mm upto 360 metres from the last connection to a larger main provided no fire service is involved.
9. In general, at every 300 metres the pipes should be inter-connected.
10. If possible two supply pipes should be provided.
11. Inter-connection valve within networks of different zones should be provided to give an emergency supply.

13. DESIGN METHODS FOR NETWORKS

Approximate Method

These methods are simple, approximate and can be used as quick check or for ascertaining preliminary pipe sizes for a new system.

Such methods include method of sections, circle method or contour method. The method of sections, the network is cut by imaginatory section lines (preferably at right-angles to the general direction of flow and for an assumed hydraulic gradient of 1 to 3 per 1000). The capacity of pipe line cut by the lines are matched with actual demand in the area to be supplied.

Equivalent Pipe Method

A network can be simplified considerably to obtain preliminary information on the flow and head losses at the important junctions where a complex system of pipes is replaced by a single pipe of equivalent capacity.

Trial and Error Method

In this method, the pipe diameters are assumed and corresponding heads or flows are obtained by using nomograms.

The closeness of assumed values is tested so that at every junction inflow is equal to outflow. The head loss to the outlet shall be equal from both sides of loop.

This assumed value is changed till head losses or the flows agree within 0.3 m or 0.2 per cent when a correct solution balance is obtained.

Hardy Cross Method

Balance Heads

In this method of balancing heads by a controlled trial and error process the correction factor for assumed flows are worked out. Necessary formulation are made algebraically consistent by arbitrarily assigning positive signs to clockwise flows and associated head losses and negative signs to anti-clockwise flows and associated head losses.

The correct factor in a circuit is calculated by

$$\Delta Q = -\frac{\Sigma \Delta H}{n \Sigma H/Q}$$

Q = Quantity of flow.

H = Head loss.

n = Constant 1.85 for Hazen-Williams formula.

The assumed flows are corrected, and procedure repeated till the required precision is had. This is an iteration process, steps of which are:

(a) Assume suitable values of flow Q in each pipe line such that the flows coming into each junction of the loop are equal to flows leaving the junction.

(b) Positive signs to all clockwise flows and negative signs to all anticlockwise flow are assigned.

(c) Compute the head loss H.

(d) Compute H (i.e. algebraic a sum of the head losses around each loop and if this is nearly equal to 0 in all loops (tolerance + 0.15) the assumed flows are correct.

If H ≠ 0 for any loop. Compute the error in flow

$$\Delta Q = -\frac{1}{1.85}\ \frac{\Sigma \Delta H}{\Sigma H/Q}$$

(e) The correction factor is of opposite sign. Add correction factor to the assumed flow with due regard to the sign of flows.

(f) Pipes operating in more than one circuit draw correction from each circuit. However, second correction is of opposite sign to that applied to the first circuit.

(g) Repeat cycle till H = Q

(h) If during correction process the head difference in an element becomes zero then pipe should be eliminated from the particular balancing operation in which it acts.

Balancing Flows

The method of balancing heads more applicable when the quantities of water entering and leaving the network are known when quantities are unknown and there are several inlets the distribution of flow amongst them can be determined by a method of balancing flows. In this method, the heads at inlet at outlets must be known and heads at junction and associated between junctions. Friction losses are then assumed and use is made of the fact that the sum of flows at a junction must be zero if flows towards junctions and away from it are given opposite sign. If for any pipe, the assumed head is $H = KQ^n$ and h is correction.

$$h = nq\ (H/Q)$$

$$q = \left(\frac{h}{n}\right)\left(\frac{Q}{H}\right) H \quad \frac{-n\Sigma Q}{\Sigma Q/H}$$ where n = 1.85 in Hazen Williams formula

(a) Assume heads at all free junctions such that the sum of head losses in clockwise direction equals sum of head losses in anticlockwise direction.

(b) Assign positive sign to head losses for flows towards the junction and negative sign for those flows which go away from junction.

(c) Compute flows use pipes nomograms if possible.

(d) Compute Q (Algebraic sum) at each free junction. If it is equal to zero with tolerance of ± 0.2 per cent) the assumed head losses are correct.

(e) If $Q \neq 0$ at any junction compute error in head loss

$$\Delta h = 1.85 \frac{\Sigma Q}{\Sigma Q/H}$$

The correction factor is of opposite sign. Add the correction factor to the assumed head losses with due regard to the sign of head losses.

(f) Pipes common to more than one loop receive correction from each loop. Correction to the companion circuit is of opposite sign to that of the first circuit.

(g) Repeat till Q = 0.

Design of a Water Supply Network for a Group of Buildings

Design of a water supply network whether it is for an individual building or for a group of buildings located in a colony, the principles remain the same i.e. the head of the water in the network should be such that all the units and outlets receive the water in the optimum quantity and at the optimum pressure— Neither the pressure should be high nor it should be low. The quantity of water should be adequate and there should be no negative pressure in any part of the network and nor any air lock formation should take place. The network should be so designed that equitable water supply results without having to manipulate valves in order to cut out and cut in some areas to provide water supply to other areas.

Basically head of water in a network, is due to difference of elevation between the network point and the starting point of water. This elevational difference causes pressure in the network which is usually indicated as in metre of water head.

Whereas in a level land the water supply network would be almost at the same level and thus the actual pressure in pipe due to the static head of water would be almost similar. The position is entirely different in a sloping site. The static head in the same network would be different in the various legs of network.

Thus the water will flow to the lower areas in larger quantity. Therefore while designing a water network, "Water zones" have to be introduced.

Zoning is also to be introduced where building heights differ considerably. For example, in a colony, there are single storeyed buildings, 4 storeyed buildings and 8 storeyed buildings would be uneconomical as well as it would be wasteful of the water designing network for pressures large enough to ensure supply in 8 storeyed building as in the case of single storeyed structures and the 4 storeyed structure, unnecessary pressures would be built up. In the case of a sloping area the building at a lower elevation would get advantage of the static pressure and thus the lower building would be receiving much more water supply. The aim in design of water supply to a group of building in one zone would be to ensure equitable water supply to all individual units.

When an upfeed water supply system is adopted, the pressure of water should be such that the consumer on the topmost storey is able to draw his requirement with adequate ease. For this purpose, buildings may have to be zoned in the network according to the height. Thus pressure in the network of 4 storeyed building would be higher than pressure in the network of 2 storeyed building.

Therefore where a down feed system of water supply is adopted, it should be seen that from the overhead tank to the tanks on the terrace, the hydraulic gradient would be same. In other words, if there is a building in a zone which is situated at a high ground the supply network shall be so designed that residual hydraulic head at the overhead tank of that building and another building which is situated at a lower elevation would be the same (a maximum difference of almost one metre). In layman's term, "the residual water pressure at the overhead tank ball valve point should be equal in all units". Wherever extra head exist due to the elevation differences it will have to be destroyed by additional pipe friction. Even though water tank may have to be at different elevation physically, hydraulically, they will be all at the same level. This is an important consideration which is often lost sight of with disasterous results in equality in water distribution. Therefore, for a design of a pipe network for a colony the following step by step procedure should be adopted.

Step 1 Obtain lay out plan of the colony.

Step 2 Super impose the water supply mains network.

Step 3 Ascertain height of various units with special reference to the level of the intended terrace level reservoir inlet point.

Step 4 Indicate elevations of all terrace level inlet points on the unit buildings.

Step 5 Ascertain correct distance from the unit rising pipe leading to the tank from the mains.

Step 6 Add the vertical length of riser pipe as in step 3 and the horizontal length in step 5. Add 50 per cent as additional equivalent length of water pipe to account for loss in fittings.

Step 7 Calculate head lost in friction in riser pipe and deduct it from the mains taking into account changes in pressure due to different elevations of the terrace tanks.

Step 8 Indicate residual pressure at the terrace level as individual unit of building.

Step 9 If the residual pressures are equal within 1 metre difference, the network is alright. Otherwise additional pressure loss will have to be introduced by constricting the riser pipe wherever residual pressures are higher than average and pressure loss will have to be reduced by increasing diameter of riser pipe wherever the residual pressure head is less than average.

Step 10 With new diameters of pipes repeat step 6 onwards till the residual pressure at tank level in all the units is reasonably similar.

14. CORROSION

Corrosion of distribution water pipe net work and of home plumping cost quite a lot. Corrosion and corrosion product causes costs of water supply distribution to rise as

1. Increased pumping costs due to increased amount of water to be pumped to neuralise loss due to leakages.
2. Increased pumping costs due to the clogging of pipe lines on account of accumulation of corrosion products.
3. Holes in pipe lines cause loss of water pressure.
4. Leaks in pipe line causes damage to the building fabric and in many cases repairs would be exhorbitant.
5. Excessive corrosion which calls for replacement of pipe networks whole-sale.
6. Coloured water due to products of corrosion, stains.
7. Bad odours caused due to corrosion which is repulsive both in terms of money and public opinion.

Corrosion is therefore one of the major problems to be faced in design construction and maintenance of water pipe networks. Corrosion could be categorised as follows:

1 Physical
2 Chemical
3 Biological

Physical corrosion or erosion occurs due to high velocity of water in pipe lines either alone or coupled with sediments. Extremely low velocity in pipe network can also cause corrosion.

Low velocities and stagnation in pipe networks including those in houses can cause tuberculosis, pitting and biological growth of organisms leading to corrosion. Therefore, the designer of a water supply system network should avoid dead ends. If the dead ends are unavoidable then there has to be a regular system for flushing dead ends.

Proper hydraulic design of water supply networks taking into consideration above factor can minimise the corrosion due to erosion or dead ends.

A maximum value of 1.1 metre/sec. velocity is recommended.

The most common types of corrosion are—

1. Galvanic Corrosion

This is caused by incorporation of different metals in the network of piping which are incompatible as per galvanic series. The thread of pipes are main points of attack.

2. Pitting Corrosion

This occurs due to action of chemicals added to water or on account of very soft water. Where the water occurring naturally is acidic in nature it has to be neutralised by additives. When chemicals are added to water either for correcting the pH imbalance or for disinfectant purpose has to be intimately mixed.

3. Crevices Corrosion

This is the phenomenon at the junction of fittings and piping. The crevices cause stagnancy and thus corrosion takes place. It is therefore necessary to have inner surface of pipes as smooth as possible. The high velocity of water can cause turbulence at the crevices and can lead to cavitation. This is a localised corrosion and is caused by oxygen deflection and acidity. It occurs at rivets, lapp joints etc.

4. Erosion Corrosion

Excessively high velocities are to be avoided. The erosion of pipe walls will take place specially at turning and bends. Cavitation corrosion is a type of erosion corrosion caused due to sudden drop in vapour pressure.

5. Biological Corrosion

There are bacterial growth which corrosion cast iron and steel pipes. Normally the thing is seen as reddish slime which sometimes gets loosened and comes out. Although it is not bad from health point of view, yet it causes stains and it is repulsive for looks. (No one would drink water if there is slight trace of reddish slime). Biological growth can also lead to bad odours being imparted to water.

Frequent complaints due to corrosion are as follows along with possible causes given.

1. Reddish water or frequent red stains or fixtures and on laundry.
2. Blue stains in laundry or on fixtures in copper pipe networks.

As against the popular notion that only iron corrodes and copper pipes do not corrode, it is to be stated that even copper piping corrodes under certain circumstances like chemicals in water.

3. Black coloured water—The cause could be sulphide attack on pipes either of copper or irons.
4. Bad taste or odours—Cause, this is due to by-products of biological activities in the pipe network.
5. Loss of pressure—Loss of pressure in a pipe network could be on account of tubers in the pipe network due to tuberculosis or it could be on account of corrosion products choking the line. In the case of hot water lines the built up of mineral deposits is fast.
6. Rapid deterioration of house-hold plumping can occur from pitting and corrosion at joints. The G.I. pipe work which is embedded in masonry with cement or lime mortar deteriorates very fast due to action of free line on G.I. pipe. Whereas the G.I. pipe can have a long life but G.I. pipe embedded in masonry may fail in 4 to 5 years also.

Tuberculosis occurs when corrosion products built up near anode. In cast iron or G.I. pipes these tubercules are of rust coloured, soft on the outside and progressively hard inside. In copper pipes the tubers could be green to bluish green in colour. Tuberculosis is possible to be broken when the pipes are hard hit.

The pipe network is therefore to be flushed with high pressure water from time to time so as to scour out the corrosion products.

7. Stray current corrosion may occur due to grounding of electrical appliances on pipe network. Corrosion otakes place at anode where the current leaves the network to return to power source or to the ground.

Therefore, the Designer and Maintenance Engineer has to take all precautions to avoid corrosion. And there should be a scour outlet provided in all net works whereby the corrosion products could be flushed out.

It will be difficult to control corrosion when the pipe network is placed in a damp, dusty environment. All pipe networks should be approachable for maintenance.

15. DESIGN OF UNDERGROUND RESERVOIR

In developed countries like USA, UK etc supply of water from municipal mains is expected to be available 24 hours a day. Whether water is available under pressure throughout 24 hours or it is available during a shorter duration does not normally change the total consumption of water. Total consumption of water depends on the applications, personal consumption habits etc and it does not vary very much. What may change slightly would be the losses in the pipe lines which would be less when water supply is intermittent.

Towns and cities go on expanding in an un-coordinated fashion. Assumptions made in design of pipe network go astray in course of time. Hence it becomes necessary to increase water supply in the pipe lines without increasing diameter. This is feasible only by increasing velocity of flow which gives rise to increasing losses, the velocity is increased by shutting of some parts of network thus increasing effectively pressure. Thus the network is now activated in parts resulting in imntermittent supply.

An underground reservoir is a must wherever the supply is intermittent. By storage of water in the underground tank water supply within given area or premises can be ensured round the clock. The water stored in the underground tank is utilised when inflow from the mains supply is less than the outgo by way of consumption. This happens when either the pressure in the mains is low during heavy withdrawl period or in general the water supply timings from corporation do not tally with the consumption pattern. For example, the water pressure and quantity in the municipal mains may be quite good during night time say from 12 midnight to 5 a.m. when other industrial requirements are low. To expect the populace to be up and filling their water cisterns during this period would be inappropriate. Under such circumstances, water supply from mains would fill the underground tank and water can be pumped during the day time when water is needed.

Location of underground reservoir should be such that it could get easily filled by from municipal mains. This is important when water supply pressure in the mains is low. The inflow of water is a function of diameter of inflow pipe and the pressure. For the same diameter if pressure is less the inflow will be less. The length of pipe line from the municipal mains to the underground tank is also of importance. High frictional loss will result in the pipeline either due to longer length or with many bends and these losses will affect adversely the ultimate quantity of water received in the tank.

The location of underground tank has to be chosen carefully with reference to the soil characteristics. A rocky strata would mean high expenses of construction. Filled up soil would mean uneven bearing capacity of soil which any result in tilting of tank. While locating the underground tank care should be taken to find out whether ground water is likely to rise above the ground level at any time. The underground tank top will have to be sufficiently above such level to avoid contamination by storm water and ground water.

While locating the underground water tank, which is utilised for fire fighting purposes approachability of municipal Fire Engine should also be taken into account.

Underground tank should be so located that it is located sufficiently away from all foul areas and contaminants. Thus an underground tank should not be located near to a soakage pit, septic tank, sewer line and municipal rubbish pit etc.

While locating the underground tank possibility of future expansion (if needed) should also be taken into account. It is not necessary that the underground tank is constructed of high capacity to cater for future expansion. Capacity of an underground sump can be easily expanded in future if in the sump a valve is kept at sufficiently low level which can serve as an interconnecting valve between old and new sump. This valve should be of sufficient size to allow adequate flow of water.

The underground reservoir should be absolutely watertight. The danger is of pollution from subsoil water or any other less satisfactory water contaminating the water supply.

From security considerations, it is absolutely necessary that the underground tank is fenced properly so that tampering of water supply by undesirable or/and unauthorised people does not result.

Underground tank should be watertight, light-tight, fly, mosquito and insect proof.

An underground tank is required to be cleaned at an interval of 3 months. Silt and other insoluble contaminants should not be allowed to remain in the tank for a long period. Cleaning operations can be carried out by emptying the tank fully and resorting to manual labour for cleaning or a special pump which will suck out a large amount of silt at the tank bottom through a special suction valve is used. Afterwards tank has to be fully disinfected before it is filled up again. Ordinary centrifugal pump is not capable of handling solids hence for the body of water below the foot valve level a special pump which can accept solids has to be used.

Calculation of capacity of underground reservoir depends on the following factors:

1. The rate of inflow of water.
2. The rate of outflow needed.

Capacity of underground tank should be such that it is able to cater for difference between the outflow and inflow during peak hours of consumption and it is in a position to store sufficient quantity of water when outflow is less than inflow till next peak outflow. For example, if the water supply from city mains is during 12 midnight to 5 O'clock in the morning, almost the entire quantity of water consumption in a day of 24 hours will have to be stored as consumption during these hours would be almost negligible. If however the water supply form municipal mains is also concurrent with the peak hours of drawl of water say from 5 a.m. to 12 noon and 4 p.m. to 8 p.m. the water required to be stored in the underground tank would be for the difference between outflow and inflow. Thus assuming a constant inflow of 20000 litres/hour and outflow of 30000 litres/hour for 11 hours a capacity of $11 \times 10000 = 110000$ litres is needed.

Thus it involves application of famous leaky tank example in secondary schools where student is asked to work out time when a tank of given capacity would get filled completely having given rate of inflow, rate of outflow and capacity of tank. The problem is still difficult in case of underground tank because the rates of inflow would vary from day to day. Rate of outflow would also vary. Pattern of consumption would also change as per seasons of heat and cold. Therefore, a good deal of great accuracy in calculation is not needed but application of common sense would be called for as no rigid rules can be laid down. Normally, 24 hours consumption is the capacity decided to cater for a prolonged shutdown in municipal supply.

16. OVERHEAD TANKS ON BUILDINGS

Water supply in building through overhead terrace tanks is normally adopted in India.

Down Feed System

In this system, the tank is provided on the terrace. A downtake pipe is taken out from the tank and laid out horizontally as a ring main on the terrace to carry the designed peak load. The down pipes to the individual consumer's take off from the ring main is laid on terrace.

Where in an overhead tank system a loop line is laid on terrace, the pressure in the loop line at the time of peak demand should not become negtive. A negative pressure may result because the loop line will work with the pressure of level difference between the water in the tank and the loop line level. This would be between 1 metre to at best 2 metres. And the downtakes from the loop line have the height of building as the head. Thus in a 20 metre high building, it would be approximately 2 kg/cm^2. Thus the water flow would be very high in the downtake if the diameter of loop line equals downtake pipe. The loop line would be working at 0.1 to 0.2 kg/cm^2. Thus a negative pressure at the junction of loop line with downtake would result which can lead to air lock.

Vertical down pipe will have to be zoned so that the water pressure is not excessive giving rise to high velocities and trouble at joints due to increase in water pressure on account of water hammer. Normally the zoning is of 8-10 metres of height. In the case of high rise building, the zoning can be done by either a break water tank system or zonal tank system wherein at 8 to 10 metres height zonal tanks are situated.

Overhead tank on the terrace and the down take pipes should be so placed that for most of the time it is in shade. When exposed to sun, the temperature of water especially in M.S. or G.I. water tank can be uncomfortably high. The water vapour can also give rise to a vapour lock. Exposed tanks are also subjected to variation in temperature on the sun side and shade side. This temperature variation may give rise to unnecessary temperature stresses and may give rise to cracking due to thermal stresses.

The tank should have sufficient clearance at bottom so that the scour valve could be operated. There is a tendency of some architects, engineers to place these tanks directly on the terrace slab on the ground that the tank should not be higher than parapat height. This may give rise to dampness in terrace as the tank bottom may not remain leakproof all throughout its life. When the tanks are placed in an enclosed space, there would be sufficient clearance at top so that manhole at top can be opened and the tank serviced.

Placement of tanks in odd position should be avoided as these tanks are required to be cleaned once in three months. Storage tank should be mosquito proof vermin proof. The normal overflow pipe without a cover can attract small birds, lizards etc. The manhole should be tight fitting and lockable. Withdrawl of water through buckets should be stopped as such operation may contaminate the supply.

Due to the moisture hardy trees like pipal etc get established near the tank in nooks and corners. The root system of these trees damages the water tightness of tank and the terrace. Sharp eye has to be kept for all such vegetation moss, etc.

Normally, separate tanks should be provided for drinking purposes and for flushing purposes. When separate tanks are not feasible at least the tank should be compartmentalised with through non communicating wall. Not that pollution would take place if non compartmentalised but the flushing of W.C. is required all the 24 hours. If water is not available for all the time for flushing malodourous and unhealthy sanitary conditions would develop which could be dangerous where as water for cultinary purposes could be stored in kitchen etc.

The capacity of overhead tank will depend upon the pattern and hours of consumption and that of pumping or inflow. A histogram over 24 hours has to be worked out for inflow and outflow characteristics.

The storage requirements are calculated on the basis of water requirements per capita per day subject to certain minimum basis storage based on the number of fitments provided like taps, showers, W.Cs bath tube etc. fed from the system. These basic storage requirements are as follows:

	Classification	*Requirement*
1.	Tenements having common conveniences.	900 litres net per W.C. seat.
2.	Residential premises other than tenements.	270 litres net per one W.C. seat and 180 litres for additional W.C. seat in the same flat.
3.	Factories, workshops etc.	900 litres per W.C. seat and 180 litres per urinal seat.
4.	Public assembly halls etc.	900 litres per W.C. seat and 350 litres per urinal.
5.	*Domestic storage*	
	(a) Premises occupied as tenements with common conveniences.	500 litres per tenement.
	(b) Premises occupied as flats etc.	800 litres per tenement.

The above storage may be provided, provided it is not less than storage calculated on the number of fittings as below:

Taps	....	70 litres each
Showers	....	135 litres each
Bath tubs	....	200 litres.

The capacity of an overhead tank is decided through a histogram of consumption. The capacity can be calculated on the basis of mass diagrams drawn for incoming water and outgoing water. While calculating capacity of overhead tank availability of electricity for pumping, pumping rate and pumping shift should also be considered.

A sample calculation for the determination of capacity of overhead reservoir could be as follows:

(a) *Consumption pattern*

If "A" is average hourly demand of water calculated over 24 hours period and if time and consumption pattern over is as follows:

Time	*Consumption of "A"*
11 P.M. to 6 A.M.	10% A
6 A.M. to 10 A.M.	250% A
10 A.M. to 4 P.M.	Average hourly demand "A"
4 P.M. to 8 P.M.	145% A
8 P.M. to 11 P.M.	50% of "A"

(b) Pumping rate = 3 A per hour

(c) Pumping timing = 6 A.M. to 2 P.M.

Period in hour	*Hourly demand and hours*	*Cumulative demand*	*Cumulative pumping*	*Deficit or surplus*
6 a.m. to 10 a.m.	2.50 A × 4 = 10A	10A	3A ××4 = 12 A	+2A
10 a.m. to 2 p.m.	A × 4 = 4A	14A	3A × 4 = 12A	+10A
2 p.m. to 4 p.m.	A × 2 = 2A	16A		+8A
4 p.M. to 8 p.m.	1.45A × 4 = 5.8A	21.8A		+2.2A
8 p.m. to 11 p.m.	0.5 × 3 = 1.5A	23.A		+0.7A
11 p.m. to 6 a.m.	0.1 × 7 = 0.7A	24A	–	–

It is clear that the tank should have a capacity of 10A in this case and tank will be empty completely by 6 a.m.

The above example is illustrative of methodology to be adopted for fixing rationally capacity of the overhead tank.

Height of the overhead tank will be decided by the water mains network design and the residual pressure.

The overhead tank is a sensitive spot therefore it should be so located and fenced then unauthorised elements can not have an access.

17. ALGAE IN WATER TANKS

Algae give rise to a variety of troubles in water suplies. They impart characteristics odours and taste to the water. They die and decay causing acute malodour trouble in the water.

Algae growth is influenced by a number of factors such as nutrients in the water, availability of the sunlight, the reservoir shape and the temperature. The best course of prevention would be to reduce the food supply, change environment and exclude the sunlight. It is possible to cover service reservoirs and small wells to exclude sunlight. With the temperature of 15 to 20 degree centrigrade blue green and a green algae make substantial growth. Shallow reservoirs are more favourable for algae growth than the deep reservoirs, because the decayed matter closer to the surface stimulates algaeial growth. Irregular margins and shallow areas encourage the growth of algae.

The algae growth is measured by a density which is expressed in terms of area which denote the number of organisms in a square of size of 20 microns. Now, when the total count reaches or exceeds 300 areal units, it has to be treated with algaecides.

Algae may be killed by treating the water with suitable chemicals. However, the procedure of allowing algae to establish themselves and then adopting algaecidal measures has disadvantages as the dosage of chemicals is required to be more. The dead algae decay and produce odour problems and the dead algae also provide a food for the second crop which makes it more prolific. Therefore, it is necessary to take all possible measures to discourage the growth of algae by suitable designs of reservoir and to reserve the use of algaecides as avoidable treatment.

The most common algaecide is copper sulphate and its action is due to the copper ion which acts as a direct protoplasmic poison. The reaction is a function of concentration of chemical and the time of exposure of the algaecal to the action of copper. The copper carbonate reacts with the bicarbonates in the water to form a basic copper carbonate which decomposes to form copper hydrate. The copper carbonate is almost insoluble in water, therefore, the copper sulphate as algaecide is effective when the temperature of water is proper and within its hardness the copper which gets added. Though copper sulphate is rendered inactive in a shortwhile, it is both an advantage and a disadvantage. It is an advantage because, content of the copper in the water rapidly gets reduced to levels below those at which copper is toxic to human beings by mere afflux of time and without any elaborate treatment for removal of the excess copper. It is a disadvantage as high dosages are needed. The dosages of copper sulphate required to kill algae are generally expressed in terms of concentration in miligram of the copper sulphate per litre. The quantity of copper sulphate is worked out on the basis of available copper at 1/5th of the weight of the copper sulphate. The lethal dosage to most of the organism are in the range of 0.1 to 0.5 miligram per litre. The copper sulphate is generally applied by enclosing in gunny bags containing the crystals. The crystals dissolve readily and the solution gets mixed with the water. When the algaecide of copper sulphate is utilised the secondary growth can be very fast therefore the action would be to repeat the treatment at intervals and to employ higher dosage of algaecides during the subsequent treatment.

Chlorine is also an effective algaecide. It has got toxic effect and causes death and disintegration of algae. The dosage of the chlorine varies from 0.3 to 2 miligrams per litre. Small reservoir are normally treated by applying a slurry of bleaching powder at the incoming end or by providing a towing bags with the bleaching powder.

Bacterial Corrosion

Several bacteria like sulphate reducing bacteria and iron consuming bacteria, sulphate bacteria and other micro organisation are responsible for bacterial corrosion. Stagnation of water as in dead ends gives rise to the development of anaerobic conditions with the production of hydrogen sulphides from sulphates in the water. These hydrogen sulphides combine with the pipe metal forming black deposits of metal sulphides which are noticed when the dead ends are flushed. Iron bacteria grow utilising the energy available in the oxidation of the metallic iron thus corroding material characteristic spongy masses that come out handpumps, tubewells are the result of this growth. Iron bacteria troubles in the tubewells can be overcome by treating the well by concentrated bleaching powder solution of 50 miligram per litre as Cl_2 and a contact period of 6 hours. It is necessary to flush out dead ends periodically so that stagnation does not take place for periods more than a month. After flushing, the dead ends, have to be disinfected by chlorine.

Chlorine compounds are most commonly utilised for disinfection of water mains. The strength of the disinfective solution should be much higher than normally utilised for water chlorination. Under normal circumstances a strength of 10 miligram per litre is recommended for a contact period of 24 hours. Application for 24 hours contact period is necessary when the chlorine has to penetrate through the organic matter coating the inner surface. In emergencies, when it is not possible to have the sections of the water supply line out of service for a long time, period of contact can be shortened by increasing the strength of the solution. Thus for a contact period of 1 hour the strength of the solution varies between 120 to 240 miligrams a litre. When strong solutions are utilised, particular attention should be paid its removal from the mains after the completion of disinfections, as illness and discomfort will result from using highly chlorinated water and corrosive action of the chlorine may damage the pipe, valves, hydrants and other plumbing. Quantity of the bleaching powder (25% available chlorine) to provide a concentration of 20 miligrams per litre in a 100 metre length of pipe line is for 75 mm pipe line = 37 grams, 100 mm pipe lines = 65 grams, 150 mm dimeter = 146 grams.

18. PUMPS

General

In a water supply system, it is necessary to inject external energy into the system to (a) compensate for the inherent friction loss associated with the piping network and (b) lift the water from lower to higher levels. This external energy would increase the pressure energy of the flowing liquid and maintain desired quantum of flow at a particular point. A 'pump' is a mechanical device meant to impart this energy to the system through conversion of mechanical energy into hydraulic energy.

A single pump may handle millions of litres of water daily with an over all loss in pumping less than 10 percent of energy supplied to it. High pressure pumps may operate again heads of over 3,000 metres.

The pumping action of all pumps is based on the same general principle. If a pump is to lift water from well/sump, it is first-necessary to exhaust the air from its working parts and also the suction length of piping. Once a partial vacuum is created within the pump, the pressure of the atmosphere on the surfaces of water in the well/sump will push it up into the evacuated chamber. Hence it will be trapped or caught by the moving member of the pump to be forced out through the discharge opening. This creation of vacuum required in all type of pumps is known as priming.

Maximum Suction Possible

Theoretically, at sea level a pump can lift water to a height equivalent to the atmospheric pressure. This, however, would require a perfect vacuum and frictionless suction line. Since these do not exist, reciprocating pump must be located within about 7 to 8 metres of the surface of the water, and a centrifugal pump, because of its slightly less positive action on creating vacuum, must not be more than about 6 metres above the surface of supply. Basic parameter known as "Net positive Suction Head" is the limiting factor in individual design as explained later in this section.

Type of Pumps

Pumps appear in a multitude of design, but most of them may be classified on the basis of principle of operation into following classes:

(i) Centrifugal Pumps
(ii) Propellar Pumps
(iii) Mixed Flow Pumps
(iv) Peripheral Pumps
(v) Rotary Pumps
(vi) Reciprocating Pumps

Applications

Centrifugal Pumps (Horizontal)

This type of pump has been perfected in design and improved in efficiency. As a result it is now used in practically all classes of pumping services. It consists of an impellar with an intake at its centre so arranged that, when it is rotated it will discharge liquid by centrifugal force into the casing around impellar leaving at a high velocity and pressure. Casing slows down the liquid gradually, thus converting the velocity head created by the impellar to the pressure head needed in the discharge pipe.

In multistage centrifugal pumps, the stages of pumps depend upon the number of impellars in a single casing, which is so designed that the discharge of one is the suction for the next and so on. Depending upon the head through which water is pushed through, the number of stages of a centrifugal pump may be decided.

A properly selected single stage horizontal centrifugal pump can give as high efficiency as 75 to 80%. The efficiency of multistage pumps will be lower depending upon the number of stages.

Advantages for Selection of Centrifugal Pumps

1. It can be directly coupled with an electric motor or a steam turbine or a diesel engine.
2. Compactness and low cost in large sizes.
3. Smooth flow of liquid through the pump and uniform pressure in the discharge pipeline.
4. In general increase in head reduces the power required, and hence by closing the discharge line, motor is not overloaded. The absence of valves and packedplungers or pistons, such as required in reciprocating pumps, allows the special types of Centrifugal pumps to handle fluid carrying solid matter.

Modified Centrifugal Pumps Turbine Pumps

It is a vertical-shaft centrifugal pump with its rotating impellers suspended from the pump head throu'h a discharge column. It is disigned primarily to deliver water from the well of small diameter. It is almost universally used in wells in areas where the ground-water level is below the suction limit of ordinary centrifugal pumps (about 6 metres).

The driving element incase of turbine pumps remains at the surface of the ground. The pumping element is located down in the well below the surface of water and the discharge column connects the driving element with the pumping element giving a support for the vertical line shaft bearing. Efficiency of these pumps is high but generally it is lower than the efficiency of horizontal centrifugal pumps. These pumps are not prone to easy installation and maintenance. The verticality of bore to very high tolerance is a primary requirement for installation of this type of pump.

Submersible Pumps

This is a modified version of deep well turbine pump and is used with great success.

In this type of pump, pumping element is directly connected to a submersible vertical water cooled/water filled electric motor. The compact assembly thus formed operates below the surface of water in the well. Delivery of water to the surface is through riser pipe on which the assembly is suspended and the electric current is conducted to the motor through a waterproof cable. The submersible pump is practically noiseless, easily installed and the intermediate bearing and larger diameter discharge column of the ordinary deep well turbine pumps are eliminated. A properly selected submersible pump can give high efficiency. As the spump is water cooled it would get over heated if run in dry environment. Even few minutes ,of such dry run will spoil the pump.

For its installation in the well, (tubewell) it may be ensured that it will supply the required discharge under all conditions because of level in the well (tubewell) may drop when the pump is in operation and due to this reason the submersible pump must be installed at a depth, where it will always be submerged in water. The water level in the summer months may be far below the level during the monsoon. The draw down due to pumping should be ascertained from the lowest level during the summer before determining the depth to which the pump is to be installed. Water level guards and/or switches are generally provided and connected in the control circuits of these pumps to guard against dry running.

The exact verticality of bore is not a very important factor for installation of these type of pumps. If it is possible to lower the pump and motor assembly bore is good enough vertical.

Jet Pumps

These are also horizontal centrifugal pumps. In the suction line a water jetting assembly is introduced thus it can draw water from larger depths due to the action of jet assembly submerged in water than what is possible in the installation of centrifugal pump. Part of the water from the delivery side of pump is drawn back from the casing to the submerged assembly for the operation the venturi nozzle creating vacuum and pushing water from the well with high pressure into the suction line. Certain minimum pressure depending upon the size is required for the operation of the Jet assembly which also governs the delivery head obtainable.

Due to its very design, there are limitations in the discharge available from such pumps and the efficiency of these pumps is as low as 30 to 35 per cent. These can be installed away from the source (bore well/open well) and easy to install and maintain. Use is thus limited to small pumping requirements where easy maintenance is the main criteria.

Propeller Pumps

For handling large quantities of water at heads below the efficient range of centrifugal pumps, propeller pumps are highly suitable. This is a straight axial flow pump which develops most its head by the propelling or lifting action of the vanes on liquid. The blades in some propeller pumps are made adjustable for different heads.

Propeller Pumps are used for:

(a) Land drainage
(b) Irrigation
(c) Storm water disposal
(d) Low-head or primary municipal pumping
(e) Unwatering of excavations

(f) Coffer dams and in many other services where large volumes at low head are required to be pumped.

Mixed-flow Pumps

It is a combination of centrifugal and propeller pump. Its head is imparted to the liquid partly by centrifugal force and partly by lift of vanes on the liquid.

These are used where the desired capacity of the pump is above that of ordinary centrifugal pump and below that of propeller pump. It is best suited for operating heads which are intermediate between the low-head propeller pumps and the higher head centrifugal pumps.

Peripheral Pumps

In peripheral pumps the fluid is pumped by vanes and total head is developed by recirculating the liquid through series of rotating vanes. It is used in Dairy Industry. Peripheral pumps can be designed so that they can be disassembled easily without disturbing the intake or discharge connections. This makes cleaning a quick and simple task. Pumps of this type used for handling milk, cream and ice-cream usually have a clamped casing, and they can be taken apart for cleaning without much effort.

Self-Priming Pumps

Most of these pumps require priming of the suction lines which means completely filling the suction side of the pump and suction pipes upto foot valve with water with no air inside. If air is trapped then with the vacuum created by running of pump it expands and cut off water flow. To avoid such a situation either there are methods of priming the suction lines or self priming pumps are used. Priming of suction line can be done through a suction cup where water can be poured till it overflows or a pipe line is connected to a small tank of water or a bye pass from the delivery line is provided. Either by opening byepass or the small tank the suction line is filled with water completely.

In a self priming pump there is a small reservoir of water inside pump and initially a mixture of water and air will be pumped out, in course of running for few minutes air will be evacuated and the suction to the pump will be established and pump would now be capable of pumping.

Rotatory Pumps/Rotary Pumps

Rotatory pumps resemble centrifugal pumps somewhat in exterior appearance but their operation corresponds more nearly to reciprocating pumps and have positive displacement which means that fluid is delivered to the discharge pipe in successive isolated quantities under pressure but the interval is kept so short that the delivery to the discharge pipe may seem to be almost continuous.

The main advantage of rotary pumps over reciprocating pumps are as under:

(a) These deliver an almost continuous flow i.e., practically free from pulsations and large air chambers to absorb the shock of intermittent discharge are not required.

(b) Simple in construction, there are no valve to be opened or closed with each successive quantity delivered.

(c) Occupy less space for a given duty.

(d) Easy to install and maintain.

Applications

(a) To pump almost any fluid that is free from abrasive materials.

(b) As the rotary pumps are displacement pumps, they are suitable for handling thick and viscous liquids, such as vegetable oils, greases, soaps, fuel oils, tars pitch, heavy lubricating oils and pressure oils in hydraulically operated governors, cranes, presses; elevators and so on. Because they have close mechanical clearance between parts, there is very little loss due to slip when these liquids of high viscocity are being pumped.

(c) Rotary pumps are not limited to the pumping of viscous liquids alone but are also widely used in pumping of lighter liquids, with high vapour pressure such as gasoline, benzene, gas oils, butane etc. Rotary pump being self priming because of its positive displacement action, usually provides insurance against interruption of pumping where these liquids are being handled.
The volumetric efficiency of a rotary/reciprocating pump (the ratio of the actual displacement to the theoretical displacement) increases as the viscosity increases because a more viscous liquid forms a better seal.

(d) Rotary pumps are in use in nearly every industry. They are used in oil refineries, soap factories, breweries distilleries, wineries and in all food processing plants.

Reciprocating Pumps

These pumps, like rotary pumps, have position displacement. Since every stroke of a reciprocating piston means definite quantity of liquid pumped, the discharge of pump will depend directly on its speed. Also since the delivery is made in successively isolated quantities, the discharge is pulsating. Making it double-acting helps to smoothen out the flow. In most installations, air chamber is connected on the discharge side of the pump to help iron as the pressure surges.

It is used to handle liquid containing gritt or abrasive materials.

Pumps Characteristic Curves

A pump is usually disigned for one speed, flow rate and head. But in actual practice, the flow rate changes due to varing heads. Due to different flow rates, the value of velocity of liquid through the impeller will be changed as a result the velocity of whirl changes, thereby changing the head developed by the pump and at the same time losses increase or decrease which ultimately affect the efficiency of the pump. In order to ascertain performance of a pump, under varying conditions, tests are performed and their results are plotted. The curves, thus obtained are known as characteristic curves of the pump.

Following are the type of curves usually dealt with in the case of centrifugal pumps:

(a) Main operative characteristics.
(b) Constant efficiency curves.
(c) Constant head and constant discharge curves.

(a) (i) Main Characteristics

In order to obtain the characteristics curve, the pump is operated at different speeds. Flow rate 'Q' is varied by means of a delivery valve and for different values of 'Q' the corresponding values of manometric head 'Hm', shaft horsepower HI, and overall efficiency are measured. The value is plotted as discharge 'Q' verses manometric head 'Hm', discharge 'Q' verses horse power 'HI', discharge 'Q' verses overall efficiency, which represent the main characteristics of a pump.

(a) (ii) Operating Characteristics

Pump is normally required to run at a constant speed, which is its design speed, (same as the speed of driving motor). Main characteristics hich correspond to the designed speed is mostly used in the operation of a pump and is therefore known as the normal (or designed) head and the designed discharge of a pump. From these characteristics it is possible to determine whether the pump will handle the necessary quantity of a water against the desired head and what will happen if the head is increased or decreased. The discharge verse Horse Power curve will show, what size of motor will be required to operate the pump at the required conditions and whether or not the motor will be overloaded under any other operating conditions. Usually 10 to 15 per cent buffer capacity in motors is desirable.

(b) Constant Efficiency Curves

These curves are useful in determining the optimum range of operation of a pump at a particular efficiency. The effect of change in speed on the efficiency can also be easily known from these curves.

(c) Constant Head and Constant Disharge Curves

These curves are helpful in finding out the performance of a variable speed pump. These curves can give speeds, required to discharge varying quantity of liquid at a constant head and to discharge a fixed quantity of liquid at different heads. Head varies as square of speed with constant discharge and discharge varies in direct proportion to speed with constant head. Power accordingly varies in proportion to cube of speed.

19. FACTORS AFFECTIVE PUMP PERFORMANCE

(a) Specific Gravity

A pump delivers the same quantity by volume independent of specific gravity but the quantity by weight will be proportional to the specific gravity. While the efficiency is unaffected by the specific gravity of the liquid pumped, the power absorbed for pumping is directly proportional to it.

The permissible suction lift also varies with specific gravity. The height of a column of a liquid corresponding to the atmospheric pressure is inversely proportional to the specific gravity and the suction lift will vary accordingly.

(b) Temperature

Temperature affects (i) specific gravity, and the performance curves, will be affected. (ii) the viscosity of the liquid at the pumping temperature. (iii) vapour pressure and hence the amount of required net positive suction head will depnd on ambient normal temperature correction to the suction head will be needed to be carried out at high ambient temperature.

(c) Viscosity

Viscosity affects the capacity and head. It increases, the power requirement due to friction losses involved and consequently reduces the efficiency. Viscosity affects the suction lift of the pump. The standard performance figure for a pump are calculated with respect to water in order to get the corresponding performance figures. When handling a liquid of known viscosity some corrections have to be applied as per correction charts available for the purpose.

(d) Cavitation

A pump working under excessive suction lift which causes a reduction in capacity, noisy operation, vibration and erosion and pitting of the impeller and other parts of the pump, is said to be in cavitation. Cavitation is that phenomenon whereby liquid is vaporized by reduction of the pressure below the vapour pressure of vapour tension point of the liquid. The bubbles of vapour so formed at the eye of the impeller, collapse. The collapse of the vapour bubbles and the resultant rush in of liquid into the cavities or spaces left by collapse causes very high local pressures resulting in serious erosion of the solid surfaces. The flow is considerably disturbed by the damage of flow passages and the efficiency is reduced.

The cavitation is also caused by the release of dissolved air in water due to reduction in pressure, forming air pockets or bubbles in the liquid. This is termed as air cavitation in contrast to vapour cavitation explained above. Though air cavitation reduces efficiency but is less damaging than vapour cavitation.

(d) Net Positive Suction Head (NPSH)

This is the head required to make the liquid flow through the suction pipe to the impeller. A distinction is to be made between the required NPSH and the available NPSH. The required NPSH is a function of pump design, its speed and capacity and is to be indicated by the manufacturer of the pump. The available NPSH is the local suction head in pump installation and should be more than the required NPSH for cavitation free operation.

Selection of Pumps for Water Supply Schemes

Basically head and required discharge are the two factors needed to decide on the type and capacity of a pump. Lest the problem should look too simple, it must be added that there is a number of important factors to be considered and pitfalls clearly identified to arrive at the most suitable choice. More often than not, the choice itself may fall on more than one type, model and size depending upon the overlapping characteristics and other factors. An extremely important consideration is the design of water supply system itself which must be examined thoroughly for possible adjustments/revisions needed to suit an optimum choice for achieving overall economy. It is to be realised that in the case of a pump, the most important factor is its running cost and hence its efficiency is the first criteria whereas, the initial investment is the overriding factor in the case of other components. The choice has, therefore, to be optimised, keeping this in mind. While it is assumed that once final data is arrived at, there should be no difficulty in making a choice based on characteristic curves and other details made available by manufacturers of pumps, some of the more important aspects which should be considered before making a selection are—

(a) Basic head components data is to be available and also the effect of system losses on the total head and whether it is overriding; other parameters such as number and size of overhead tanks, rate of consumption, sizes of pipelines are to be considered for this purpose so as to decide on the rate and schedule of pumping. If permitted by other factors such as peak demand, simultaneous pumping to all the receiving tanks will be more economical as it will give minimum friction losses. This, however, may not be feasible with different heights, capacities and consumptions in the case of more than one tank.

(b) Optimum, minimum and maximum pump discharge obtainable and role of system net work (whether critical or not) in determining these limits. It is to be borne in mind that if the head available is lower than calculated for selection, while the discharge will increase with or without overloading the motor but the efficiency will be reduced and running may be uneconomical and even risky, apart, from energy lost due to higher velocity. On the other hand, if head obtainable is higher than calculated the discharge will be reduced with motor underloaded but the efficiency will be again reduced. In the case of a critical choice with no sacrifice in discharge permitted, the head calculations should be a bit liberal and possible overload should be covered by higher motor rating. In any case, it will be preferable to operate the pump close to the maximum efficiency point.

(c) SUCTION head must ensure cavitation free operation in the case of centrifugal pumps.

(d) Buffer capacity in the rating of the motor to be provided (atleast 10 to 15%). For this purpose if it is necessary to select next higher size, its effect on other parameters is to be examined. It may be preferable to go only for a higher size motor as explained in (b) above.

(e) In the case of parallel running of pumps, the effect of higher discharge through common header and delivery line is to be considered for selecting a pump. Such a situation will have the effect of increasing the head and the pump must be capable of catering to it close to the maximum efficiency point. This may not be always possible without increasing the size of piping system, thereby increasing the cost and hence a balance has to be struck to achieve overall economy taking into consideration the frequency of such parallel running.

(f) Where the pumps are located at different points feeding either a common net work or a single point through a common net work, more precise calculations would be necessary. Different pumps in such a case are likely to affect the delivery head of others and pressure at critical points in the system has to be equalised for optimum choice of pump head. This is a very ticklish problem in the case of jet pumps where the head generated is predecided. Radial feeds should be preferred in such cases with pumps selected accordingly unless the cost of pipe line prohibits this.

(g) The voltage conditions available and whether stabiliser, single phasing preventer and other protective equipment would be necessary here also to be considered, (IS:585 give voltage limits of + 10% for the equipment to be connected on medium voltage system.)

(h) Due consideration is also to be given for standby capacity requirements individually or collectively for a number of installations in an area, ease of maintenance and overhauling, replaceability and availability of spare parts, outage time and its effects on the service as a whole. Normally electric motor driven pumps are to be used where electricity is available but the need for diesel engine driven pumps or provision of standby generators are also to be considered taking the importance of service and frequency of failure of power supply into account.

(i) Due consideration should be given to the type of motor frame viz. SPDP or TETC. SPDP frames are economical where damp conditions do not prevail.

(j) The speed of motor is also important. Here also local bye-laws are required to be checked.

20. PROCUREMENT OF PUMPS

(A) Centrifugal Pumps

Information to be furnished by the purchaser

When enquiring or ordering pumps, the user must furnish the following information to the prospective supplier

(a) Name of purchaser
(b) Address
(c) Installation site
(d) Number of pumps required
(e) Spare parts required
(f) Type of drive (electric motor/internal combustion engine)
(g) Optional fittings required
(h) Pump operating conditions:
  (1) Capacity..........litres per minute, and
  (2) Total head..........metres

If total head is not known, then details of the following shall be provided.

(i) Static head
  (1) Minimum depth of water..........metres from pump level.
  (2) Variation in water level..........metres.
  (3) Ground level to maximum water depth..........metres.
  (4) Ground level to delivery point..........metres.
  (5) Pressure in the suction tank..........kg/cm^2.
  (6) Pressure in the delivery tank..........kg/cm^2.

(ii) Pipes and Fittings
  (1) Length and size of suction pipe..........metres diameter in mm
  (2) Numbers and sizes of bends, tees valves and other fittings on the suction side.
  (3) Length and size of delivery pipe..........metres diameter in mm.
  (4) Numbers and sizes of bends, tees valves and other fittings on the delivery side.
  (5) Material and condition of pipes and fittings.
  (6) Sketch of pipeline.

(j) Drive arrangement—This can be any of the following
  (1) Direct through coupling,
  (2) Flat/Vee belt,
  (3) Gear,
  (4) Propeller or splicer shaft, and
  (5) Hydraulic/Magnetic coupling.
(k) Drive data—This can be any of the following
  (1) Electric Drive:
    (i) Type of current (AC/DC, single phase/three phase),
    (ii) Frequency (cycles per second)
    (iii) Voltage,
    (iv) Preferred speed in r.p.m.,
    (v) Rating.
(l) If pump is to be coupled to an existing prime mover complete details of prime mover are to be given.
(m) Site conditions:
  (1) Height above mean sea level in metres,

(2) Maximum and minimum temperature during the year (^{0}).
(3) Humidity (percent).
(4) Nature of atmosphere.
(5) Details of quality of water.
(6) Water free from sand or not, and
(7) Water corrosive or not.

(n) Any other information or requirement.
Under this the purchaser is required to give metallurgical requirement of pump parts i.e. of casing, impeller, sleeves, bearing, and shaft dependings upon the physical/chemical properties of liquid to be pumped.

21. TESTING OF PUMPS

Testing of pumps may be carried out as per IS : 1520 as detailed below:

Pump Tests are Made to Determine the Following:

(a) The discharge against a specified head when running at a specified speed under a specified suction lift or head,
(b) The power absorbed by the pump at the pump shaft (BI) under the above specified conditions, and
(c) Efficiency of the pump under the above specified conditions.

Observations During Pump Test

During the whole period of the pump test, careful observations shall be made in regard to the following:

(a) Undue shock, hammering, vibrations or other mechanical defects;
(b) Bearing temperature, which shall not exceed the limits specified by the manufacturer;
(c) Lubrication of the bearings;
(d) Operation of stuffing box and water sealing device;
(e) Operation of the balancing device in multi-stage pumps, when provided; and
(f) Any loss of discharge between the pump and the point of measurement of discharge.

Unless otherwise specifically agreed to between the purchaser and the supplier, the temperature of the water during the test should not exceed 30°C.

The water to be handled should be reasonably free from air and gases.

Duration of Test

The duration of test should be sufficient to secure accurate and consistent results. To verify the mechanical conditions, of the pump, it shall be run continuously for not less than one hour.

Where a specification covers a range of performance, a minimum of five sets of readings shall be taken approximately equidistant on the characteristic curve.

Measurement Speed

The speed should be measured by a revolution counter or by an accurately calibrated Tachometer, or by means of Stroboscopic arrangement.

Effect of Variation in Speed

When the speed during the test is within ± 5% of the specified speed, the following relations should be taken into account for finding the corresponding discharge, head and power at the specified speed:

(a) $$\frac{\text{Actual discharge}}{\text{Specified discharge}} = \frac{\text{Actual speed}}{\text{Specified speed}}$$

(b) $$\frac{\text{Actual discharge}}{\text{Specified head}} = \left(\frac{\text{Actual speed}}{\text{Specified speed}}\right)^2$$

(c) Assuming the efficiency curve to be the same,

$$\frac{\text{Actual power}}{\text{Specified power}} = \left(\frac{\text{Actual speed}}{\text{Specified speed}}\right)^3$$

Measurement of Discharge

The discharge of the pump may be measured by means of volumetric tank, vee notch, rectangular weir, standard venturimeter, pitot tube, orifice plate or a water meter. The method adopted for discharge measurement shall be suitable, for the size of the pump, its duty and situation. The pump manufacturer shall, if required, give evidence of the proper calibration of the apparatus used.

Volumetric Method

The water should be pumped directly into one or more vessels of known or easily measurable capacity by volume or weight, the time to fill such vessels carefully noted and the discharge calculated.

Limit of Accuracy

The accuracy of the result by this method will depnd on the length of time for which the flow is recorded, the accuracy of the stop watch as well as the method of measuring the height of water in the tank of given cross section. Provided, every precaution is taken and the rise and fall is not less than 300 mm, this method will give discharge correct to within + 1%.

Measurement of Head

In the laboratory test, the head is created artificially by throttling the sluice valve placed beyond the delivery flange of pump, at least six diameters downstream of the pressure gauge connection.

The standard method of measuring head should employ a water column gauge glass giving a direct or surface elevation. Where this cannot be used, indirect methods may be employed, such as the use of mercury or other fluid gauge or a Bourden type gauge.

It is recommended that water or mercury manometers be used in preference to Bourden type gauges when the head to be measured is 7.5 m or less.

22. GAUGES—PRECAUTIONS AND CONNECTIONS

When water columns are used, care should be taken to avoid errors due to the difference between the temperature of the water in the gauge connection and that of the water in the pump by frequently draining the connection or determining the necessary correction.

When Bourden type gauges are used, they should be of suitable range for the heads to be measured (the gauge range should be about twice the maximum head to be measured). It is recommended that the drain cocks be placed immediately below the gauges and that frequent tests be made to determine whether pipe connections of the gauges are filled with water. With this form of gauge, care shall be taken to eliminate any leaks in the connecting pipes, and to avoid the trapping of air in the connecting pipe or hose.

The gauges should be calibrated prior to/or after the test and when calibrated and used, shall be in an upright position. On no account should any Bourden type gauge be fixed so that any strain is placed on its case, as its readings may thereby be seriously affected.

The end of the connecting tube or pipe should be flush with the inside of the conduit in which the pressure to be measured and shall have its axis at right angles to the direction of flow.

Limits of Accuracy

With the above precautions, and provided the head to be measured is reasonably steady, an accuracy within ± 1% may be expected.

Measurement of Power Input

The measurements of power input fall into two general classes:

(a) Some measurements are those which themselves determine the actual power or torque delivered to the pump and are, therefore, made entirely during the test, using some form of transmission dynamometer.

(b) Other measurements are those which involve measurement, during the pump test, of power input to the driving element, and the previous or subsequent determination of the relation the power input to the power output of this driving element under indentical conditions of the pump test, thus deriving the efficiency of the driving element.

Corrections and Allowances

Power delivered to the pump shaft when directly connected shall be the power output of the driving element. When not directly connected, corrections shall be made for the losses between the driving element and the pump. In the case of flat belt and V-belt drives, the allowances for belt losses may be taken as 5% and 2% respectively.

Guarantees

The efficiency of a pump should be guaranteed at the specified point of rating only and shall not be guaranteed to cover the performance of the pump under conditions varying therefrom nor for a sustained performance of any period of time. However, pump discharge may be guaranteed for the range of head + 10% and –25% from the specified head.

Unless specified otherwise, pump performance figures shall be deemed to be applicable for 4.5 m suction lift at mean sea level and at water temperature of 30ºC.

Suction lift is to be reduced for higher altitudes at the rate of 1.5 m for every 1000 m above mean sea level and for higher temperature at the rate of one metre for every 5ºC rise above 50ºC.

Information to be Furnished by the Supplier

When offering pumps, the supplier is required to furnish the following informatin to the purchaser:

(a) Code designation of pump.
(b) Type of pump (giving number of stages and type of suction).
(c) Suction flange connection....................mm.
(d) Delivery flange connection....................mm.
(e) maximum permissible total suction lift....................metres.
(f) Type of casing.
(g) Type of impeller.
(h) Type of fitting—standard.
fitted/bronze
fitted/all iron
(i) Type of drive.
(j) Direction of rotation.
(k) Speed of pump in rev/min.
(l) Total head....................metres.
(m) Discharge....................litres/min.
(n) Pump input at the specified point....................kW.
(o) Maximum pump input for the working range between +10 per cent and –25 per cent from the specified head.
(p) Recommended power of the prime mover.
(q) Additional information to be supplied with the supply:
(1) Certified drawings giving leading dimensions;
(2) Certified performance figures, or performance curve and
(3) Instructions for installation and maintenance.

(r) Additional information to be supplied on request:
 (1) Efficiency of the pump;
 (2) Maximum power consumed by the pump; and
 (3) Design details, such a:
  (i) Bearing arrangement,
  (ii) Sealing arrangement,
  (iii) Axial thrust arrangement,
  (iv) Approximate dimensions, and
  (v) Approximate weight.

Possible Causes of Trouble in Pumping Installation

(a) Suction troubles

(1) Pump not primed.
(2) Pump or suction pipe not completely filled with liquid.
(3) Suction lift too high.
(4) Insufficient margin in between suction pressure and vapour pressure is insufficient available N.P.S.H.
(5) Excessive amount of air or gas in liquid.
(6) Air pocket in suction line.
(7) Air leaks into suction line.
(8) Air leaks into pump through stuffing box.
(9) Foot-valve too small.
(10) Foot-valve partially clogged.
(11) Inlet of suction pipe insufficiently submerged.
(12) Water pipe plugged.
(13) Seal cage improperly located in stuffing box preventing sealing fluid entering space to form the seal.

(b) System trouble

(14) Speed too low.
(15) Speed too high.
(16) Wrong direction of rotation.
(17) Total head of system higher than design head of pumps.
(18) Total head of system lower than pump design head.
(19) Specific gravity of liquid different from design.
(20) Viscosity of liquid differs from that for which designed.
(21) Operating on very low capacity.
(22) Parallel operation of pumps unsuitable for such operation.

(c) Mechanical trouble

(23) Foreign material in impeller.
(24) Misalignment.
(25) Foundation not rigid.
(26) Shaft bent.
(27) Rotating part rubbing on stationary part.
(28) Bearing worn.
(29) Wearing ring worn.

(30) Impeller damaged.
(31) Casing gasket defective permitting internal leakage.
(32) Shaft or Shaft sleeves worn or scores at the packing.
(33) Packing improperly installed.
(34) Incorrect type of packing for operating conditions.
(35) Shaft running off centre because of worn bearing misalignment.
(36) Rotor out of balance resulting in vibration.
(37) Gland too right resulting in no flow of liquid to lubricate packings.
(38) Failure to provide cooling liquid to water cooled stuffing boxes.
(39) Excessive clearance bottom of stuffing box between shaft and casing, causing packing to be forced into pump interior.
(40) Dirt or grit in sealing liquid, leading to scoring of shaft or shaft sleeve.
(41) Excessive thrust caused by a mechanical failure inside the pump or by the failure of the hydraulic balancing device, if any.
(42) Excessive grease or oil in antifriction bearing housing or lack of cooling causing excessive bearing temperature.
(43) Lack of lubrication.
(44) Improper installation of antifriction bearing (damage during assembly, incorrect assembly of stacked bearings use of unmatched bearings as a pair etc.)
(45) Dust getting into bearings.
(46) Rusting of bearings due to water getting into housing.
(47) Excessive cooling of water cooled bearing resulting in condensation in the bearing housing of moisture from the atmosphere.

Do not Run the Pump

(1) Outside the recommended range.
(2) Without lubricating the bearings with grease or oil as the case may be.
(3) With liquid other than specified.
(4) With less N.I.S.H. than recommended.
(5) With delivery valve fully shut for longer period.
(6) When misaligned.
(7) Without lubricant to the stuffing box either external or internal.
(8) Unless periodically checked as suggested.
(9) With undue weight on suction and delivery pipe flanges.
(10) When strainer is removed from suction.

Tolerances

In all commercial acceptances tests of pumps, a certain tolerance should be allowed to the manufacturer on his guarantee to cover inaccurancies of the equations for discharge, errors of observations and unavoidable minor inaccuracies of the instruments employed.

(i) A tolerance of ± 2.5 per cent shall be permissible on the discharge. However, of small discharges upto 900 litres per minute, a tolerance of ± 2.5 per cent of 24 litres per minute whichever is higher, is allowed, while the negative tolerance of 2.5 per cent is maintained.

(ii) The pump efficiency shall be not less than the specified value by more than 2.5 per cent. This tolerance may be raised to –5 percent in case the prime mover does not overloaded.

Submersible Pumps

Information to be Furnished by the Purchaser.

When enquiring or ordering submersible pumps, the user shall furnish the following information to the supplier.

(a) Name of purchaser
(b) Address
(c) Installation site
(d) Number of pumps required
(e) Spare parts required
(f) Pump operating conditions
  (1) Capacity..........1/min. 1/s, or m³/h
  (2) Speed..........rev/min
  (3) Total head below ground level at rated capacity..........m
  (4) Total head above ground level at rated capacity..........m and
  (5) Details of delivery conditions. Sketch of pipe line giving information such as delivery pipe diameter and length, method of connection, distance between point of discharge, ground level, total head, etc. may be given.

Description of Well

1. Installation of the pump in:
   (i) Open well
   (ii) Tube well
   (iii) Open well with a boring; and
   (iv) others.
2. Minimum inside diameter of well or casing pipe
3. Total depth of the open well..............m.
4. Total depth of casing pipe for tubewell..............m.
5. Well slantness..............mm, cut at..........m (if verticality test is carried out, the test results should be furnished)
6. Static water level below ground surface.........m. Highest-Lowest
7. Pumping draw-down (D)..........m at.........min 1/s, m³/h
8. Well developed to..........1/min. at.........metres of draw down.

Site Conditions

1. Height above mean sea level in metres, and
2. Details of quality of water.

Power Supply

1. Type of current (single-phase/three-phase).
2. Frequency (Hz).
3. Voltage (V).
4. Preferred speed in rev/min, and
5. Variations in voltage/frequency.

Accessories

(State whether the following items are required):

1. Starter (indicate starting method),
2. Sluice valve,
3. Reflux valve,
4. Pressure gauge,
5. Voltmeter,
6. Ammeter,
7. Rising main pipes and delivery bend,
8. Depth gauge or water level relays,
9. Automatic starting and stopping device,
10. Isolating switches,
11. Single-phase preventor,
12. Water level guard, and
13. Low voltage protector.

Information to be Furnished by the Supplier

When offering pumps, the supplier is required to furnish the following to the purchaser:

(a) Code designating of pump and submersible motor:

(b) Type of pump, giving:

(1) Method of lubrication (normally the parts of the submersible pumpset are lubricated by the pumped liquid itself. If any other type of lubrication is adopted, it should be indicated).

(2) Suitability in tubewell of size.........mm diameter

(3) Number of stage;

(4) Outside diameter of the bowl, the maximum dia of the pump fitted with non-return valve and maximum overall diameter of the pumpset including the cable:

(5) Discharge............l/min, m^3/h

(6) Total head............m;

(7) Speed............rev/min;

(8) Pump-input at duty point...............kW;

(9) Overall efficiency at duty point............percent; and

(10) Minimum submergence required..........m.

Details of Motor

(1) Rating.........kW;

(2) Type................squirrel cage induction type, whether wet or dry winding type;

(3) Lubrication..........(method adopted for lubricating the thrust bearing, rotor shaft journal bearings, etc.)
(4) Details of power supply; and
(5) Revolutions per minute.

Assessories

(1) Suitable starter;
(2) isolating switch;
(3) Ammeter and voltmeter;
(4) Pressure gauge;
(5) Water level indicating relays;
(6) Automatic starting and stopping device;
(7) Reflux valve and sluice valve; and
(8) Erection clamps and special spanners, if any.

Additional Information to be Furnished with the Supply, if Required

(1) Performance curves:
- (i) head vs discharge curve;
- (ii) discharge vs power input; and
- (iii) discharge vs overall efficiency.

(2) Instructions for installation and maintenance; and
(3) Weight of the pump, motor and cables and rising main pipe weight for a specific setting.

Tolerances

Tolerances permissible for overall efficiency and discharge.

(i) Overall efficiency – 4.5%
(ii) Discharge ± 5%

Material of Construction

Number of materials of construction is available to meet the needs for pumping sets handling clear, cold, fresh water. Typical materials for a few parts are indicated below:

	Name of Part	*Relevant Specification*
(i)	Bearing sleeve	Grade 3, 4 or 5 or IS:318—leaded tin bronze ingots and casting (revised) or 12 per cent chromium steel (Grades 07 Cr 13, 15 Cr 13 and 22 Cr 13), conforming to IS:1570 (Part–V)—Schedules for wrought steels: Part–V Stainless and head-resisting steels (first revision).
(ii)	Casing wearing	Grade 3, 4 or 5 of IS:318 or Grade 20 of IS:210 'Grey iron castings (second revision)'.
(iii)	Discharge casing	Grade 20 of IS:210

(iv)	Impeller	Grade 3, 4 or 5 of IS:318 or Grade 20 of IS:210 or 12% chormium steel (Grades 07 Cr 13, 15 Cr 13 and 22 Cr 13).
(v)	Pump bowl	Grade 20 of IS:210
(vi)	Pump Shaft	12% chromium steel (Grades 07 Cr 13, and 22 Cr 13) conforming to IS:1570 (Part–V) or Grades C 40 or C 45 of IS:1570—'Schedules for wrought steels for general engineering purposes'.
(vii)	Suction casing	Grade 20 IS:210.

23. PUMP ROOM LAYOUT

Besides selection of pumps, the size of pump room layout of the installations and the type of controls are very important.

The pumps, valves which ar provided in pump room do require maintenance from time to time hence the first criterion would be provision of adequate space for movement of persons along with tools and also adequate clearances when machinery is required to be taken out.

The pumps, delivery lines etc. some times leak. With the electrical energy also being used it is necessary that all such water is quickly drained out. This precaution is very much necessary for pumps which are installed in basements. Where pumps are provided over the underground tank care has to be taken while designing that all rubbish, grease, oils spilled water do not find its way into the underground tank. This is all the more necessary where diesel pumps are used.

Noise level when pumps are operated can be very high. Proper noise proofing is needed to avoid trouble specially where over the pumproom normal living accommodation is provided.

Some of the points to be considered in the planning of pump room are:

(a) The underground tank has to be as near the pump room as possible in order to have minimum length of suction line. The suction line has to be as straight as possible. Longer suction lines and suction lines with many bends always create priming problems.

(b) Width and length of the pump room—Except for very small (less than 3 HP) pumps, the length of the pump room should be preferably 7.5 metres and width 5 metres for two pump istallation (one working and one standby) Additional 3 metres in length is needed for each additional pump. These sizes are sufficient for pumps upto a rating of 50 HP. For higher sizes of pumps, the size of pump room has to be increased.

(c) The height of pump room should be 3 metres, clear. Beams upto 40 cm depth can be neglected.

(d) Drainage arrangements should be made.

(e) Normally the height of cement concrete foundation for pumps should not exceed 200 mm.

(f) The layout of pumps are piping should be so as to be easy in operation and maintenance.

(g) Cables from motor control panel to motor should be taken on cable trays neatly preferably suspended from ceiling. This makes pump room neat and unobstructed.

(h) The delivery header should be taken not on floor. But on the suspenders from wall or ceiling or at least on raised masonry pillars.

(i) The suction foot valve requires more maintenance. The connection to the vertical pipe containing foot valve from the horizontal pipe could be a flanged connection thereby the foot valve length of pipe can be uncoupled quickly and lifted out.

(j) Pump room should be well lighted and ventilated.

24. HYDRO-PNEUMATIC SYSTEM

In any water supply the water has to be subjected pressure head to make it flow through piping. This head may be provided through an overhead reservoir creating pressure by static head or the difference in levels. Second method would be to apply pressure on the water through any medium like air. Hence name "Hydro-pneumatic".

The system consists of the following:

1. Underground tank.
2. Pumps (a) Lead pump,
   (b) Supplementary pump.
3. The hydro-pneumatic vessel. This is an air-tight vessel. The capacity of the vessel is equivalent to about 3 minutes water requirement. The vessel is provided with manholes, water level gauge, pressure gauge, and automatic controls for pumps etc.
4. Air compressor—An air compressor keeps the air vessel charged with the correct ratio of air to water.
5. Electrical control panel to enable the pumps to start automatically when pressure in the hydro-pneumatic vessel falls below a predetermined level due to drawl of water and stops when the deficiency is made up.

The hydro-pneumatic system works as follows:

In the hydro-pneumatic vessel certian levels of volumes of air and water are fixed. When water is drawn for consumption, the water level falls and air pressure on it gets reduced due to expansion of air volume. The water pumps starts and pumps water into vessel. This raise water level and air gets compressed. At a predetermined pressure of air the electrical panel cuts off the pump. When the consumption of water is high, the lead pump may not be capable of satisfying the demand then the supplementary pump also helps. As demand falls, the supplementary pump stops and with further fall in demand, the lead pump may also stop.

All pumps work with control switches and relays. In course of time some amount of air gets dissolved in water hence replenishment takes place through air compressor.

Fire and Water Provision

Literally and actually nobody digs well for water when there is a fire. One has to be prepared for its well in advance in a prudent and economical way.

Most fire fighting involves use of water. Water may be used as a fire extinguishing medium in case of carbonacious fire or it may be used as a cooling or drenching liquid to save further property being affected by fire.

Fire requires immediate attention hence depending upon importance of building, of occupants, etc, Bureau of Indian Standards lay down certian minimum criteria which are mandatory.

For the water supply for wet riser system a storage tank should be available with arrangement for replenishment of water supply through city mains or by an alternate source of supply at the rate of 1000 litres/minute. Where this is not possible the capacity of the static tank will have to be increased in consultation with local fire authorities.

A pressure of atleast 3 kg/cm should be available at the highest hydrant outlet.

Some categories of public buildings (these have been indicated in the following paragraphs), which have generally low fire loads but higher personnel hazards, require to be provided with portable appliances when the total area of the floors exceeds 1000 sq. metres so that the whole of the floor is protected. It should be ensured that no part of the floor is more than 6 metres from the hose nozzle when the hose reel is fully extended. There has to be adequate constant supply of water which will ensure supply of not less than 23 litres per minute through a nozzle of not less than 6.5 mm size for half an hour when upto 3 hose reels are operated. The hose shall be or rubber of rubber lines, having a bore of 12 or 20 mms diameter. The water supply should be independent of the domestic supply connections.

(a) Hotels, boarding houses, restaurants and similar establishments;

(b) Schools and buildings used for educational and/or training purposes;

(c) Hospitals, nursing homes, sanatoria, asylums and dispensaries, including all associated offices, plants and equipments;

(d) Buildings for devotional congregations, such as temples, mosques and churches;

(e) Public halls;

(f) Museums, art galleries, public libraries, record rooms and similar buildings;

(g) Commercial offices, banks and government offices;

(h) Club houses;

(i) Retail shops, emporia and stores; and

(j) Theatres, cinemas and places of public entertainment.

TABLE 5
Typical Fire-Fighting Installations/Requirements

Sr. No.	Type of Building Occupancy	Type of Installation	Requirements			
			Water Supply		Pump Capacity	
			Under-ground Static Tank	Terrace Tank	Near the Under-ground Static Tank	At the Terrace Level
(1)	(2)	(3)	(4)	(5)	(6)	(7)
1.	**Residential Building** (a) Lodging or room houses (A-1)' dormitories (A-3) and hotels (A-5).					
	(i) Upto 15 mts. in height *Note*: No provisions are necessary for dormitories housing less than 25 persons.	Nil	50,000 litres	Nil	Nil	Nil
	(ii) Above 15 mts. in height but not exceeding 24 mts.	One wet riser-cum-down-comer per 1000 m^2 floor area. The riser shall be fully automatic in operation.	100,000 litres	20,000 litres	2,400 litres per minute, giving a pressure of not less than 0.3 N/mm^2 (3 kgf/cm^2) at the top most hydrant.	900 litres per minute, giving a pressure of not less than 0.3 N/mm^2 (3 kgf/cm^2) at the top most hydrant.
	(iii) Above 24 mts. in height but not exceeding 35 mts.	One wet riser-cum-down-comer per 1000 m^2 floor area. The riser shall be fully charged with adequate pressure at all times,	100,000 litres	20,000 litres	(i) 2400 litres per minute, giving a pressure of less than 0.3 N/mm^2 (3 kgf/cm^2). The pump provided will be of multi-stage type with	900 litres per minute, giving a pressure of not less than 0.3 N/mm^2 (3 kgf/cm^2) at the topmost hydrant.

(1)	(2)	(3)	(4)	(5)	(6)	(7)
		and shall be automatic in operation.			suction and delivery sizes not less than 15 cm. in dia., with low-level riser upto 10 storeys and high-level riser delivery for upper floors. (ii) A stand by pump of equal capacity shall be provided on alternative source of supply.	
(iv) Above 35 mts. in height but not exceeding 60 mts.		One wet riser-cum-down-comer per 1000 m^2 floor area. The riser shall be fully charged with adequate pressure at all times, and shall be automatic in operation.	150,000 litres	20,000 litres	(i) 2400 litres per minute, giving a pressure of less than 0.3 N/mm^2 (3 kgf/cm^2). The pump provided will be of multi-stage type with suction and delivery sizes not less than 15 cm. in dia., with low-level riser upto 10 storeys and high-level riser delivery for upper floors. (ii) A stand by pump of equal capacity shall be provided on alternative source of supply.	Nil

(1)	(2)	(3)	(4)	(5)	(6)	(7)
	(v) Above 60 mts. in height but not exceeding 92 mts.	One wet riser-cum-down-comer per 1000 m^2 floor area. The riser shall be fully charged with adequate pressure at all times, and shall be automatic in operation.	200,000 litres	Nil	(i) 2400 litres per minute, giving a pressure of less than 0.3 N/mm^2 (3 kgf/cm^2). The pump provided will be of multi-stage type with suction and delivery sizes not less than 15 cms. in dia., with low-level riser upto 15 storeys and high-level riser delivery for upper floors. (ii) A stand by pump of equal capacity shall be provided on alternative source of supply.	Nil
	(vi) Above 92 mts. in height	One wet riser-cum-down-comer per 1000 m^2 floor area. The riser shall be fully charged with adequate pressure at all times, and shall be automatic in operation.	250,000 litres	Nil	(i) 2400 litres per minute, giving a pressure of less than 0.3 N/mm^2 (3 kgf/cm^2). The pump provided will be of multi-stage type with suction and delivery sizes not less than 15 cms. in dia., with low-level riser upto 15	

(1)	(2)	(3)	(4)	(5)	(6)	(7)
					storeys and high-level riser delivery. for upper 60 mts. Another pump of equal performance with a break tank of 12,000 litres capacity at 75 mts. level and a set of ball valves to supply the tank with at least 2,400 litres per minute from the first pump. Alternatively, a multi-state multi-outlet pump may be installed. (ii) A stand by pump of equal capacity shall be provided on alternative source of supply.	
	(b) One or two-family private dwellings (A-2) and apartment houses (flats) (A-4)					
	(i) Upto 15 mts. in height *Note* : One or two family dwelling above 15 mts. in height shall not be permitted.	Nil	Nil	Nil	Nil	
	(ii) Above 15 mts. in height	One wet riser-cum-	Nil	10,000 litres	Nil	450 litres per minute,

(1)	(2)	(3)	(4)	(5)	(6)	(7)
	but not exceeding 24 mts.	down-comer with a provision of fire service inlet only ground level per 1,000 m^2 floor area.				giving a pressure of not less than 0.3 N/mm^2 (3 kgf/cm^2) at the top most hydrant.
	(iii) Above 24 mts. in height but not exceeding 35 mts. With shopping area upto 250 m^2 restricting the area to the ground floor only.	One wet riser-cum-down-comer per 1000 m^2 floor area. The riser shall be fully charged with adequate pressure at all times, and shall be automatic in operation.	50,000 liters	20,000 litres	1,800 litres per minute giving a pressure of not less than 0.3 N/mm^2 topmost hydrant. (3 Kgf/cm^2) at the tompost hydrant.	900 litres per minute, giving a pressure of not less than 0.3 N/mm^2 (3 kgf/cm^2) at the top most hydrant.
	With shopping area exceeding 250 m^2	One wet riser-cum-down-comer per 1000 m^2 floor area. Riser shall be fully charged with adequate pressure at all times, and shall be automatic in operation.	100,000 litres	20,000 litres	2,400 litres per minute, giving a pressure of not less than 0.3 N/mm2 (3 kgf/cm^2) at the topmost hydrant.	900 litres per minute, giving a presure of not less than 0.3 N/mm^2 (3 kgf/cm^2) at the topmost hydrant.
	(iv) Above 24 mts. in height but not exceeding 45 mts.	One wet riser-cum-down-comer per 1000 m2 floor area. The riser shall be fully charged with adequate	50,000 litres	20,000 litres	1,800 litres per minute giving a pressure of not pressure of not less than 0.3 N/mm^2 (3 kgf/cm^2) at the topmost hydrant.	450 litres per minute, giving a pressure of not less than 0.3 N/mm^2 (3 kgf/cm^2) at the topmost hydrant.

(1)	(2)	(3)	(4)	(5)	(6)	(7)
		pressure at all times, and shall be automatic in operation.				
	(v) Above 50 mts. in height but exceeding 60 mts.	One wet riser-cum-comer per 1000 m^2 floor area. The Riser shall be fully charged with adequate pressure at all times, and shall be automatic in operation.	100,000 litres	20,000 litres	2,400 litres per minute giving a pressure of not less than 0.3 N/mm^2 (3 kgf/cm^2) at the topmost hydrant.	900 litres per minute, giving a pressure of not less than 0.3 N/mm^2 (3 kgf/cm^2) at the topmost hydrant.
	(vi) Above 60 mts. in height but not exceeding 92 mts. *Note* : Apartment house (flats) above 92 mts. shall not be permitted.	One wet riser-cum-down-comer per 1000 m^2 floor area. The riser shall be fully charged with adequate pressure at all times and shall be automatic in operation.	150,000 litres	20,000 litres	2,400 litres per minute, giving a pressure of not less than 0.3 N/mm^2 (3 kgf/cm^2) at the topmost hydrant. The pump provided should be of multistage type with suction and delivery sizes not less than 15 cms in dia with low level riser upto 15 storeys and high level riser delivery for upper floors.	450 litres per minute, giving a pressure of not less than 0.3 N/mm^2 (3 kgf/cm2) at the topmost hydrant.
2.	**Educational (B) Institutional (C) Building**					
	(i) Upto 15 mts. in height	Nil	50,000 litres	Nil	Nil	
	(ii) Above 15 mts. in heigh but	One wet riser-cum-	Nil	20,000 litres	Nil	450 litres per minute,

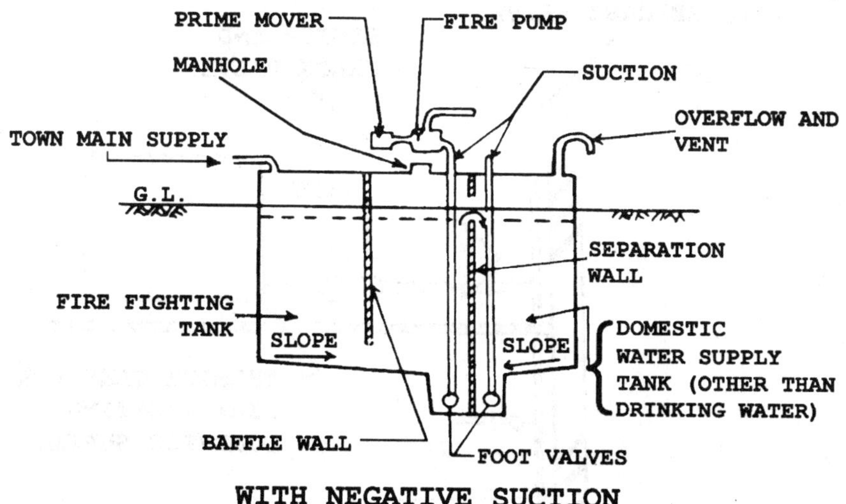

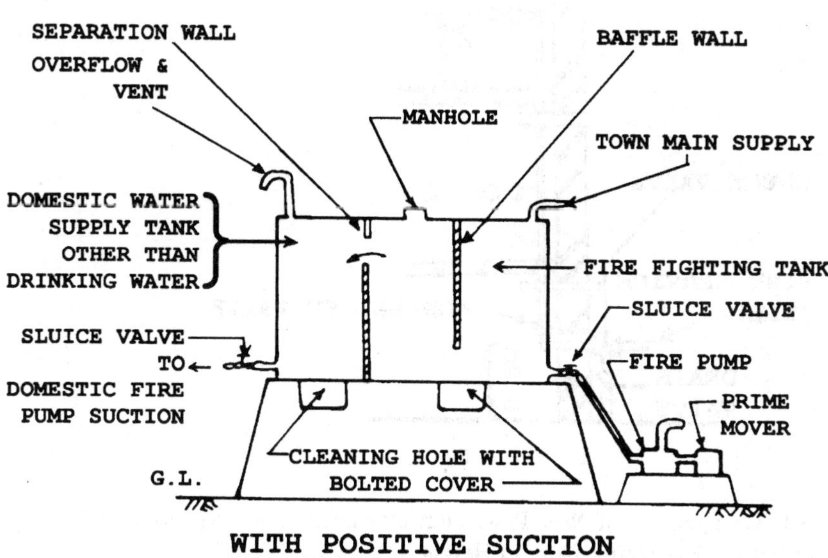

Fig. 10

With Positive Suction Typical Arrangement for Providing Combined Fire: Fighting and Domestic Water Storage.

Note:

1. Negative suction can give trouble on ingress of air creating suction lock.
2. Foor Valve can give problem. These factors can be very detrimental in fire fighting. Hence use of positive suction arrangement is always to be insisted upon.

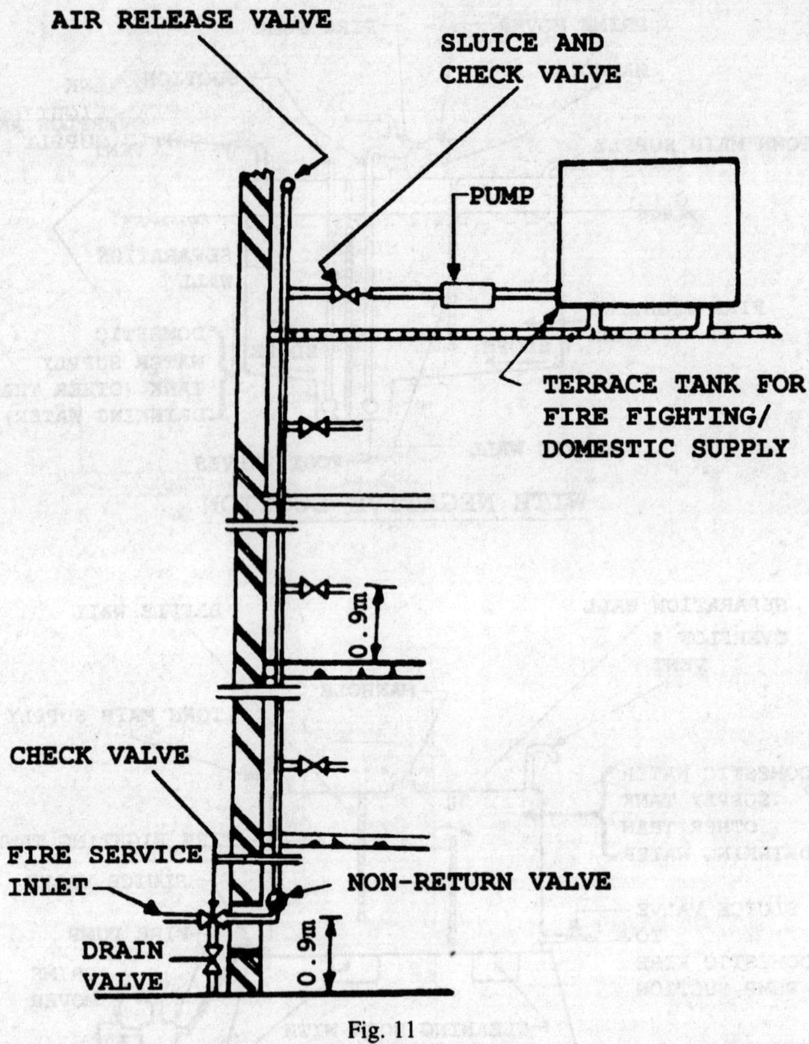

Fig. 11

Typical Arrangement of Wet Riser-cum-Downcomer for Appartment Houses Above but not Exceeding 24 m in Height.

Notes:

1. Only down pipe from tank would not create desired pressure for the fighting. Hence a terrace pump is needed.
2. Air release valve is needed for removal of air when water is pumped to terrace tank.
3. The filling of tank cannot be done when terrace pump is in operation.
4. No underground tank is provided.
5. It is desirable to have one fire outlet at terrace level for purposes of fire fighting on the next building.

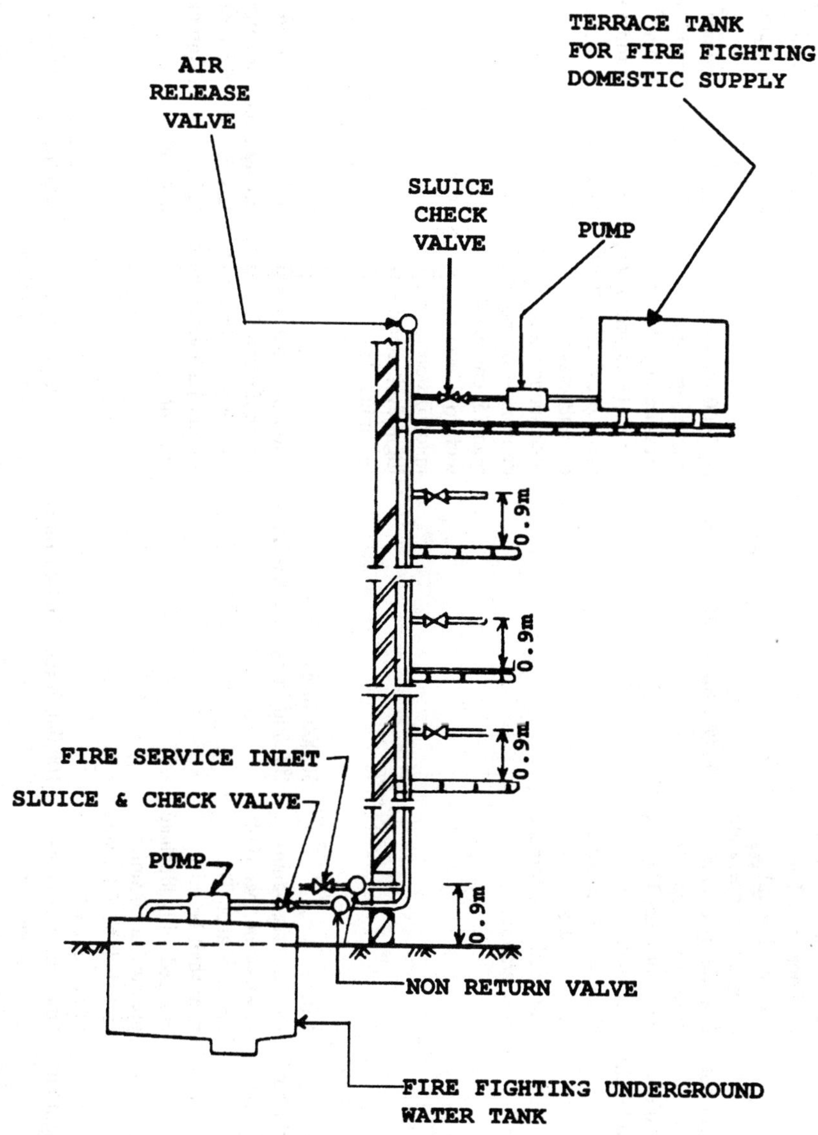

Fig. 12

Typical Arrangement of Wet Riser-cum-Downcomer for Apparent House Exceeding 24 m in Height.

Note:

For extra height water supply is augmented by underground tank pump.

(1)	(2)	(3)	(4)	(5)	(6)	(7)
	not exceeding 24 mts.	down-comer per 1000 m^2 floor area. The riser shall be fully automatic in operation.				pressure of giving a not less than 0.3 N/mm^2 (3 kgf/cm^2) at the topmost hydrant.
	(iii) Above 24 mts. in height but not exceeding 35 mts. *Note*: Education and institutional buildings above 35 mts. in height shall not be permitted.	One wet riser-cum-down-comer per 1000 m^2 floor area. The riser shall be fully charged with adequate pressure at all times, and shall be automatic in operation.	100,000 litres	20,000 litres	(i) 2400 litres per minute, giving a pressure of less than 0.3 N/mm^2 (3 kdg/cm^2). The pump provided will be of multi-stage type with suction and delivery sizes not less than 15 cm. in dia., with low-level riser upto 10 storeys and high-level riser delivery for upper floors.	900 litres per minute, giving a pressure of not less than 0.3 N/mm^2 (3 kgf/cm^2) at the topmost hydrant.
3.	**Assembly (D) Building**					
	(i) Upto 15 mts. in height	Nil	50,000 litres	Nil	Nil	Nil
	(ii) Above 15 mts. in height but not exceeding 24 mts.	One wet riser-cum-down-comer per 1000 m^2 floor area. The riser shall be fully charged with adequate pressure at all times and shall be automatic in operation.	100,000 litres	20,000 litres	2,400 litres per minute, giving a pressure of not less than 0.3 N/mm^2 (3 kgf/cm^2) at the top most hydrant.	900 litres per minute, giving a pressure of not less than 0.3 N/mm^2 (3 kgf/cm^2) at the top most hydrant.
	(iii) Above 24 mts. in height but not exceeding 92 mts. *Note* : Assembly building above 35 mts. in height shall not be	One wet riser-cum-down-comer per 1000 m^2 floor area. The riser shall be fully	100,000 litres	20,000 litres	2400 litres per minute, giving a pressure of less than 0.3 N/mm^2 at the topmost hydrant. The	900 litres per minute, giving a pressure of not less than 0.3 N/mm^2 (3 kgf/cm^2) at the topmost

(1)	(2)	(3)	(4)	(5)	(6)	(7)
	permitted.	charged with adequate pressure at all times and shall be automatic in operation.			pump provided will be of multi-stage type with suction and delivery sizes not less than 15 cm. in dia., with low-level riser upto 10 storeys and high-level riser delivery for upper floors. (ii) A stand by pump of equal capacity shall be provided on alternative source of supply.	hydrant.
4.	Business (B) Mercantile (F) and Industrial (G) Building					
	(i) Upto 15 mts. in height but not exceeding 24 mts.	Nil	50,000 litres	Nil	Nil	Nil
	(ii) Above 15 mts. in height but not exceeding 24 mts.	One wet riser-cum-down-comer per 1000 m^2 floor area. The riser shall be fully charged with adequate pressure at all times and shall be automatic in operation.	100,000 litres	20,000 litres	2,400 litres per minute, giving a pressure of not less than (3 kgf/cm^2) at the topmost hydrant.	900 litres per minute, giving a pressure of not less than 0.3 N/mm^2 (3 kg/cm^2) at the topmost hydrant.
	(iii) Above 24 mts. in height but not exceeding 35 mts. *Note* : Education and institutional buildings above 35 mts. in height	One wet riser-cum-down-comer per 1000 m^2 floor area. The riser shall be fully charged	100,000 litres	20,000 litres	(i) 2400 litres per minute, giving a pressure of less than 0.3 N/mm^2 (3 kgf/cm^2). The	900 litres per minute, giving a pressure of not less than 0.3 N/mm^2 (3 kgf/cm^2) at the topmost

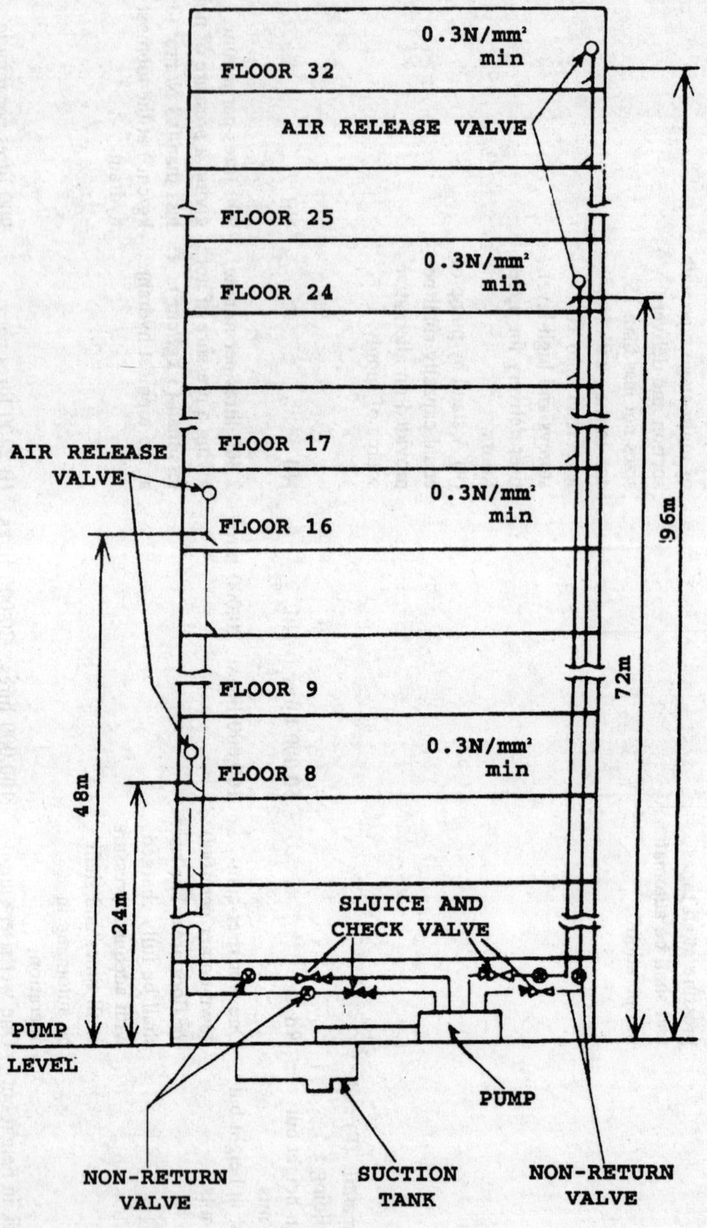

Fig. 13

Typical Arrangement of Wet Riser System for Buildings other than Apartment Houses above 35 m in Height.

Notes:

Pumps to cater for different zones (each zone approximately 24 metre)

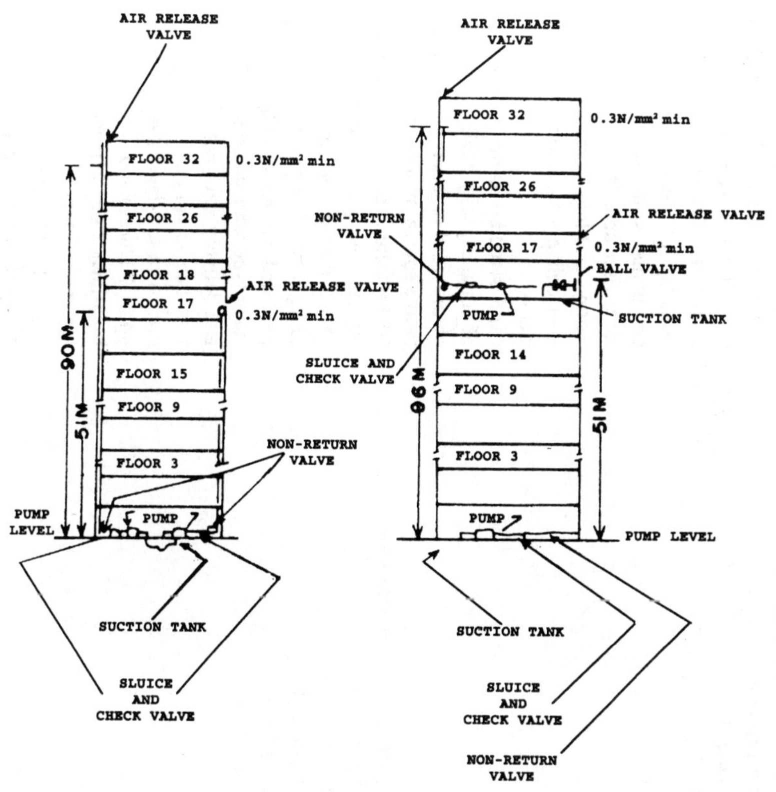

Fig. 14

Typical arrangement of Wet-Riser System for Bldgs other than Appartment Houses Above 35 m in Height.

1. Two separate pumps provided to cater for different heads of water.

2. A terrace level fire outlet is desirable.

Typical arrangement of Wet-Riser System for Bldgs other than Appartment Houses Above 35 m in Height.

1. Where service floor is provided advantage can be taken to reduce very high head pumping.

2. Terrace level fire outlet is desirable.

(1)	(2)	(3)	(4)	(5)	(6)	(7)
	shall not be permitted.	with adequate pressure at all times, and shall be automatic in operation.			pump provided will be of multi-stage type with suction and delivery sizes not less than 15 cm. in dia., with low-level riser upto 10 storeys and high-level riser delivery for upper floors. (ii) A stand by pump of equal capacity shall be provided on alternative source of supply.	hydrant.
	(iv) Above 35 mts. in height but not exceeding 60 mts.	One wet riser-cum-down-comer per 1000 m² floor area. The riser shall be fully charged with adequate pressure at all times, and shall be automatic in operation.	150,000 litres	Nil	(i) 2400 litres per minute, giving a pressure of less than 0.3 N/mm² (3 kgf/cm²). The pump provided will be of multi stage type with suction and delivery sizes not less than 15 cm. in dia., with low-level riser upto 10 storeys and high-level riser delivery for upper floors. (ii) A stand by pump of equal capacity shall be provided on alternative source of supply.	Nil

(1)	(2)	(3)	(4)	(5)	(6)	(7)
	(v) Above 60 mts. in height but not exceeding 92 mts.	One wet riser-cum-down-comer per 1000 m^2 floor area. The riser shall be fully charged with adequate pressure at all times, and shall be automatic in operation.	200,000 litres	Nil	(i) 2400 litres per minute, giving a pressure of less than 0.3 N/mm^2 (3 kgf/cm^2). The pump provided will be of multi-stage type with suction and delivery sizes not less than 15 cms. in dia., with low-level riser upto 15 storeys and high-level riser delivery for upper floors. (ii) A stand by pump of equal capacity shall be provided on alternative source of supply.	Nil
	(vi) Above 92 mts. in height	One wet riser-cum-down-comer per 1000 m^2 floor area. The riser shall be fully charged with adequate pressure at all times, and shall be automatic in operation.	250,000 litres	Nil	(i) 2400 litres per minute, giving a pressure of less than 0.3 N/mm^2 (3 kgf/cm^2). The pump provided will be of multi-stage type with suction and delivery sizes not less than 15 cms. in dia., with low-level riser 15 storeys and high-level riser delivery for upper 60 mts. Another pump of	Nil

(1)	(2)	(3)	(4)	(5)	(6)	(7)
					equal performance with a break tank of 12,000 litres capacity at 75 mts. level and a set of ball valves to supply the tank with at least 2,400 litres per minute from first pump. Alternatively, a multistate multi-outlet pump may be installed. (ii) A stand by pump of equal capacity shall be provided on alternative source of supply.	
5.	Storage (B) and Hazardous (J) Buildings					
	(i) Upto 15 mts. in height *Note* : Hazardous building above 15 mts. in height shall not be permitted.	One wet riser-cum-down-comer per 1000 m^2 floor area. The riser shall be fully automatic in operation.	100,000 litres	20,000 litres	1,800 litres per minute, giving a pressure of not less than 0.3 N/mm^2 (3 kgf/cm^2) at the topmost hydrant.	450 litres per minute, giving a pressure of not less than 0.3 N/mm^2 (3 kgf/cm^2) at the topmost hydrant.
	(ii) Above 15 mts. in height but not exceeding 24 mts. *Note* : Storage building above 24 mts. in height shall not be permitted.	One wet riser-cum-down-comer per 1000 m^2 floor area. The riser shall be fully charged with adequate pressure at all times, and shall be automatic in operation.	100,000 litres	20,000 litres	(i) 2400 litres per minute, giving a pressure of less than 0.3 N/mm^2 (3 kgf/cm^2) at the topmost hydrant.	900 litres per minute, giving a pressure of not less than 0.3 N/mm^2 (3 kgf/cm^2) at the topmost hydrant.

Note 1 : Any of the above categories may incorporate an automatic sprinkler/drencher systems, if the risk is such that it requires the installation of such protective devices. Where a sprinkler/drencher system is installed, water requirements for such installations shall be in addition to those indicated in this table.

Note 2 : A minimum of two hydrants shall be provided in the countryard.

Note 3 : The wet riser-come-down comer is an arrangement for fire fighting within the building by means of vertical riser mains not less than 100 mm internal dia., with hydrant outlets reel on each floor/landing connected to an overhead water storage tank for fire-fighting purposes with a booster pump, check valve and a non-return valve near the tank-end and a fire pump, gate and non-return valve shall also be provided to the rising main for charging it by fire services pump in case of failure of static fire pump over the underground static tanks.

Note 4 : The performance of pumps specified above shall be at revolutions per minute not exceeding 3,000.

Note 5 : The terrace tank and pump need not be provided if the automatic pump at ground level can be maintained to the satisfaction of the local fire brigade.

Note 6 : The above quantities of water shall be exclusively for fire-fighting and shall not be utilised for domestic or other use.

Note 7 : The size of the riser shall be as under (internal diameter)

(a) Apartment buildings:

- (i) Upto 45 mts. —100 mm with single/twin hydrant outlets and hose reel on each floor.
- (ii) Above 45 mts to 85 mts —150 mm with twin hydrant outlets and hose reel on each floor.
- (iii) Above 85 mts upto 165 mts. —250 mm with two hydrant outlets and hose reel on each floor.

(b) Non-appartment building:

- (i) Upto 24 m —10 cms with single hydrant outlet and hose reel on each floor.
- (ii) Above 24 m —15 cms with twin hydrant outlets and hose reel on each floor.

Note 8 : A facility to boost water pressure in the riser directly from the mobile pump shall also be provided to the wet riser system with suitable fire service inlets (collecting breaching with 2 numbers of 63 mm inlets for 10 cms rising main and 4 number of 63 mm inlets with check valves for 15 cm dia rising main), and a non-return valve and a gate valve.

Note 9 : Hose Reel: Internal diameter of rubber hose for hose reel shall be at least 12 mm. A shut-off branch with nozzle of 5 mm size shall be provided.

Source : National Building Code of India 1983. ISI. for details refer National Building Code of India.

25. HOT WATER AND CHILLED WATER

In this book the hot water system which are simplest and in normal use in a house or offices would be discussed. Complicated continuous flow loop type system which is utilised for hotels and such uses is kept outside the scope of discussion. Presently, electrical geysers are the most commonly used equipment. The first question to be answered would be what capacity of storage and what capacity of electrical heating. In a colder climate of U.K. the following rate of power is recommended.

	In watts per person
School (Hostel)	750
(Day)	90
Houses	1200
Flats	750
Hospitals	1500
Office	120

In estimating the power needed about 20 per cent heat loss should be added. Thus, in a flat with 4 person the boiler power would be

$$\frac{4 \times 750 \times 100}{80} = 3750 \text{ watts}$$

Volume of hot water used for each use would also vary yet for estimation following figures would be useful.

	Litres
Wash basin	1—5
Hand wash	3
Wash	6
Hair wash	13
Shower	70
Bath	70

It would now depend on the frequency of use and the interval between use to decide upon the storage capacity of geyser installation. The geyser should be preferably fed from an overhead tank and it should not be directly connected to mains.

In India the temperatures of various regions would vary substantially. Thus, in Jammu & Kashmir, where winter is severe, the above estimation would be fair and it could be suitably adjusted for more warmer climate.

The hot water storage vessel may be preferably not less than 40 litres per head when bath tubs are used and 25 litres per head when bath tubs are not used. When small capacity heaters of 10 to 25 litres capacity are used there would be a time gap between use of hot water by one person for bath and the next bather.

Instantaneous Electric Heaters

These heaters are designed for direct connection to the mains and the electric heating element is to be switched on after water flow is established.

An electrical loading of 6 kW will give water for showering at 3 litres a minute and Electrical load of 3 kW will give warm water of appr. 1.4 litres a minute.

However, these heaters require very good earthing to avoid shocks. Substandard instantaneous heaters can lead to fatal shocks. Hence, it would be preferable to insist on storage type of heaters only.

Explosions

Water when heated forms steam and heated water which occupies more volume. Provision has to be made for expansion of water and steam to escape by provision of vent pipes, pressure relief valve.

Development of high pressure or steam in a geyser represents an emergency condition and it is not normal.

Hot water geyser explosions are dangerous to life and property.

Water at atmospheric pressure boils at 100°C and if the pressure is above atmospheric then the water boils at higher temperature. Due to blocking of vents and nonfunctioning pressure relief value the pressure over the water in geyser increases due to steam thus even though the water stops boiling and the steam continues to form and the temperature of water rises further. At sufficiently elevated temperature the weak places like solder at seams of vessel, etc. melts and water which is superheated at a high pressure with release of pressure turns into steam with explosive violence. Many times, when hot water taps are opened the overheated water coming from taps immediately turns into steam sometimes with explosive violence. Hot water geysers depending on roof expansion tanks for pressure relief are safest if explosion or generation of steam is to be avoided.

26. TUBEWELLS

Water is vital to mankind and easy availability of water has always made region prosperous. In the water which is available to the mankind, part comes as surface water and rest from the underground water table where tremendous quantity of water are stored in the earth crust. The total volume stored under land areas may be around 80 million km^3 which is about 35 times the quantity of fresh water available on the surface of the earth. Surface water is easy and economical to harness, but its availablity varies with the season. Ground water on the other hand is obtainable all the year round.

The ground water is normally taken out through open wells and tubewells. Open wells are nothing but pits in the earth surface in which water percolate. It is just like a tank which is deep in the earth. Technical problems involved in an open well are very few like steining to be provided where strata of earth requires support, occasional desilting etc. The tube well has different types of technical problems and it will be those problems which will be discussed in this chapter.

Tube wells are of three types:

(i) Screen wells
(ii) Screen wells with gravel packing
(Gravel packed wells)
(iii) Cavity wells

Cavity wells are tubewells which draw water from fissures and cavities in rock strata and therefore of limited application. Screen well with or without gravel pack are of more common application.

Tubewell design should be efficient and economical with a service life of 50 thousand to 70 thousand hours, which may mean more than a decade. The aim of a tubewell should be to draw clear water from acquifer without excess head loss and at the same time to keep the acquifer material out. In the case of a tubewell design the effective grain size D50 (50 per cent fines) and the uniformity co-efficient D60 over D10 of acquifer material are important factors.

Screen Wells

These wells are possible when the acquifer material is well graded and coarse. In the development of such wells, the finer material adjacent to the well is removed and a natural envelop of coarse fractions is formed. Screens of size slots can therefore be used (larger than the size of the finest particle of the acquifer removed). Basically the screen wells can be provided when the effective grain size of the aquifer is more than 0.25 mm and uniformity co-efficient is greater than 3. Where the uniformity coefficient of acquifer is greater than 6 which is a heterogeneous and the materials lying over acquifer are fairly firm and will not cave. D70 size is selected as a slot size. If the materials overlying acquifer is soft, well will cave in such case D50 size is selected.

When the uniformity co-efficient is between 3 to 6 the D60 grain size is selected where no caving is expected and a D40 grain size where the acquifer are soft and will easily cave.

Gravel Packed Wells

Gravel packed wells are utilised where the acquifer is homogenous and has a uniformity coefficient of less than 3 and an effective grain size of less than 0.25 mm. In case of gravel packed well, the development is rather limited as the coarse material of the gravel packing is a material which is denuded of fines. The delvelopment of such wells is for breaking up and removing the mud cake deposited on the walls of the hole during boring operation. Normally river gravel is utilised so that it gives passage to the various materials without undue friction.

The gravel envelope should be as thin as possible. Normally, 15 to 23 cm thickness is recommended. The minimum thickness is 12.5 cms. The uniform acquifer should have the D50 of pack and D50 of acquifer ratio between 9 to 12.5 which means D50 of the pack should be 9 to 12.5 times more than D50 of the acquifer. In the case of a graded acquifer where uniformity co-efficient is more than 2, D50 of the pack over D50 of the acquifer should be between 12 to 15.5. The slot size of the screen should be equal to D10 size of the pack and in the case of non-homogenous acquifer, the slot sizes should vary. The screen entrance velocity should be kept low and in Northern India a screen velocity of 3 cm per second is generally utilised. The diameter of the well does not make much of the difference and it should be 10 cm larger than the pump size and it should be vertical and straight. A 12 metre long pipe fitted with 3 flanges of 30 cms diameter on both ends in the middle should be able to move fully up to the depth of the lowest pumping. The alignment of a tube well should be tested by use of a plungers 6 mm smaller in the diameter than the inside diameter of the well casing and it is suspended by the wire. The wire should pass through the centre of the top of the casing and plunger is lowered in the steps of 3 metres and deviations are noted.

The draw down of the tubewell should be the smallest one so that the entrances velocity is limited. Whenever a tubewell has functioned for a long time with extended pumping hours it behaves better than a tubewell which is drawn at a very high rate for a lesser period of time.

Failure of Tubewells

The tubewells fail earlier than normal economic life on account of:

(i) Incorrect design such as incorrect size of the gravel pack.
(ii) Poor construction,
(iii) Depletion of ground water,
(iv) Collapse of the screen due to subsidence of the soil,
(v) Inadequate development, and
(vi) Chemical action of water which produces corrosion and incrustation.

Inadequate development means the acquifer is not flushed and its all fines removed. The fine progressively move out along with pumped water and turbulence pockets are created and sand movement increases by time. In the early stages of the trouble the well can be redeveloped and the gravel pack material D90 is spread around the well.

Incrustation and corrosion is due to the chemical action of water on the screen of casing. Incrustation is usually hard and cement like. It clogs the screen opening and pores due to which yield of the well is reduced. Incrusted wells should be cleaned by acids, chlorine and other dispersing agents. Chlorine is mostly effective in removing becteria growth and slime. It is necessary that type of corrosion should be determined before deciding the treatment to be given and it can be done by analysing water pumped by the well and taking samples of acquifer around the well screen. Hydrochloric and sulphuric acids are effective in removing carbonate and partially effective in removing iron and manganese oxide.

The treatment is by effective contact between chemical and deposit on the well screen. It is very necessary to agitate the solution and to surge it. A treatment may have to be repeated two or three times. Hydrochloric acid dissolves calcium and magnesium carbonate. The acid attacks the steel well lining but when the inhibiter is put in the damage due to the treatment is not serious. Gelatine is a good inhibiter and 0.7 k.g. or gelatine in warm water to 100 litres of acid of 28 strength is good enough. The acid is added to the screen through a plastic pipe which is long enough to reach the bottom of the well. A large T should be fitted on the top for the overflow as the gases which get created can explosively come out alongwith the acid. It takes one or 2 hours with the surge plunger to get the entire acid agitated. The acid should be taken out until almost clear water runs out. Acid treatment should not be attempted on agricultural strainers which consist of a brass wire mesh wrapped over iron pipe for perforated screen because of the rapid electrolysis corrosion of the screen during the process. During acid treatment of a tubewell other tubewells within another 60 metre diameter should be closed. Instead of the sulphuric or hydrochloric acid sulphamine acid NH_2SO_3H is sometimes utilised because it attacks metal more slowly than hydrochloric or sulphuric acid and its corrosive action is less. Normally 15°C dry acid in 20 kg. per 100 litres of water utilised.

The chlorine treatment is utilised where wells get choked by the bacterial growth and slime deposit. Chlorine is introduced in the form of calcium hypochlorite $CaOC_{12}$ which is containing 70 per cent chlorine. 20 to 25 kg. is adequate for a well. Sodium hypochlorite can also be utilised. The corrosive waters attacks the metal if the water is acidic and the chlorides are present in excess of 500 PPM. Hydrogen sulphide also corrodes steel and copper if it is present in quantities more than 1 PPM.

Therefore the sick tubewell are on account of either water or the corrosion or the bad design. All said and done the tubewell having a life of 50,000 hours should be utilised properly within its life time.

Essential Tools Needed in Plumbing Work

Plumbing is a specialized art. Without proper tools, plumbing can not be proper. The essential tools needed in the plumbing works can be categorised as follows:

1. **Plouring Ladle**
   This is for pouring lead into the lead joints. The size of the ladle should be such that it should be possible to complete the needed jointing in one go.
2. **Cold Caulking Iron**
   These are chisels which are bent. These are available either as inside cauking chisels or outside caulking chisels.

3. **Yarning Iron**
   In most of the piping joints to be prepared yarn is placed below the joint, whether it is a lead joint or a cement joint. In order that yarn compressed properly. Yarning iron bent to the proper shape is utilised.
4. A melting pot for melting lead.
5. A blow torch is utilised, in the plumbing, specially in lead work.
6. **A Pipe Vice**
   This is utilised for holding the pipe for cutting the threads etc.
7. Die and stock for threading.
8. Pipe reamer.
9. Pipe cutter.
10. 35 cm pipe wrench.
11. Ordinary adjustable pipe wrench 20 cm.
12. Iron files of sorts.
13. Hacksaw and hacksaw blades.
14. Measuring tape.
15. Spirit level.
16. Metallic tape.
17. Marking chalk.

27. PLASTICS

Plastics in building construction in general and in water supply and sanitary installations in particular is a rather recent phenomenon. Plastic pipes PVC started in 1927 in U.S.A. These pipes have many desirable properties like corrosion resistance ease of handling, less weight in transportation etc. Plastics have properties by which it can be moulded in various complex shapes.

Plastics have limitations also and they have to be correctly designed and installed. Specially integration with other product is rather complex on account of some properties of plastics. Plastics in generally very much less in tensile strength which is comparable to wood and much less than steel. Plastics deflect much more under an applied load when compared to steel.

Plastics are resistant to impact when compared with glass or wood but they are not hard as glass or steel and can get scratched quickly. Because of their molecular structures plastics do exhibit creep at normal ambient temperatures and deformation can be large. This is particularly true of thermo-plastics. Thermo-setting plastics, reinforced plastics have better resistance to creep but under prolonged load they can exhibit high creep.

Plastics in general have got high values for coefficient of expansion. It could be as 150 × 10 × cu/in/F which is very high when compared with wood or steel or concrete. The value is 3 to 15 times more than that of concrete.

Inflamability is another concern which has to be taken into consideration in buildings. Being organic in nature plastics would burn and some plastics like polyethylene is inflamable. The flamability can be soemwhat controlled by additives but basically these products can be problem in a fire. The fumes which result would be highly toxic. The plastics are not more inflamable than thin wood sections, fabric etc. which is organic in nature but when compared with metal they are seriously a fire hazard and have to be handled with caution.

Compared to metals, the plastics are more corrosion-resistant. They are not subject to electro-chemical corrosion as they are bad conductors. The plastics can be therefore by a good choice where the soil is corrosive in nature or there are many stray currents.

Environmental stress cracking is another way of degradation of plastics. The process is believed to occur when surface active agent like alcohol or detergent acts. The plastics are vulnerable to stresses caused by forced alignments which can take place due to poor workmanship or changes in the levels of building component due to settlement, shrinkage, thermal expansion and contraction etc.

The plastics which are in common use and their properties in general is given in the following table for guidance.

TYPICAL PROPERTIES OF PLASTICS

Meterial	*Density Kg./m*	*Linear expansion per Occ*	*mm/m*	*Max. temp. recommended for continuous use*	*In fire*
1. Polythene					
Low Density	910	20×10^{-5}	0.2	80	Melts and burns like parafin wax.
High Density	945	14×10^{-5}	0.14	104	"
2. Polypropylene	900	11×10^{-5}	0.11	120	"
3. UPVC (Rigid PVC)	1395	7×10^{-5}	0.07	65	Melts, burns with difficulty.
4. CPVC (Post chronated)	1300-1500	7×10^{-5}	0.7	100	"
5. Plasticised PVC	1280	7×10^{-5}	0.7	40-65	Melts, burns according to plasticiser
6. ABS	1060	7×10^{-5}	0.07	90	Melts & burns readily with while flame.
7. Nylon	1120	8×10^{-5}	0.08	80-12	Melts, burns with difficulty.

All product with density less than 1000 kg/m float in water.

In specifying use of plastic piping in a building specially in a hot country like India much care has to be taken.

Most of the places in India may have a shade temperature exceeding 45° C in summer and if piping network is exposed on the exterior then the temperature can be very high much beyond 45° C. Thus if such pipes are laid on the outside there could be problems of pipes buckling etc. due to high coefficient of expansion.

The horizontal runs of pipes have to be carefully done and most of these pipes require clamps/support at closer intervals when compared to steel pipes. This is because of low modulus of elasticity of these pipes.

All structures are subject to substantial temperature changes. The difference between the coefficient of expansion between brick-work/concrete etc. which are common building materials and plastics can give rise to the pipes buckling as substrata of masonry/concrete would be less expansive when compared to pipes of plastics. These pipes could be used in shade like in a shaft etc.

When plastic pipes are used, they have to be cleaned very carefully with special tools as the scratch resistance is fairly low.

Care have to be taken not to exceed the service temperature which can be low as much as 50 to 60 C. Thus flow of hot water may damage piping.

The stresses created by water hammer can also be very high.

Some of the plastics cannot be threaded like G.I. pipes. This facture has also to be taken into account while specifying.

28. SPRINKLER INSTALLATIONS IN A BUILDING

A sprinkler installation for fire fighting is important equally to a water-supply engineer and a fire engineer. Hence some knowledge about its installation is necessary.

Automatic sprinkler systems are designed to hold a fire in check and to give warning of danger. They do not necessarily extinguish a fire all the times but many times they do.

The requirements for water supplies for automatic sprinklers are very stringent and for all installations the local fire officer should always be consulted.

The water supply should be of sufficient quantity, pressure and flow to be capable of meeting the requirements for different classes of hazards as laid down. The network should not be subject to freezing. It must be under direct control of occupier. The water should be free from fibrous or other materials in suspension that might cause sedimentation and/or corrosion in pipe work. Use of brackish water is not allowed.

The supplies of water for sprinklers depned on the fire hazards of the occupancy of the premises. There are three main classes of occupancy which are—

1. Extra Light Hazard

This is for hospitals, hotels, offices etc. In parts of premises like attics, basements boiler rooms, kitchen, laundries, storage spaces, work-rooms. The density of water discharged is increased by spacing the sprinkler heads closer.

2. Ordinary Hazard

This is sub-divided into four distinct sub-groups.

(a) Light ordinary hazards like breweries, cement works and restaurants.

(b) Medium ordinary hazard as in bakeries confectionery, light engineering works, medium sized retail shops (less than 50 assistants).

(c) High ordinary hazard as in boot & shoe manufacture, large stores.

(d) Special Hazard—This is basically C classification but where there is a danger of flash fires, such as cotton mills, photo studios, oil mills etc.

3. Extra High Hazard like Aircraft Hangers, Fire Works, Foam Plastic, Paint and Varnish, Wood, Wool Manufacture.

Sources of water supplies for sprinkler system could be.

1. Mains
2. Elevated tank
3. Automatic pumps
4. Pressure tanks.

1. Mains

The mains should be not less than 150 mm and the source must have at least 1000 m^3.

2. Elevated Tank

It must have a constant capacity of atleast 500 m if used for an extra-light hazard, 1000 m^3 if used for ordinary hazard and for extra high hazard it should be at least 1000 m^3 plus extra capacity for design density of that particular hazard.

3. Automatic Pumps

Automatic pumps should have a positive suction. The pump should have a direct drive and automatic start. Once started the pump must run continuously until stopped manually.

A test for the automatic starting of the pump must be carried out weekly.

Means should be provided to reduce the applied water pressure to the starting device to simulate the condition of automatic starting at the requisite pressure and test must be for at least 10 min. When the pump is powered by I.C. engine then the capacity of fuel tank should be sufficient to allow the engine to run on full load for atleast

Extra light hazard	3 hours
Ordinary hazard	4 hours
Extra high hazard	6 hours.

4. Pressure Tanks

Pressure tank can be accepted as a sole supply in case of extra-light hazard and ordinary hazard group 'A' only and for the rest they can be accepted as a duplicate water supply.

In case of pressure tanks there should be an audible warning device if there is a failure of the devices to restore the correct air pressure and water level within reasonable period.

Minimum quantity of water to be maintained in tank.

Extra light hazard	7 m
Ordinary hazard group A	23 m
When duplicate supply	
Extra light hazard	7 m
Ordinary hazard	23 m

Pipe Work

The layout of pipe work and the sizes necessary should be rationally calculated.

It must be sloped to allow for drainage. Where this is not feasible subsidiary drain points are required. Pipes must not be embedded neither they should be in a position where it is difficult to work upon it for extension or alterations or repairs.

Where corrosive condition exists the pipe work must be thoroughly cleaned and protected by suitable means. Where pipe work is liable to mechanical damage it must be protected by adequate guards and vertical risers and guards protected by guard rails.

Flushing points mut be installed at the end of distribution pipes.

There should be ample hangers to support sprinkler piping and nothing should be hung from sprinkler pipes. There should be no undue strain on pipe work.

Alterations and repairs to the installation or its water suplies should be carried out during normal working hours and done expeditiously so that system is inoperative for as short time as possible. Where work cannot be completed in one day as much of the installation as practicable must be kept operative during progress of the work. Before water is turned off it should be seen that there is no fire or fire-like situation in any part of the structure. Smoking should be prohibited in the structure when the system is being repaired. Where the system is inoperative, the shop floor manager should be kept informed so that for fire emergency additional hand held extinguishers could be arranged.

When there is a drought in the town mains special pre-caution should be taken to arrange other supplies.

It is laid down as one of the principles that warning should be given of danger. This warning is given by means of loud sounding gong which is actuated by flow of water. Before the gong water motor the water passes through a strainer which should be examined and cleaned at frequent intervals.

A test of the alarm gong should be made every week.

PART II—DESIGN AND CONSTRUCTION OF SANITARY INSTALLATION

1. SANITARY PIPE WORKS ABOVE GROUND

Upto the middle of 19th century, even in the developed countries only a few buildings had a supply of water under pressure which could reach first floor. Water used to reach to the ground floor level only. Water closets used to be either inside the house or outside the house at the ground floor level only and washing water was carried by water jugs. It is only when better plumbing and pumps were available that the water could be had in the water mains at a pressure by which it could reach upper floors.

Earlier to the 20th century waste water from basins and baths was not considered foul by sanitary engineers and the waste water was allowed to go through even rain water pipes and through a gulley grating (to separate out rough solids) to the soak ways. The W.C.'s were connected to the septic tanks or sewers through a system of traps. The waste water from bath and basins used to discharge into an open hopper head which many times also collected the rain water. The hopper heads drained to an open gulley trap. The gulley trap acted as a water seal against odours arising from drains. The advantage of the system was simplicity. As the bath and wash basin waste would discharge over the hopper head they did not need a trap.

The disadvantage of the system was that in course of time the hopper head used to collect muck, become smelly and used to get finally blocked. With two storeyed building it was a relatively easy matter to clean first floor hopper head. However, with construction going more than two storeys cleaning of hopper heads became difficult and flooding of hopper heads and smellyness of the system led to the abandonment of hopper head gulley trap system.

Thus came the two pipe system wherein the excreta matter (solid matter) was collected through one system and waste matter through another. Both pipe systems were independent of each other and finally were led to the sewer or septic tank.

Even introduction of continuous vent pipe is a phenomenon which developed much later.

To prevent siphonage or loss of water in a trap it is necessary to maintian equal pressure on both sides of the trap to an appliance. The most straight forward way for doing this is to connect a short length of pipe from the out go side of the trap to the open air.

The short length of pipe was called a puff pipe because it drew puffs of air to stabilize pressure. The use of puff pipes was later abandoned because of fear of sewer gas and other malodours rising up from soil pipe and through puff pipe to the open window or any opening nearby. The puff pipe type vents were replaced by vent pipes. Thus came up to two pipe fully vented system.

The terminology used in case of sanitary pipes above ground is as follows:

(a) Discharge from watercloset and urinals is called soil water and the pipe which carry that discharge is called soil pipe.

(b) Discharge from basins, baths and sinks is called waste water and the pipe which carry that discharge is called waste pipe.

There are following main systems of sanitary pipe work above ground.

(a) Hopper head system (discarded)

(b) Two pipe vented system

(c) Single pipe vented system

(d) Single stack system

Under certain circumstances the changeover can be effected from two pipe vented system at S.No. (b) to S.No. (c) and (d) which leads to economy as well as doing away with unsightly webbing of pipes.

Basically two pipe vented system has four pipes—two pipes for carrying waste and soil discharge and two pipes for venting; single pipe vented system has two pipes one for carrying the soil and waste pipe discharge and one for venting and single stack system where there is only one pipe carrying soil and waste plus venting, the economics of single stack stystem which uses only one pipe over two pipe vented system which uses four pipes is obvious.

Prevention of Blockages

In a sanitary installation poor design is often signified by a large number of inspection fittings. The aim should be to reduce as far as possible numerous short radius bends and horizontal pipes. Every time and access door is removed for rodding there is inevitable spill of dirt and dirty water which is a health hazard. Wherever possible long radius bends should be used.

Long horizontal piping should be avoided by installing more vertical stacks. Batter grouping of sanitary fittings will go a long way in reducing the blockages.

Where spillage due to rodding is inevitable and the building is a sterile building like a hospital, the access doors for rodding should not be in sterile areas but in dirty areas.

2. THE TRAP

According to the dictionary meaning, a trap is a device to catch something or a pit. In sanitary installations, however, the word trap is utilised to mean entirely different functions according to the context in which the word is utilised.

First, installation of a trap is for catching something like, a sand trap which is utilised to avoid sand flowing into the sewer lines; in case of a combined system where sewer and drainage is combined, a grease trap by which the grease particles get separated is utilised by the side of a kitchen to take out the grease from drainage, a petrol trap which is utilised by the side of a petrol pump wherein it is so arranged that the petrol which is highly inflammable does not flow into the sewer lines creating an explosive mixture. Thus, traps are correctly to be called interceptors and are to be provided when the liquid waste containing grease and such objectionable flowable waste, sand and other ingredients harmful to the building sewer drainage system public sewer and sewage treatment plant is to be handled. The basic idea is to separate out these harmful ingredients from the flow and take them out from time to time for safe disposal.

In sanitary installation design, a trap is a fixture which is utilised to keep out foul air from the sewer line and at the same time allow water and solids to pass through only in one direction to another, i.e., from inlet to outlet. This type of trap allows flow of liquids but prevents a flow of air.

In this chapter, the second type of trap which keeps out foul air from the sewer line is discussed.

The basic requirement of trap design is that it must be self-cleansing, i.e., it must permit the passage of liquid conveying solids, in suspension, without segregating them and solids getting deposited in the trap. The trap must maintain water seal under all conditions, i.e., when the water flow is there and when the water flow is not there. Thus, the two basic requirements of a trap are self-cleansing design and the water seal. These two requirements of being self-cleansing and retention of water seal are compulsory when the design of trap is considered. These requirements are contradictory to each other. For maintaining the water seal the passage of water has to be complicated and in this arrangement the trap is more likely to get clogged due to deposition of solids due to low velocity of flow and a clogged trap is useless. When the water passage becomes simple and straightforward, the danger of water seal getting broken increase. A self-cleansing trap means that when the water is flowing along with the solids, there is no deposition of solids due to changes in direction of flow or due to changes in velocity. The self-cleansing trap of improper design may break its water seal when it is being utilised due to self-siphonages or induced siphonage. One fear which is sometime expressed is that the water seal would get evaporated in summer. Normally the evaporation of water takes place at a fairly low rate in a building which is occupied. The problem may occur only in buildings which are vacant for periods of 2-3 months or more. The self siphonage takes place due to velocity of flow and for this usually a small trailing flow is ensured by all flushing systems which refills the trap. If, however, a deluge of flow exist like a bucket of water dumped there then there could be a chance of self siphonage. The induced siphonage takes place due to the fixtures or their trap being over-flooded and negative pressures are created. If the outlet pipes from trap are of sufficiently large dimension as per standards chances of induced siphonages are very remote. The design of the trap has to fulfil the following requirements:

1. It should be able to pass freely the water and the solid without any mechanical aid.
2. It must be able to retain the trapped water to prevent passage of foul air.
3. When it is functioning the foul air should not be permitted to cross the current of the water flowing.
4. It must be strong and proof against all leakage of gas or liquids.
5. It should have no recesses, cavities or pockets which are not covered by the flow of water through the trap.
6. It should not have any internal projections or partitions which will cause resistance to the flow, therefore, it should have smooth surface which will be scoured by the velocity of water. It must not employ any washer connected to retain the seal of water.

The trap should not have the vent at the top called a crown vented trap and no fixture should be double trapped. The trap of 38 mm of water seal is sufficient when the variation of air pressure either positive or negative in the sanitary pipelines does not exceed 25 mm of water. Normally, the sizing of sanitary branches and vertical stacks is made with the limitation of air pressure variation of 25 mm of water. Normally, the trap sizes provided are:

Minimum Internal Diameter of Trap

Wash basin		32 mm
Bidet		32 mm
Sink		40 mm
Bath		40 mm
Shower		40 mm
Wash-tub		50 mm
Kitchen		40 mm
Urinal	1 or 2	50 mm
	3 to 4	64 mm
	5 to 6	75 mm

The internal diameter of trap and whether the fitment is ventilated or not decide the water seal of trap, usual rule is,

Trap Water Seals

—Traps upto 64 mm internal diameter not provided with ventilatity pipe should have 75 mm seal

—Traps upto 64 mm diameter provided with ventilating pipe may have 38 mm seal.

—Traps from 75 to 100 mm internal diameter with or without ventilating pipe should have 50 mm seal.

In ordinary terms, the water seals provided are:

1. W.Cs.	50 mm
2. Wash basin	75 mm when wash basin is used after making it full 38 mm when wash basin is used with water taps running flow.
3. Floor trap	38 mm.
4. Bath tub	75 mm.

More than one fitment like wash basins, kitchen sink are sometimes clubbed and only one common trap is provided. If two such fitments are connected together, one trap compartment should not be more than 15 cm deeper than the other and should not be more than 75 cm apart. The trap to the fixture distance shall not exceed 60 cm in any case.

3. LOSS OF WATER SEAL IN TRAPS

There could be three situations in which there could be loss of water seal in traps of appliances. These three situations are induced siphonage, back pressure and self siphonage.

Induced siphonage may be caused by a heavy discharge from a fitment situated at a higher elevation than the trap under consideration. The discharge may carry air from the branch pipe serving the trap creating a partial vacuum which may cause breaking of seal. Thus induced siphonage is a result of air being sucked out. Thus induced siphonage is result of air being sucked out. This will be happening more a frequently wherever the flow is non laminar and turbulent. Wherever the flow is less turbulent then there is less chances of induced siphonage. Thus where W.C. branch is swept in the direction of flow the danger of induced siphonage is reduced. Offset in the vertical pipeline cause quite a lot of turbulence and the flow will be non laminar containing much of air mixed with water. This can give rise to induced siphonage. Offset in the pipelines should be avoided as far as feasible and the stacks should run as vertical as feasible without any offset. Wherever offset is provided venting may be needed.

Back pressure occurs at the junction of a branch waste near the base of stack. When a discharge reaches the base of a stack, the change of direction of flow by almost 90° from vertical to horizontal coupled with fact that velocity of flow is vertical pipe in decidedly more than what is possible in a nearly horizontal pipe, formation of a hydraulic jump is inevitable leading fullbore to turbulence and flow at some stage or other. When bend is full of the water and another plug of flow shoots down the stack leads to compression of air column between the base and the upper plug of flow. The increased pressure caused by the discharge may over turn the water seal. Similar situation would be created by the offsets in the pipeline which are provided. The way to reduce chances of back siphonage is to make transition from vertical flow to horizontal flow as smooth as possible. Therefore to limit back pressure the bend in the base of stack should have a large radius.

Where a branch waste is connected close to W.C. branch a discharge from the W.C. may cause back pressure in the waste. Therefore branch waste should not be connected to the stack for a depth of 20 cm below the centre line of W.C. branch.

Self siphonage may occur where the discharge from an appliance runs fullbore in the waste pipe at the end causing a reduction in pressure and possible loss to water seal in trap. When loss of water seal to wash basin traps occur due to self siphonage, the trap will not be filled because there is too little trail flow. To reduce the possibility of self siphonage, the wash basin waste should not be longer than 1.7 metre. Which in other terms means that wash basins should be within 1.7 metres of Stack. In case of baths and sinks even if the self siphonage occurs from the flat bottom of these appliances there is sufficient trail flow to fill and therefore no need to limit the length or slope of waste against self siphonage.

In two pipe fully vented network of piping soil pipes are utilised to drain soil appliances and waste pipes are utilized to drain waste appliances. A separate system of vent pipes is connected to traps of all soil fitments which is called soil vent pipe and a separate network of vent pipes is connected to vent all waste appliances. This fully vented two pipe system is commonly installed in building irrespective of hieght. Now with the advent of further research two pipe fully vented system is used for very tall buildings or a complicated network of pipe when siphonage (induced or back) is feared.

The two pipe fully vented system is a jumble of pipes of soil, soil vent, waste and waste vents which pipes criss-cross with pass over fitments etc. This system is efficient yet costly and many time complicated. In case of not so large installations and where both soil and waste waters discharge in the same outfall like a septic tank or sewer line, it has been experimentally established that there is no need for separate waste pipe and this gave rise to single pipe fully vented system where all traps were vented but the soil and waste were drained by one pipe only.

Building research in flow of fluids through sanitary piping established that the air column which is always present in the flow through sanitary vertical pipes can be made use of for venting. It was further established that by careful arrangement of branches to a soil vertical pipe there would be no loss of seal to the trap of appliances therefore there will be no need of a separate vent system to be provided. One pipe will carry soil, waste, water and at the same time provide air for venting. The single soil pipe system without vent pipe system is called single stack system.

Main Requirements of a Single Stack System for its Proper Functioning.

(a) Sanitary fittings should be very close to the stack in order to limit the length of branch pipes.

(b) To avoid induced siphonage, sanitary fittings should be individually connected to the main stack.

(c) An offset should not occur in the "Wet" part of the stack. This is to avoid compression of air in the stack.

(d) The foot of stack should be connected to the drain by a large radius (15 cm minimum radius) or by two large radius 130 bends. This prevents compression of air at the base of stack.

(e) Ground floor fitments should be connected directly to the drain.

(f) W.C. Connection should be swept in the direction of flow with a radius at invert of atleast 50 mm. A swept connection helps to prevent turbulant flow of water with a resultant reduction in air pressure at the highest part of stack. Unvented W.C. branches up to 1.5 metre only are possible. Beyond this venting is necessary.

(g) A branch pipe from bath should be so connected that its centre line and centre line of stack meet at a level higher than W.C. branch. Where it is lower it should be 20 cm lower.

(h) Waste fittings should have P traps with 75 mm deep seals.

(i) Branch waste pipe should not exceed:

Basin Bidet	1.7 meters in length
Bath Sink Shower	2.3 metres in length

The pipes should be laid to a fall of minimum 1¼ to 5° only. Or from 1:10 slope maximum slope to a minimum slope of 1:50.

4. VENTS AND VENTING

The discharge through a sanitary pipe is a combined flow of air, solids and water. The characteristics of flow also differ from a horizontal branch to a vertical stack. Even in the flow in the vertical stack, the type of flow of the waste and soil water differ when a fitment is discharging or not discharging. With all these changes of flows of water, the changes in the pressure of the air column take place. These changes in the pressure of the air column are normally of the order of 25 mm water guage. Care is taken to even out fluctuations of pressure by providing access to the outside air from inside the system by which the pressure gets stabilised for this purpose vents or vent pipes are utilised.

The vent pipes protect the seals provided to the various fitments, from siphonage. It is accomplished by the appropriate use of soil and vent stacks, vents revents, back vents, loop vents or continuous vents or combination thereof. The objective of providing the vent is to prevent a balance of air within the branch system so that at no time positive and negative pressure by greater than 25 mm water at the seal of the fixtures.

The vent pipe has to be necessarily open at the outer end. Location of the top vent terminal should be such that no vent terminal from a drainage system shall be directly angled towards any door opening, window or ventilator of the building or of an immediately adjacent building is provided. Nor any such vent shall be provided within 3 metres, horizontally, of such opening, unless it is 1.6 metre above such opening. The vent terminal should not terminate under the overhang of the building. Where in cases, such as roof gardens, it is not desirable to extend a vent through the roof, then the vent terminal should be taken on the side. This precaution is necessary as the excess air when it is driven out from vent pipe system is necessarily a polluted air and most of the time malodourous.

The vent pipe terminal provided on the top of the building is likely to be subjected to variations in air pressures, on account of wind flows. It is common knowledge that wind causes pressure on windward side and a suction on leeward side. These pressures and suction due to wind flow can interfere with small variations of pressure changes which occur due to stack flow. The cowl design has to be such that such variations in windflow will nto cause violent variation of pressure. While designing the soil stack vent system, in a multi-storeyed building, this factor of suction and pressure zones around the building should be considered.

All vent and branch vent pipes should be so laid to a grade and connected so that no water stagnates and small amount of condensate water if there is condensation flows to the soil or waste pipe by gravity. Wherever vent pipe connects to horizontal soil or waste pipe, the vent shall be taken of above the central line of the soil pipe and it shall be at an angle not more than 45 from the vertical to a point atleast 15 cm above the floor level, against the fixtures, (it is venting), before being placed horizontally or connected to the branch vent. (Horizontal means nearly horizontal laid to a grade and not truely horizontal).

The connection between a vent pipe and a vent stack or stack vent shall be made atleast 15 cm above the float level rim of the highest fixtures, served by the vent. The horizontal vent pipes forming the branch vent, relief vent or the loop vent shall be at least 15 cm above the float level rim above the highest level served.

The vent opening from a soil or vent pipe except for water closet, or similar fixtures shall not be below the weir of the trap. To have an effective vent, the distance of the fixtures trap, from the vent, shall not exceed the following. Size of the fixtures drain = 35 mm, Distance = 1.05 metres, size of the fixtures drain 75 mm = 2 metres, size of the fixtures drain 100 mm = 3.3 metres.

A common vent may be utilised for 2 sets of fixtures fixed on the same floor level. The fixtures drain shall be vented between the hydraulic gradients and a vent connection provided.

The diameter of the individual vent shall not be less than 30 mm and in any case not less than 1/2 of the diameter of the drain to which it is connected.

The single stack system and single pipe system can function, by taking air from the air column, inside the soil stack. For this purpose there are certain restrictions in placement of the fitments and various types of fixtures, which could be utilised. These are dealt with, in greater detail on the chapter on the single pipe and 2 pipe systems.

5. FLOW THROUGH SANITARY STACKS

The sanitary piping system of a building is, without exception, a non pressure system. This means that the hydraulic pressure does not exist in the system as against water supply piping which is basically a pressure system. In case of water supply piping there is always a full bore flow where as it is essential that the sanitary pipe should not have flow more than 1/4 to 1/3 of its full bore capacity if noise in the system and excessive air pressure fluctuations are to be avoided.

The flow in the vertical stack finally becomes nearly horizontal at the bottom point through a heel rest bend or a long turn bend.

If the picture of the flow in the sanitary piping is mentally sketched, it will be seen that from sanitary fitment a nearly horizontal pipe is provided to connect the fitment to the vertical pipe and the vertical pipe is finally connected to the sewer through a manhole by a horizontal pipe. Thus the flow of water (waste or soil) is first horizontal, then vertical and then horizontal. Before an attempt is made for understanding the phenomenon of change of direction of flow of water, it is interesting to study as to how in the vertical piping of sanitary network water flows.

Water in the piping as soon as it comes in the vertical section accelerates rapidly by action of gravity and it assumes form of sheet of water around the walls of the stack. This sheet of water continues to accelerate. The thickness of the sheet is roughly proportionate to its velocity until the friction by the walls of the stack on the flowing sheet of water equals the gravity. From this point on, the water sheet will remain unchanged in thickness and velocity until it reaches the bottom of the stack. The ultimate vertical velocity that the sheet attains is called the "terminal velocity" and a distance through which the sheet of water passes from the start at which flow enter vertical pipe to the point when it reaches terminal velocity is called "terminal length". The distance of the terminal length is approximately 4 to 5 metres. This is so because the stacks even though they might differ in roughness in the initial stages when it is new get a coating of slime around it in course of time. The slime coating is very much smoother than original surface as the pitting in original surface is filled with slime.

When the water is falling through, as a sheet of water, along the wall of the stack at a centre of the stack is a core of air, which is tagged along with the water by friction and air supply if not provided to account for this loss of air alongwith the water an excessive pressure reduction in the stack results. The usual means of supplying this air is through a pipe called a vent pipe. The sucking of the air into the stack requires that the pressure reduction exists inside the stack and it is provided by the extraneous air. In most of the cases sheet of water which will be flowing would be devoid of solid materials and the solid materials fall freely in the core area which is an air column from the top till it reaches the bottom of the stack.

When the water is rushing from higher level of the stack to the lower level and any sanitary fitment discharges into the stack in the meantime the water flow which is in a form of sheet gets deflected to cater for the incoming water and after some time it becomes an integral part of the sheet of the water. When the stack gets discharge from intermediate fittings there are areas where suction pressure which get developed.

It is to be understood that with the normal sizes of fittings and the rules for combining fittins the vertical stack will never have a plug of water flowing. (A plug of water means entire section of pipe filled). Even if a plug of water may flow for a small distance yet after a certain point of time in the run downward it gets converted into a sheet of water.

When this sheet of water reaches the bend at a bottom of the stack or anywhere there is an offset and it is turned at approximately right angle, and if the quantity of water flow is not very large, the sheet of water will make the turn without leaving the wall of the pipe even at a top surface at a cross section. This water is sufficiently of high velocity because it has been coming from a vertical stack and the slope of building drain will not be adequate to maintain the velocity that existed in the sheet when it reached the bottom of the stack. The result is that the velocity of the water flowing alongwith the building drain will decrease slowly with a corresponding increase in the surface cross section of water till the time of hydraulic jump take place and then the horizontal drain will tend to flow full with large air bubbles being carried at a top of the section.

When the particular horizonatal drain is free from any sediments, once the hydraulic jump takes place and it settles, the drain will carry the discharge properly but partly full. Any partial chokage of the cross section of the building drain will have an important effect on the existing pressure in the lower part of the stack. As the water will not be able to flow along with air bubble and positive pressure will start building up in the bend and the vertical stack. A similar effect will be produced if the drains is flowing so full that the end of the building drain is flooded and that air is carried alongwith water in the drain can not pass freely into the street sewer.

Thus apart from the point of change of direction there is substantial change in the flow characteristics of the water. This change in flow characteristics is accompanied by turbulence of water. If the water which is flowing contains certain detergent, they have a tendency to foam further due to turbulence and the detergent foam does not break quickly, therefore, it will rise back in the space available in the vertical stack. If the outlet from the fitments to the vertical stack is very near, then there is a tendency for the detergent foam to come out with force to the fitments and may even flow out on to the ground floor through fitments. There is no way to prevent this phenomenon occurring. A good engineering practice is that the ground floor fittings (and first floor fittings, if the height of the building is very high) should be independently connected to the manhole. This solves two purposes. Vertical stack which has a tendency to collect muck like sticks rags etc. at the bend on account of various reasons will have sufficient water pressure to carry away the muck. Incidentally, the static pressure of water upto Ist floor level is sufficient to drive detergent foam back to the sewer.

This problem of foaming is a recent phenomenon as the soap suds break fairly quickly and form part of water bubble but the detergents have a very strong foam which does not break quickly and has a long life.

Birds and Children have an uncanny tendency to put inflatable objects like balls, rags, sticks etc. into the vertical stack and these objects get struck at the bend point. If the distance between the heel rest bend to the starting manwhole is very long, it is very difficult to clean this particular bend portion and it can remain as a trouble point for all the times to come. Therefore, where the starting manhole is fairly separated from the heel rest bend, a Y junction could be introduced which would be normally remain plugged, so that it can be opened whenever there is any such problem of chokage.

The water which is flowing alongwith the stack causes substantial changes in the pressure, the rules of design for the stack so dictate that this air pressure changes shall not be exceeding 25 mm. The flow traps and other water traps have normally a depth of 38 mm and thus under the normal circumstances there is no possibility of a trap being broken.

If vertical stacks top is closed, then sucking of air due to the changes in the pressure does not take place. Therefore, it is absolutely necessary that under no circumstances the top of the stack should be closed.

If the top of the stack is closed then violent changes takes place in air pressure as the air present in stack gets drawn out due to suction and there is always a possible of trap seals getting broken. Such violent air pressure changes also take place if the pipe from heel rest bend to first manhole is choked. These air pressure changes may even break trap seal specially in ground floor fitments. Hence it is absolutely essential that no flooding or choking of the pipe branches to the manhole takes place.

6. FLUSH—HOW IT WORKS

A layman is apt to think that the flushing system works by pull of a handle and the matter in the water closet (W.C.) bowl gets evacuated automatically. He is apt to think that the flushing system can be of any size and so long as there is water, the flushing will take place. In the paragraph to come an attempt has been made to indicate how the simple flush system works and what are its intricacies.

The discharge of W.C. is a very complicated phenomenon. The inflow of water is controlled by a tank or a valve called a flushing tank or a flushing valve W.C. bowl in conjunction with the tank or the valve operate together as a total system. Therefore both W.C. bowl and flush tank/valve have to be considered as an integral part of the flushing system.

Flush water should be adequate enough to remove the contents of the bowl completely and refill the water in the trap which may be an integral part of the bowl or otherwise. It should be economical in the use of water. A layman when he tries to flush out the contents of a bowl of W.C. by throwing almost a bucket of water would be surprised to observe even though the bucket of water contains almost the same quantity of water which an overhead cistern contains i.e. 10-12 litres, the contents of the bowl do not go but settle where they are. This is because the carriage of matter during the flushing process from the bowl is a very complex process.

The flushing action which takes place as a result flushing cistern discharge is a combined action of self-syphonage of water with the jet action and also the refill due to the trail flow.

When the flush chain is released the flush water starts coming from the flushing cistern and rushes through the orifices of the W.C. bowl and also through the rim of the orifices which take care of the matter which has settled on the side of bowl. The jet orifice is directed into the up leg of the syphon and by mixing with the water in the leg, it imparts, momentum to the water body in minimum time, in the direction of the discharge thus tending to produce a quick priming of the syphon. The syphonic action is started when the water reaches slightly above the level of the weir of the bowl. The water in the initial stages is mixed with air and there is turbulence because of friction of the downleg. When the air pocket is filled with water the syphon begins to act in discharging water at a much higher pace when it enters the bowl. There are 3 basic stages, therefore, in the flushing part of it (a) the flush water starts coming in flushes and fills up the down leg of the syphon thus starting the syphon to the flushing of the sides and matter in the bowl takes place. (b) During this syphonic action and later through the inflow from the flushing cistern reduces and thus the level of water falls below the weir and air starts entering into syphonic legs and the syphonic action stops. (c) The trail flow from cistern fills up the trap again and now the W.C. bowl can be flushed again.

The entire operation of flushing and refilling of trap occupies a time interval of 10-15 seconds depending on the valve and the device utilised. The most certain method of efficient cleaning of W.C. bowl occurs when there is a strong syphonic action in the first 2-3 seconds followed by a weak syphonic action when the bowl is practically emptied followed by second syphon. If the rate of supply of water to the bowl is too low, complete break in the syphonic action will occur and the result is uncertain and sluggish working of the flush cistern. If the rate of supply of water to the bowl is rather too high then syphonic action continues till the end of the flush and the matter in the bowl does not flush out.

The flushing cistern when the chain is pulled starts working by syphonic action discharging water in the bowl. When the syphonic action of the flushing cistern is in progress there is an inflow of water into the flushing cistern. The rate of inflow being dependent on the line pressure. Thus the actual amount of flush water is utilised is always slightly more than the capacity of the flushing cistern by its exact tank volume measurement.

It is impossible to find a definite value either for the rate of supply or the total quantity of water needed, which will give the best results for water closets as the water requirement will differ with different bowls. Normally a wash down closet which requires a strong flushing requires a mean rate of discharge and approximately mean rates of supply of about 123 to 135 litres per minute. For syphon jet closets the range is between 110 litres to 165 litres in a minute. Therefore on an average about 125 to 150 litres in a minute rate of discharge is needed.

A wash down closet is inferior in action when compared to syphon closet as in the case of wash down closet the water cleanses by sheer force of flow whereas in the syphonic closet, the syphonic action of closet adds to the force of water thus cleaning action is very certain. But the cost of the syphonic closet is very much higher than the wash down closet.

When a water closet is utilised and flushed out it would mean total bowl will be emptied at a time of the end of the flush and thus certain amount of water will be required for completing the water seal. This is normally provided by what is known as trail flow. This trail flow has to be equal to the amount of water required for filling the trap completely. Trail flow results when the bowl is flushed out yet cistern, action is still in progress.

It will thus be clear that the flushing of a W.C. is a very much complicated phenomenon and it is better to rely on well known brands of sanitary fitments.

Many firms therefore produce flushing system by assembling all components, especially in the case of low level cisterns. These should be utilised as a composite unit.

The flushing cistern using 8-12 liters of water are available and it would depend on the availability of water as to how much and what type of flushing cistern is to be designed. However water is also vehicle for transport of faecal matter. It should be rechecked that lower quantity of flush water is good enough to create self cleansing velocities and there is no unwanted deposition of solids in the horizontal piping due to less quantity of flush water.

However, a high level flushing cistern should not be utilised as a low level flushing cistern and vice-a-versa. Even though a high level flushing cistern will be very much cheaper than a low level flushing cistern as the rates of flow in both would differ.

It will be better to have correct combination of fitments of WC bowl and cistern as recommended by manufacturer.

7. DESIGNS OF SANITARY LINES—BASIC PHILOSOPHY

In the case of sanitary installations, the basic design philosophy is that the sanitary system should serve the primary purposes of convenience and comfort. The aim of any sanitary system should cover normal possible contingency arising from its use. The system is to be optimal and economical.

The aim of designing a drainage system is to provide a system of conduits which are designed to be self cleansing while conveying soil, waster water speedily to the sewer or outfall efficiently without risk of nuisance and hazard to health.

(a) The drainage system has to carry waste and soil water rapidly away from the fixtures without any leakage.

(b) The foul gases from the sewer line should not get an access to the interior of the building, whether the system is functioning or not functioning and provision for the escape of the gases, which get created within the drainage system, should also be made.

(c) The drainage pipe lines should be water tight, gas tight and air tight.

(d) The drainage pipe lines should be suitably installed so that slight movement of the building, or of the pipes due to thermal changes, ground movement etc. will not cause leakage.

(e) There should be no air lock, siphonage, proneness to obstruction deposit and damage.

(f) There should be easy access for cleaning. Adequate and easy access for clearing obstructions should be a major consideration from the maintenance angle. This point is many times forgotten for various considerations, either intentionally or unintentionally, whereby pipes get buried without any provision for cleaning them or the cleaning outlets are embedded in the masonry or in many cases they are turned towards masonry by which it is impossible to clean the outlets.

The materials for the pipe line should be selected for strength, durability and should be corrosion free.

All the pipe lines should be designed by the standard hydraulic formulae. The vertical stacks and the horizontal branch will have certain capacity of carriage of water. In any case horizontal branches have got a surge flow i.e. whenever any fitments discharges, there is a surge of water which may fill in the entire pipe, the floating of the surge occurs when water alongwith the solids pass along the horizontal branch and when it comes down the vertical stacks, the entire method of flow changes from surge flows to an annular flow along walls of stack.

The horizontal branches will have to have certain minimum velocity of flow. At about 1/2 metre velocity of flow per second greases will not be carried and at about 1 metre per second, as a velocity of flow, the drain will have a self-cleansing velocity. As it is already stated, most of the horizontal branches do not have a flow, which is constant, but have a surging flow. It is, therefore, needed that these surges of flow should be utilised for cleaning of the pipe.

The sanitary fitments are utilised at certain intervals of time and they are not under continuous use. The frequency of use of fixtures varies from the number of users as well as the average time intervals between uses. For example, the water closet is going to be utilised not continuously, but there is going to be a certain time interval between the uses. Similar is the position for a lavatory or a kitchen or a bath. Therefore, if the system is designed taking into consideration that all fittings are going to be in use simultaneously the capacity of the branch and stack required, will be very high thereby, leading to an uneconomical design. It is not only an uneconomical design, which is objectionable, here, but the very fact, that the total quantity of the sewerage flowing in it will not be as much as it will be on the basis that all the fitments are functioning. Therefore, the velocity of flow will be less as the quantum of sewage will be less. When the velocity of flow is less than the self cleansing velocity solids will get deposited. Therefore the system will be more prone to chokages. It is, therefore, necessary to find out the probabilities for simultaneous discharge of fixtures very approximately. The probabilities of simultaneous discharge of fixtures is as follows:

0 in 10	Probability	=1.000
1 in 10	" "	= 0.1534
2 in 10	" "	= 0.0124
3 in 10	" "	= 0.00068
4 in 10	" "	= 0.00002

The design of the sanitary system, therefore, is a combination of probabilities and, may be, that once in a while, there will be slight over loading however, when compared to the probabilities factor. This is going to be a very very remote happening. For example, the probability of 4 fitments out of 10 functioning at a time is hardly 2 in 1 lakh.

In the case of vertical stacks, the probable number of fixtures will be high enough and, therefore, the possibility of their usage simultaneously, is going to be less.

Thus the sanitary system design, besically, boils down to a fairly empirical design. Table 6 (page 109) will be good guide for residential buildings. In the case of office buildings, where large number of fitments would be available, the size could be as given below.

The layout of the piping should be as simple and direct as possible. In the case of sanitary systems, the water closet and connected pipes are the costliest system and water supply pipings is the cheapest. W.C. Pipes are also prone to chokages more than the water supply line, therefore while laying the system, it should be seen that as far as possible W.C.s drains discharge directly into the stack close to it without any unnecessary bend, the waste water from washbasins and such other installation is taken, also, without any bends; as at each bend, there is a likelyhood of reduction of its velocity. When compared to the above, the water supply pipes could be taken through any bends and only precaution should be taken in such cases is that no air locks get formed. For this purpose even the water supply of pipes should fall from the highest point of the tank to the outlet point properly and no reverse slope should ever be provided as a 'U' bend form with the reverse flow is prone to air leakage.

The installation of sanitary fittings and a piping should not introduce crevices which should not be possible to be inspected and cleaned readily. With the introduction of reinforced concrete as a major building material places where water stagnants or even minor stagnation and condensation takes place, there the corrosion occurs faster.

Pipes should be approachable all the times and as far as possible should these not be embedded into the masonry. Pipes when not embedded should run well clear of all the wall. Holes, through the walls to take the pipes should be made good on both sides, to prevent entry of insects. Materials used for embedded pipe should be rodent proof and passage of rodent from rim to rim or from floor to floor or from sanitary shaft to the interior of the building should be prevented by suitable sealing. Any unused drain sewer line pipe should be demolished to keep it free from the rodents.

Wherever sanitary pipes are utilised, the rodents can climb on them with ease. Therefore a rodent protection device of provided at about 2 metre level from the ground will effectively avoid the rodents climbing on the pipes.

What is applicable to a rodent is equally appliacable to a thief. A thief can climb a sanitary pipe or a G.I. pipe with ease because of fairly rough surface. Therefore it should be made non climable by wrapping it with barbed wire or similar material. If the pipes are plastered then the problem is reduced. In any case pipes should be sufficiently away from any open windows or ventilate and where it is not feasible to do so the window and ventilate should have necessary security grills and bars.

Floors and walls for toilets, bathrooms and kitchens or wherever sanitary fixtures are installed should be of impervious materials that can be easily washed. The space between the fixtures and the walls should be closely filled and pointed so that there is no chance of dirt or worms to collect. Plumbing fixtures are generally of impervious material and have somooth surfaces so that soap and water is all that is needed to produce clean and rustless surface.

The wall or the floor where these fixtures are provided, therefore, should be such that with soap and water a clean rustless surface is possible. The surface of the plumbing fixtures, in contact with the wall or the floor should be such that the water cannot penetrate through the edges.

TABLE 6
Vent Stack Sizes (Dia in mm) for Office Buildings

Diameter of Drainage Stack		100 *mm*			150 *mm*				
Number of Floors:		4	8	12	8	12	16	20	24
	WC/Basin								
(a) 10-min interval	1 + 1	0	0	30	0	0	0	0	0
	2 + 2	0	0	30	0	0	0	0	0
'Public' use	3 + 3	0	30	40	0	0	0	0	0
	4 + 4	0	40	40	0				
	5 + 5	0	40	see note	0		see note		
(b) 5-min interval	1 + 1	0	0	30	0	0	0	0	0
	2 + 2	0	50	50	0	0	0	0	0
'Peak' use	3 + 3	0	50	0	0	0	0	50	65
	4 + 4	30		see note	0				
	5 + 5	30			0				

0 means no vent stack needed

		WC/Urinal/Basin		*WC/Basin*
Main assumptions:	No offset in 'Wet' part of drainage stack	2 + 1 + 2	equipments	2 + 2
	Large-radius bend at foot stack	2 + 2 + 3		3 + 3
	Surcharging of the drain connection at the base of the stack is unlikely	3 + 3 + 4		4 + 4
	No intercepting trap in the drain adjacent to the stack	4 + 4 + 5		5 + 5

TABLE 7
Minimum Stack Sizes and Vents Required for Various Loading Conditions

Type	*Stack diameter mm*		*Requirements*
Houses (one-family)			
Up to 3 storeys	90	Single-stack	
Flats		Stack serving one group on each floor	Stack serving two groups on each floor
Up to 10 storeys	100	Single-stack	Single-stack
Up to 15	100	50 mm vent stack with connection on alternate floors	50 mm vent stack with one connection on alternate floors
Up to 20	100	65 mm vent stack with connection on alternate floors	65 mm vent stack with one connection on alternate floors
Up to 12 storeys	125	Single-stack	Single-stack
12 to 15	125	Single-stack	50 mm vent stack with one connection on alternate floors
16 to 25 storeys	150	single-stack	Single-stack
Mainsonettes		Stack serving one group on alternate floors	Stack serving two groups on alternate floors
Up to 10 storeys	100	Single-stack	Single-stack
11 to 15	100	Single-stack	50 mm vent stack with one connection on alternate (bathroom) floors
16 to 20	100	50 mm vent stack with one connection on alternate (bathroom) floors	50 mm vent stack with one connection on alternate (bathroom) floors

Each group consists of a WC, bath, basin and sink. Where dwelling contain more appliances it may be necessary to provide more vents.

N. B. The above recommendations apply to systems with swept inlet WC branches. With straight inlet branches, a 100 mm stack with no vent has been found satisfactory up to 4 storeys; a 150 mm stack with no vents had been found satisfactory up to 15 storeys.

In a nutshell the performance criteria for drainage could be laid as follows:

Performance Criteria for Drainage Installation

Requirement	*Achieved by means of*
1. Watertight	Appropriate selection of pipe material and joining system and by satisfactory workmanship.
2. Non-blocking	Adequate minimum diameter. Smooth internal surfaces properly aligned joints. No reduction in diameter in direction of flow.
3. Adequate discharge capacity	Flows in pipe depend on diameter, gradient, internal surface and alignment of pipes.
4. No nuisance, overflowing should not occur.	Traps at all entries to drainage pipework. Pipe installation designed to avoid violent air pressure fluctuations which might unseal the traps.
5. Durable. Durability of drain installation is the problem. Very durable materials may not necessarily provide a long life due to effects of moisture, building settlement and ground movement of drain. Deterioration of pipes and joints due to chemical nature of flow. Deterioration of pipes and joints due to surroundings (e.g.: soil, chemical) Mechanical damage or crushing. Rust penetration.	Selection of pipe material. Selection of jointing system. Support of bedding. Workmanship for above.
6. Traceable and accessible for maintenance.	Pipe work arranged in straight lines between access points. Access point provided so that all sections may be inspected and if necessary cleared by flexible lines and rods.
7. Economic	Grouping of sanitary appliances to give short pipe runs.

Drainage and Sanitation Requirement

The requirement of sanitation would vary from person to person and affluence. However, for all practical purposes, some sort of a minimum requirement is to be given. There should be atleast one water tap and arrangement for drainage in the vicinity of each water closet or group of water closets in all buildings. Dwellings with individual conveniences shall have atleast the following fitments:

1. One bathroom provided with the tap.
2. One water-closet.
3. One Nahni or sink in the floor or raised from the floor with tap.

Where only W.C. is provided, the bath and water closet should be separately accommodated. Dwellings without individual conveniences shall have the following fitments:

1. One water tap with draining arrangement in each tenement.
2. One water closet and one bath for every two tenements.
3. Water taps in common bathrooms and water closets.

For structures, other than the residences, the requirement of fitments for drainage and sanitation other than residences shall be in accordance with Tables 1 to 13 of National Building Code, Sections 9-28. These tables are reproduced below. In the case of traffic terminals, the adequate arrangement should be made to separately dispose off water containing kitchen waste. The minimum sanitary convenience provided at any traffic terminal stations like Railway station, Bus station, Bus terminal shall consist of non-service type latrine, one for male and one for female and non-service type of urinals for males, for a daily passenger volume upto 300 people. For large stations and airports, sanitary arrangements given in Table 13 would apply. In the case of airports the following provisions shall be made in addition to those given earlier.

Wash Basin Domestic Airports

Minimum of 2 each for males and females with a scale of provision as per international airport. For International Airport 10 for 200 persons, 15 for 400, 20 for 600, 25 for 1000 persons. Shower stall with washbasin in the enclosure shall be provided. Four stalls each in the male and female toilets in the transit and departure lounge and 4 stall each in the male and female toilet in the main concourse. Adequate scavenging arrangement should be provided so that each terminal is kept free of refuse. Refuse container should be provided.

8. HOSPITAL PIPE NET WORKS FOR SANITATION

In the case of hospitals and dispensaries where patients are treated for the diseases plumbing and sanitation is very important.

Most of piping is installed internally. Many times these piping take a torturous path through the structure on account of poor planning of services. The main reason in this is the lack of coordinated planning for services in hospitals where large number of piping has to be run for various services. The network of piping is over the entire hospital building and little thought is given

TABLE 1
Office Buildings

Sl. No. (1)	*Fitments* (2)	*For Male Personnel* (3)	*For Female Personnel* (4)
(i)	Water-closets*	1 for every 25 persons or part thereof	1 for every 15 persons or part thereof
(ii)	Ablution taps	1 in each water-closet	1 in each water-closet
		1 water tap with draining arrangement shall be provided for every 50 persons or part thereof in the vicinity of water-closet and urinals.	
(iii)	Urinals	Nil, up to 6 persons 1 for 7-20 persons 2 for 21-45 persons 3 for 46-70 persons 4 for 71-100 persons From 1C1 to 200 persons add at the rate of 3 percent For over 200 persons add at the rate of 2.5 percent	
(iv)	Wash basins	← 1 for every 25 persons or part thereof →	
(v)	Drinking water fountains	1 for every 100 persons with a minimum of one on each floor	
(vi)	Cleaner's sinks	1 per floor, *Min,* preferably in or adjacent to sanitary rooms	

* This may include adequate number of water-closets of European style, where desired

TABLE 2
Factories

Sl. No.	*Fitments*	*For Male Personnel*	*For Female Personnel*
(1)	(2)	(3)	(4)
(i)	Water-closets*	1 for every 1-15 persons 2 for 16-35 3 for 36-65 persons 4 for 66-100 persons From 101 to 200 persons, add at the rate of 3 percent For over 200 persons, add at the rate of 2.5 percent	1 for 1-12 persons 2 for 13-24 persons 3 for 26-40 persons 4 for 41-57 persons 5 for 58-77 persons 6 for 78-100 persons From 101 to 200 person, add at the rate of 5 percent For over 200 persons, add at the rate of 4 percent
(ii)	Ablution taps	1 in each water-closet	1 in each water-closet
		1 water tap with draining arrangement shall be provided for every 50 persons or part thereof in the vicinity of water-closets and urinals.	
(iii)	Urinals	Nil, up to 6 persons 1 for 7-20 persons 2 for 21-45 persons 3 for 46-70 persons 4 for 71-100 persons From 101 to 200 persons, add at the rate of 3 percent For over 200 persons, add at the rate of 2.5 percent	
(iv)	Washing taps with draining arrangements	← 1 for every 25 persons or part thereof →	
(v)	Drinking water fountains	1 for every 100 persons with a minimum of one on each floor	
(vi)	Baths (preferable showers)	As required for particular trades or occupations	

Note 1— For many trades of a dirty or dangerous character, more extensive provisions are required by law.

Note 2— Creches, where provided, shall be fitted with water-closets (one for 10 persons or part thereof) and wash basins (one for 15 persons or part thereof) and drinking water tap with draining arrangements (one for every 50 persons or part thereof).

* Some of the water-closets may be of European style, if desired

TABLE 3
Cinemas, Concert Halls and Theatres

Sl. No. (1)	*Fitments* (2)	*For Male Public* (3)	*For Female Public* (4)	*For Male Staff* (5)	*For Female Staff* (6)
(i)	Water-closets	1 per 100 persons upto 500 persons For over 400 persons, add at the rate of 1 per 250 persons or part thereof	3 per 100 persons up to 200 persons For over 200 persons, add at the rate of 2 per 100 persons or part thereof	1 for 1-15 persons 2 for 16-35 persons	1 for 1-12 persons 2 for 13-25 persons
(ii)	Ablution taps	1 in each water-closet	1 in each water-closet	1 in each water-closet	1 in each water-closet
		1 water tap with draining arrangements shall be provided for every 50 persons or part thereof in the vicinity of water-closets and urinals			
(iii)	Urinals	1 for 25 persons or part thereof	1 for 7-20 persons 2 for 21-45 persons	Nil, up to 5 persons	
(iv)	Wash basins	1 for every 200 persons or part thereof	1 for every 200 persons or part thereof	1 for 1-15 persons 2 for 16-35 persons	1 for 1-12 persons 2 for 13-25 persons
(v)	Drinking water fountain	← 1 per 100 persons or part thereof →			

Note 1—Some of the water-closets may be of European styles, if desired.
Note 2—It may be assumed that two-thirds of the number are males and one-third females.

TABLE 4
Art Galleries, Libraries and Museums

Sl. No. (1)	*Fitments* (2)	*For Male Public* (3)	*For Female Public* (4)	*For Male Staff* (5)	*For Female Staff* (6)
(i)	Water-closets	1 per 200 persons up to 400 persons For over 400 persons, add at the rate of 1 per 250 persons or part thereof	1 per 100 persons up to 200 persons For over 200 persons, add at the rate of 1 per 159 persons or part thereof	1 for 1-15 persons 2 for 16-35 persons	1 for 1-12 persons 2 for 13-25 persons
(ii)	Ablution taps	1 in each water-closet	1 in each water-closet	1 in each water-closet	1 in each water-closet
		1 water tap with draining arrangements shall be provided for every 50 persons or part thereof in the vicinity of water-closets and urinals			
(iii)	Urinals	1 per 50 persons or part thereof		Nil, up to 6 persons 1 for 7-20 persons 2 for 21-45 persons	
(iv)	Wash basins	1 for every 200 persons or part thereof. For over 200 persons, add at the rate of 1 per 250 persons or part thereof	1 for every 200 persons or part thereof. For over 200 persons, add at the rate of 1 per 150 persons or part thereof	1 for 1-15 persons 2 for 16-35 persons	1 for 1-12 persons 2 for 13-25 persons
(v)	Cleaner's sinks	← 1 per floor, *Min* →			
(vi)	Drinking water fountain	← 1 per 100 persons or part thereof →			

Note 1—Some of the water-closets may be of European styles, if desired.
Note 2—It may be assumed that two-thirds of the number are males and one-third females.

TABLE 5
Hospital Indoor Patient Wards

Sl. No. (1)	*Fitments* (2)	*For Male and Female* (3)
(i)	Water-closets	1 for every 8 beds or part thereof
(ii)	Ablution	1 in each water-closet plus one water tap with draining arrangements in the vicinity of water-closets and urinals for every 50 bed or part thereof
(iii)	Wash basins	2 up to 30 beds; add 1 for every additional 30 beds or part thereof
(iv)	Baths	1 bath with shower for every 8 beds or part thereof
(v)	Badpan washing sinks	1 for each ward
(vi)	Cleaner's sinks	1 for each ward
(vii)	Kitchen sinks and dish washers (where kitchen is provided)	1 for each ward

Note 1—Some of the water-closets may be of European style, if desired.
Note 2—Additional and special fitments for specific needs of hospitals may be provided.

TABLE 6
Hospitals Outdoor Patients Wards

Sl. No. (1)	Fitments (2)	For Males (3)	For Females (4)
(i)	Water-closets	1 for every 100 persons or part thereof	2 for every 100 persons or part thereof
(ii)	Ablution taps	1 in each water-closet	1 in each water-closet
		1 water tap with draining arrangements shall be provided for every 50 persons or part thereof in the vicinity of water-closets and urinals	
(iii)	Urinals	1 for every 50 persons or part thereof	
(iv)	Wash basins	1 for every 100 persons or part thereof	1 for every 100 persons or part thereof
(v)	Drinking water fountain	1 per 500 persons or part thereof	

Note 1—Some of the water-closets may be of European style, if desired.
Note 2—Additional and special fitments for specific needs of hospitals may be provided.

TABLE 7

Hospitals (Administrative Buildings, Medical Staff and Quarters and Nurses' Homes)

Sl. No.	*Fitments*	*For Administrative Buildings*		*For Medical Staff Quarters (Hostel Type)*		*For Nurses Homes (Hostel Type)*
		For Male Personnel	*For Female Personnel*	*For Male Staff*	*For Female Staff*	
(1)	(2)	(3)	(4)	(5)	(6)	(7)
(i)	Water-closets*	1 for every 25 persons or part thereof	1 for every 15 persons or part thereof	1 for 4 persons	1 for 4 persons	1 for 4 persons or part thereof
(ii)	Ablution taps	1 in each water-closet	1 in each water-closet	1 in each water-closet	1 in each water-closet	1 in each water-closet
		1 water tap with draining arrangements shall be provided for every 50 persons or part thereof in the vicinity of water-closets and urinals				
(iii)	Urinals	Nil, up to 6 persons 1 for 7-20 persons 2 for 21-45 persons 3 for 46-70 persons 4 for 71-100 persons From 101 to 200 persons, add at the rate of 3 per cent For over 200 persons, add at the rate of 2.5 percent				

(1)	(2)	(3)	(4)	(5)	(6)	(7)
(iv)	Wash basins	1 for every 25 persons or part thereof	1 for every 25 persons or part thereof	1 for every 8 persons or part thereof	1 for every 8 persons or part thereof	1 for every 8 persons or part thereof
(v)	Bath (with shower)	—	—	1 for 4 persons or part thereof	1 for 4 persons or part thereof	1 for 4-6 persons or part thereof
(vi)	Drinking water fountains	1 per 100 persons or part thereof with a minimum of 1 on each floor				
(vii)	Cleaner's sinks 1	← 1 per floor, *Min* →				

* Some of the water-closets may be of European style, if desired

TABLE 8
Hotels

Sl. No.	*Fitments*	*For Residential Public and Staff*	*For Public Rooms*		*For Non-Residential Staff*	
			For Males	*For Females*	*For Male Staff*	*For Female Staff*
(1)	(2)	(3)	(4)	(5)	(6)	(7)
(i)	Water-closets	1 per 8 persons omitting occupants of the room with attached water-closets minimum of 2 if both sexes are lodged	1 per 100 persons up to 400 persons For over 400 persons add at the rate of 1 per 250 persons or part thereof	2 per 100 persons up to 200 persons For over 200 persons add at the rate of 1 per 100 persons or part thereof	1 for 1-15 persons 2 for 16-35 persons 3 for 36-65 persons 4 for 66-100 persons	1 for 1-12 persons 2 for 13-25 persons 3 for 26-40 persons 4 for 41-57 persons 5 for 58-77 persons 6 for 78-100 persons
(ii)	Ablution taps	1 in each water-closet	1 in each water-closet	1 in each water-closet	1 in each water-closet	1 in each water-closet
		1 water tap with draining arrangements shall be provided for every 50 persons or part thereof in the vicinity of water-closets and urinals				
(iii)	Urinals	1 per 50 persons or part thereof	—		Nil, up to 6 persons 1 for 7-20 persons 2 for 21-45 persons 3 for 46-70 persons 4 for 71-100 persons	—
(iv)	Wash basin	1 per 10 persons omitting the wash basins installed in the room suite	1 per water-closet and urinal provided	1 per water-closet provided	1 for 1-15 persons 2 for 16-35 persons 3 for 36-65 persons 4 for 66-100 persons	1 for 1-12 persons 2 for 13-25 persons 3 for 26-40 persons 4 for 41-57 persons 5 for 58-77 persons 6 for 78-100 persons

(1)	(2)	(3)	(4)	(5)	(6)	(7)
(v)	Baths	1 per 10 persons omitting occupants of the room with bath in suite	—	—	—	—
(vi)	Slop sinks	1 per 30 bedrooms; 1 per floor, *Min*	—	—	—	—
(vi)	Kitchen sinks and dish washers	← 1 in each kitchen →				

Note 1—Some of the water-closets may be of European style, if desired.

Note 2—It may be assumed that two-thirds of the number are males and one-third females.

TABLE 9
Restaurants

Sl. No. (1)	*Fitments* (2)	*For Male Public* (3)	*For Female Public* (4)	*For Male Staff* (5)	*For Female staff* (6)
(i)	Water-closets	1 for 50 seats up to 200 seats. For over 200 seats, add at the rate of 1 per 100 seats or part thereof	1 for 50 seats up to 200 seats. For over 200 seats, add at the rate of 1 per 100 seats or part thereof	1 for 1-15 persons 2 for 16-35 persons 3 for 36-65 persons 4 for 66-100 persons	1 for 1-12 persons 2 for 13-25 persons 3 for 26-40 persons 4 for 41-57 persons 5 for 58-77 persons 6 for 78-100 persons
(ii)	Ablution taps	1 in each water-closet	1 in each water-closet	1 in each water-closet	1 in each water-closet
		1 water tap with draining arrangements shall be provided for every 50 persons or part thereof in the vicinity of water-closets and urinals.			
(iii)	Urinals	1 per 50 seats	—	Nil, up to 6 persons 1 for 7-20 persons 2 for 21-45 persons 3 for 46-70 persons 4 for 71-100 persons	—
(iv)	Wash basins	← 1 for every water-closet provided →			
(v)	Kitchen sinks and dish washers	← 1 in each kitchen →			
(vi)	Slop or service sinks	← 1 in each restaurant →			

Note 1—Some of the water-closets may be of European style, if desired.
Note 2—It may be assumed that two-thirds of the number are males and one-third females.

TABLE 10
Schools and Educational Institutions

Sl. No.	Fitments	Nursery Schools	Educationals Institutions (Non-Residential)		Educational Institutions (Residentials)	
			For Boys	For Girls	For Boys	For Girls
(1)	(2)	(3)	(4)	(5)	(6)	(7)
(i)	Water-closets	1 per 15 pupils or part thereof	1 per 40 pupils or part thereof	1 per 25 pupils or part thereof	1 for every 8 pupils or part thereof	1 for every 6 pupils or part thereof
(ii)	Ablution taps	1 in each water-closet	1 in each water-closet	1 in each water-closet	1 in each water-closet	1 in each water-closet
		1 water tap with draining arrangements shall be provided for every 50 pupils or part thereof in the vicinity of water-closets and urinals.				
(iii)	Urinals	—	1 per 20 pupils or part thereof	—	1 for every 25 pupils or part thereof	
(iv)	Wash basins	1 for 15 pupils or part thereof	1 per 60 *Min* 2	1 per 40 *Min* 2	1 for every 8 pupils or part thereof	1 for every 6 pupils or part thereof
(v)	Baths	1 bath-sink per 40 pupils or part thereof			1 for every 8 pupils or part thereof	1 for every 6 pupils or part thereof
(vi)	Drinking water fountains	1 for every 50 pupils or part thereof	1 for every 50 pupils or part thereof	1 for every 50 pupils or part thereof	1 for every 50 pupils or part thereof	1 for every 50 pupils or part thereof
(vii)	Cleaner's sink	← 1 per floor, *Min* →				

* For teaching staff, the schedule of fitments to be provided shall be the same as in the case of office buildings (see Table 1)
** Some of the water-closets may be of European style, if desired.

TABLE 11
HOSTELS

Sl. No.	*Fitments*	*For Residents and Residential Staff*		*For Non-Residential Staff*		*Rooms Where in Outsiding are Received*	
		For Males	*For Females*	*For Males*	*For Females*	*For Males*	*For Females*
(1)	(2)	(3)	(4)	(5)	(6)	(7)	(8)
(i)	Water-closets*	1 for every 8 persons or part thereof	1 for every 6 persons or part thereof	1 for 1-15 persons 2 for 16-32 persons 3 for 36-65 persons 4 for 66-100 persons	1 for 1-12 persons 2 for 13-24 persons 3 for 26-40 persons 4 for 41-57 persons 5 for 58-77 persons 6 for 78-100 persons	1 per 100 persons up to 400 persons for every 400 persons, add at the rate of 1 for 250 persons or part thereof	2 per 100 persons up to 200 persons For over 200 persons, add at the rate or 1 for 100 persons or part thereof
(ii)	Ablution taps	1 in each water-closet	1 in each water-closet	1 in each water-closet	1 in each water-closet	1 in each water-closet	1 in each water-closet
		1 water tap with draining arrangements shall be provided for every 50 persons or part thereof in the vicinity of water-closets and urinals					
(iii)	Urinals	1 for 25 persons or part thereof	—	Nil, up to 6 persons 1 for 7-20 persons 2 for 21-45 persons 3 for 46-70 persons 4 for 71-100 persons	—	1 per 50 persons or part thereof	—

(1)	(2)	(3)	(4)	(5)	(6)	(7)	(8)
(iv)	Wash basins	1 for 8 persons or part thereof	1 for 6 persons or part thereof	1 for 1-15 persons 2 for 16-35 persons 3 for 36-65 persons 4 for 66-100 persons	1 for 1-12 persons 2 for 13-25 persons 3 for 26-40 persons 4 for 41-57 persons 5 for 58-77 persons 6 for 78-100 persons	1 per each water-closet and urinals provided	1 per each water-closet provided
(v)	Baths	1 for 8 persons or part thereof	1 for 6 persons or part thereof				
(vi)	Cleaner's sinks	←		1 per floor, *Min*			→

* Some of the water-closets may be of European style, if desired.

TABLE 12
Fruit and Vegetable Markets

Sl. No. (1)	*Fitments* (2)	*Requirements* (3)
(i)	Urinals	Not less than 2 for every 50 persons
(ii)	Water-closets*	2 *Min,* and an additional 1 for every 50 persons
(iii)	Ablution taps	2 *Min,* and an additional tap for every 50 persons
(iv)	Bathing places	Suitable numbers with bathing platforms

Note 1—For layout for regulated market yards for fruit and vegetables, reference may be made to accepted standards IX-2 (1)**

Note 2—Separate and adequate provision of water-closets shall be made for females.

Note 3—Adequate washing places for fruit and vegetables shall be provided.

*Some of the water-closets may be of European style, if desired.

** In this section where reference is made to accepted standards, in relation to material specification, testing or other information, the appropriate document listed at the end of this section may be used as a guide to the interpretation of the term.

TABLE 13
Sanitary Requirements for Large Stations and Airports

Sl. No.	*Place*	*WC for Males*	*WC for Females*	*Urinals for Males only*
(1)	(2)	(3)	(4)	(5)
(i)	Junction stations, intermediate stations and bus stations	3 for first 1000 persons and 1 for every subsequent 100 persons	4 for first 1000 persons and 1 for every additional 1000 persons	4 for every 1000 persons and 1 for every additional 1000 persons
(ii)	Terminal stations and bus terminals	4 for first 1000 persons and 1 for every subsequent 1000 persons or part thereof	5 for first 1000 persons and 1 for every subsequent 2000 persons or part thereof	6 for first 1000 persons and 1 for every additional 1000 persons or part thereof
(iii)	Domestic airports, *Min*	2*	4*	2*
	for 200 persons	5	8	6
	for 400 persons	9	15	12
	for 600 persons	12	20	16
	for 800 persons	16	26	20
	for 1000 persons	18	29	22
(iv)	International airports			
	for 200 persons	6	10	8
	for 600 persons	12	20	16
	for 1000 persons	18	29	22

Note—Separate provision shall be made for staff and workers at these traffic terminal stations.

*At least one Indian style water-closet shall be provided in each toilet. Assume 60 males to 40 females in any area.

to the access to the pipe work when the original planning and execution is being done.

The complexity of pipe layout is directly in relation to the blockages and stoppage. More simple and in straight line the pipe network is there would be less of chokages and blockages. These chokages and blockages cost money for cleaning. Not only it costs money but the disturbance caused and possibility of infection spreading is high. Most chokages occur where the pipe work has knucklebends, sharp offsets, 92½° junctions. No or very few chokages are reported when the pipes are straight vertical (100 to 150 mm pipes).

Stoppages and chokages also result from mis-use of the services.

While there is some construction or repair is going on then builders malba is found in the drainage system. What is required is improved site supervision and blocking of sanitary inlets when the builders work is going on in that area.

Special appliances like sluices, bed pan cleaners, slop-hoppers are available to the ward staff for disposal of so called "disposable hand gloves, syringes etc." Dressings, sanitary towels, floor cloth etc. find way into the sanitary system, most of it intentionally. One of the reason is non-availability of a closed container to put in these disposable items.

The floor and urinal traps get blocked by tea-leaves, cigarette butts etc.

The disposable materials like spatulae, syringes, gloves etc. have to be incinerated and not put into the drainage system.

Kitchens in hospitals have to be scrupulously clean and hygenic. The grease traps require frequent cleaning.

In case of hospitals regular rodding programme has to be drawn out to clean all drainage systems and it has to be adhered to.

Access to drainage pipe work is very important. There should be sufficient number of cleanouts for cleaning the pipes and the size of shaft etc. should be sufficient to allow for rodding. The lighting of pipe work has to be properly designed. No plumber can work under a small torch light.

Where pipes are encased in masonry or it is in cramped duct, then the removable of chokages would be difficult and costly.

The horizontal pipe work encased in false ceiling is sometimes adopted. It many times means that instead of one now two levels are disturbed, when stoppage occurs.

In case of hospital wherever cleanouts or inspection doors are provided they should be in an unclean areas from medical angle.

General recommendations for hospitals sanitary layout are:

(a) Adequate service space is fundamental.
(b) The position of sanitary appliances and the maintenance schedules should be kept in view.
(c) The service space should be well lit and capable of being cleaned.
(d) Bends should be avoided as far as possible. Where they are unavoidable in place of sharp bends, large radius bends should be used.
(e) Oblique junctions should be preferred to 'T' junctions.
(f) Access doors and cleanouts should be provided in all changes of directions.

(g) Planned maintenance is a necessity and the maintenance staff should be able to work without disturbing the ward routine or hygiene.

9. SANITATION FOR EATING PLACES

Many times almost every one takes a meal or bites an eatable outside his house. These places may be canteens in offices, or restaurants, etc. The condition of sanitation in some eating places is so horrible that it is nauseating.

Most of the problems which arise in food cutting, preparation, and serving are man-made. The food-handlers have to be scrupulously clean and healthy. Proper method of handling food, dishes, glass-ware have got to be taught to all staff along with the emphasis on good personal hygiene.

A system of relying on routine medical examination is not sufficient enough. These examinations are many times cursory and spread at long intervals of time.

Day to day health of the persons handling food is of great importance. Exclusion of sick persons and persons with infected wound is absolutely necessary.

Hot and cold water under pressure are a necessity in all eating establishments and the supply of water should be whole-some and potable. The water supply system should be from an approved source.

Where it is not possible to have potable water in large quantity and an alternate supply which may not be safe has to be used for flushing and gardening etc. then entirely separate piping system should be designed and painted separately to indicate that this is an unsafe supply. Any outlet on the non-potable system should be clearly labelled that it is not for drinking or any other culianary purpose. No out of non-potable system should be there in kitchen, dining rooms or pantry etc.

Dish Washing

In case of eating places dish washing is a major problem. Prior to washing the dishes are scraped manually to remove remnants of food etc. The scraping table should be impervious water-tight and fitted with a sprayhose for cleaning. The scraped material should be kept in garbage cans with closed lid.

Pre-washing machines with hot water at 36°C to 60°C and which retain the garbage on specially designed racks are practical.

The importance of clean and hygenic utensils for food preparation, serving etc. cannot be over emphasised. The use of mechanical dish washing machines have supplanted the practice of washing by hand.

The dish washing is done at 60°C to 72°C followed by a clean water at a temperature not less than 83°C and with a flow of not less than 30 litres/minute.

All dishes and utensils should be stacked properly in the machine without crowding and in a manner that will permit the wash and rinse water to reach all surfaces of articles.

Maintenance of dish-washers is important which requires frequent cleaning of spray jets, detergent, dispensers and sides of the machine, pipes.

Washing by Hand

When dishes and utensils are washed in hot water by hand at 50°C containing sufficient detergent to remove grease and solids until clean to sight and touch. Then it is rinsed in clear water at 60°C and immersed finally in hot water at 75°C. This procedure calls for a three compartment sink. Immersion in hot water at 75°C is for atleast 3 minutes only through wire baskets as these temperatures will scald the hand. Pouring of scalding water on dishes etc. is not proper solution.

The dishes and utensils should be checked for bacterialogical tests. Normally immersion in warm chlorine solution with 50 ppm chlorine will be sufficient.

Dishes and utensils should be air-dried if drying cloth is used then they must be clean and used for no other purpose.

Adequate hot water is a necessity. Booster local heaters will be needed. Water temperatures should be checked by thermometers.

The efficiency of washing is usually determined by SWAB Test. This is based on the formation of number of bacteria on the surfaces after they have been sanitised. Standard procedure is that 4 utensils of the same type are swabbed and the average plate count of bacterial colony should not exceed 100 t 37°C.

Garbage is a major problem in eating places whether it is the kitchen or the washing place. The garbage should be in tightly lidded containers and cans should be cleaned daily. The sewer lines should not pass through kitchen, dining etc. and never in a overhead way.

Good maintenance and house-keeping is necessary.

Hand washing facilities for food handlers should be available in adequate numbers and convenient in location.

Toilets

Toilets and lavatory facilities should be provided for the staff. No one should be permited to work without thoroughly washing his hands and feet. Toilet rooms should not open directly in the food preparation rooms or storage.

Toilet doors should be self closing and windows should have fly screens. The toilet and lavatory facilities for public should be different from those for staff.

10. DESIGNS OF PIPING FOR A LARGE NUMBER OF SANITARY FITMENTS

In case of small residential houses and offices the number of fixtures is necessarily limited hence in one horizontal branch of waste and soil pipe not many appliances of one type would drain and with probability of simultaneous use being remote, the horizontal branch would not get overloaded.

However in a large establishment large number of fitments of one type may have to be installed in a row and the probability of simultaneous use is also high hence separate discussion on the subject would be needed.

The discharge of soil and waste in intermittent and limited and comes in surges. Therefore, accumulation of solids does take place and there is gradual shifting of deposits as discharges take place. Gradients should be sufficient to prevent undue accumulation of these solid thereby blocking drain.

The self cleansing velocity of 0.75 m/s should be aimed. Where gradient is not feasible the practice of using pipes of larger diameter than required in order to justify laying at a flatter gradient is to be deprecated as increase of pipe diameter does not increase velocity of flow but it reduces the depth of flow and with increased frictional losses due to larger area of pipe being in contact with flow reduces velocity substantiallv which leads to accumulation of solids at a much faster rate.

Gradients and Pipe Sizes

Gradients

The discharge of water through a domestic drain is intermittent and limited in quantity and, therefore, small accumulations of solid matter are liable to form in the drains between the building and the public sewer. There is usually a gradual shifting of these deposits as discharges take place. Gradients shall be sufficient to prevent these temporary building up and blocking the drains.

Sanitary lines

The approximate gradients which give this velocity for the sizes of pipes likely to be used in building drainage and the corresponding discharges when flowing half-full are as follows:

Diameter mm	*Gradients*	*Discharge m³/min*
100	1 in 57	0.18
150	1 in 100	0.42
200	1 in 145	0.73
230	1 in 175	0.93
250	1 in 195	1.10
300	1 in 250	1.70

In cases, where it is practically not possible to conform to the ruling gradients, a flatter gradient may be used but the minimum velocity in such cases shall on no account be less than 0.16 m/s.

On the other hand, it is undesirable to employ gradients giving a velocity of flow greater than 2.4m/s. Where it is unavoidable, cast-iron pipes shall be used. The approximate gradients which give a velocity of 2.4 m/s for the various sizes of pipes and the corresponding discharge when flowing half-full are as follows:

Diameter	*Gradient*	*Discharge m³/min*
100	1 in 5.6	0.59
150	1 in 9.7	1.32
200	1 in 14	2.4
230	1 in 17	2.98
250	1 in 19	3.60
300	1 in 24.5	5.30

The problem of design of pipes and stacks could be approached in an empirical way and a somewhat rational way. In the rational way discharge expected from fixture unit configuration can be found out from Fig. 15 and pipe size decided on hydraulic formula.

Empirical Findings for Horizontal Branch

Branch pipes serving W.C.s are normally 100 mm in diameter and do not run full. It has been established by laboratory studies that upto 8 W.C.s can be connected to a straight branch of 100 mm laid at 2.5% slope. Similarly 8 wash basins may be discharged into one branch of 75 mm.

Normally wash basin branches are more prone to chokage and regular cleaning is necessary.

Urinals in a Row

Similar to washbasin, however, deposit of harder variety will be encountered requiring regular and vigorous cleaning.

The maximim flow in a branch on stacks depends on the simultaneous probable use of the appliances. All appliances do not have similar discharge rates and characteristics. Hence one way of approaching problem would be to assign some weightage to each appliances and indicate the maximum weightage which can be drained off by a branch or stack.

The loading units to be adopted are as given below:

Fixture Units for Different Sanitary Appliances or Groups

Sl. No.	*Type of fixture*	*Fixture unit value as load factors*
(1)	(2)	(3)
(i)	One bathroom group consisting of water-closet, wash basin and bath tub or shower stall:	
	(a) Tank water-closet	6
	(b) Flush-valve water-closet	8
(ii)	Bath tub*	3
(iii)	Bidet	3
(iv)	Combination sink-and-tray (drain board)	3
(v)	Drinking fountain	½
(vi)	Floor traps**	1
(vii)	Kitchen sink, domestic	2
(viii)	Wash basin, ordinary***	1
(ix)	Wash basin, surgeon's	2
(x)	Shower stall, domestic	2
(xi)	Showers (group) per head	3
(xii)	Urinal, wall lip	4
(xiii)	Urinal, stall	4

(xiv)	Water-closet, tank-operated	4
(xv)	Water-closet, valve-operated	8

* A shower head over a bath tub does not increase the fixture unit valve.
** Size of floor trap shall be determined by the area of surface water to be drained.
*** Wash basins with 32 mm and 40 mm trap have the same load value.

Fixture Unit Values for Fixtures Based on Fixture Drain or Trap Size

Sl. No.	*Fixture drain on trap size*	*Fixture unit value*
(1)	(2)	(3)
(i)	30 mm and smaller	1
(ii)	40 mm	2
(iii)	50 mm	3
(iv)	65 mm	4
(v)	75 mm	5
(vi)	100 mm	6

After calculating branch wise and stackwise loading units, the size of branches and stacks can be found out as per the following table:

Maximum Number of Fixture Units that can be Connected to Branches and Stocks

Sl. No.	*Diameter of pipe*	*Maximum Number of fixture Units that can be connected connected*			
		*Any horizontal fixture branch***	*One stack of in height or 3 intervals*	*More than 3 storeys in height Total for sack*	*Total at one storey or branch interval*
(1)	(2)	(3)	(4)	(5)	(6)
(i)	30	1	2	2	1
(ii)	40	3	4	8	2
(iii)	50	6	10	24	6
(iv)	65	12	20	42	9
(v)	75	20	30	60	16
(vi)	100	160	240	500	90

(vii)	125	360	540	1,100	200
(viii)	150	620	960	1,900	350
(ix)	200	1,400	2,200	3,600	600
(x)	250	2,500	3,800	5,600	1,000
(xi)	300	3,900	6,000	4,800	1,500
(xii)	375	7,000	—	—	

* Depending upon the probability of simultaneous of appliances considering the frequency of use and peak discharge rate.

** Does not include branches of the building sewer.

Maximum number of Fixture Units that can be Connected to Building Drains and Sewers

Sl. No.	*Diameter of pipe*	*Maximum number of fixture units that can be connected to any portion* of the building drain or the building sewer for gradient*			
(1)	(2)	(3)	(4)	(5)	(6)
(i)	100	—	180	216	250
(ii)	150	—	700	840	1,000
(iii)	200	1,400	1,600	1,920	2,300
(iv)	250	2,500	2,900	3,300	4,200
(v)	300	3,900	4,600	5,600	6,700
(vi)	375	7,000	8,300	10,000	12,000

* Includes branches of the building sewer.

11. VARIOUS TYPES OF SANITARY FITTINGS AVAILABLE IN THE MARKET

What is Fire Clay, Earthen Ware and Vitreous China

Sanitary equipment may be made from one of the three ceramic materials—Fire clay, earthen-ware or vitreous china. These materials have different qualities and characteristics.

Where rough or heavy usage is expected and strength is needed, fire clay or vitreous china is needed. Where good appearance is also needed, vitreous china is used.

Earthern-ware

Ball and china clay are the important constituents of earthen-ware which is lighter in weight than fire-clay. The articles manufactured have clean lines and sharp edges. Earthen-ware has a white porous body protected by glaze. These articles are cheaper than fire clay or vitreous china.

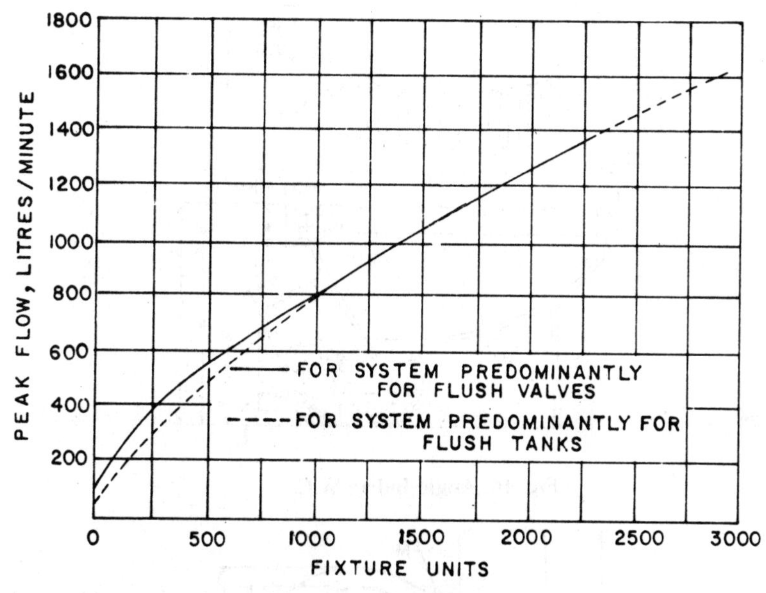

Estimate Curves

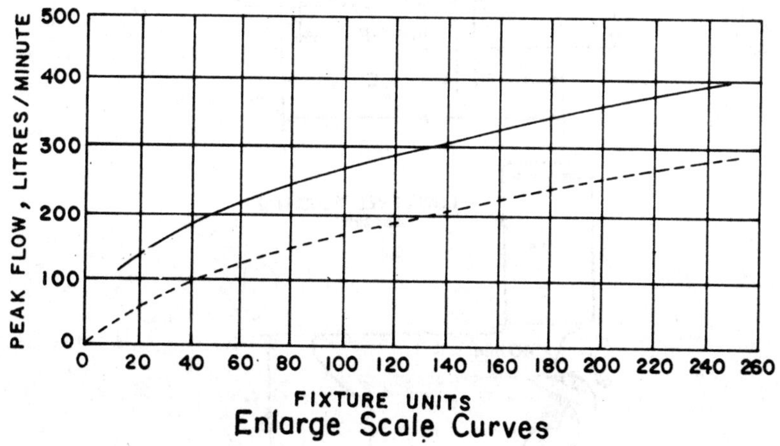

Enlarge Scale Curves

Fig. 15. Peak flow load curves.

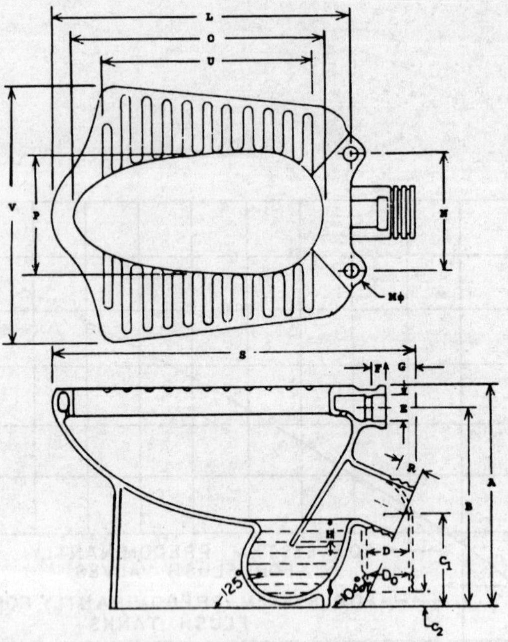

Fig. 16. Anglo Indian W.C.

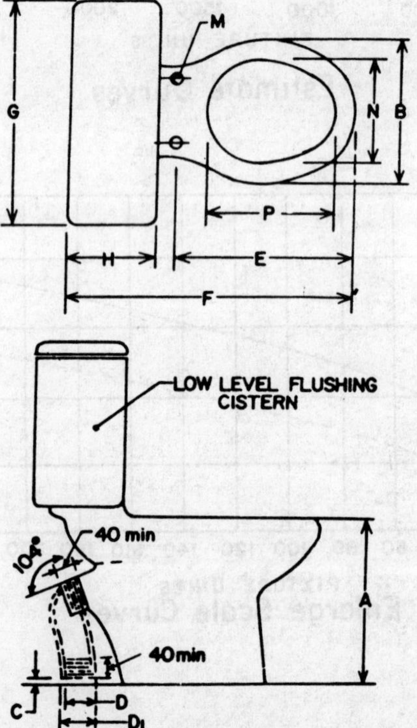

Fig. 17. European type W.C. with flushing cistern

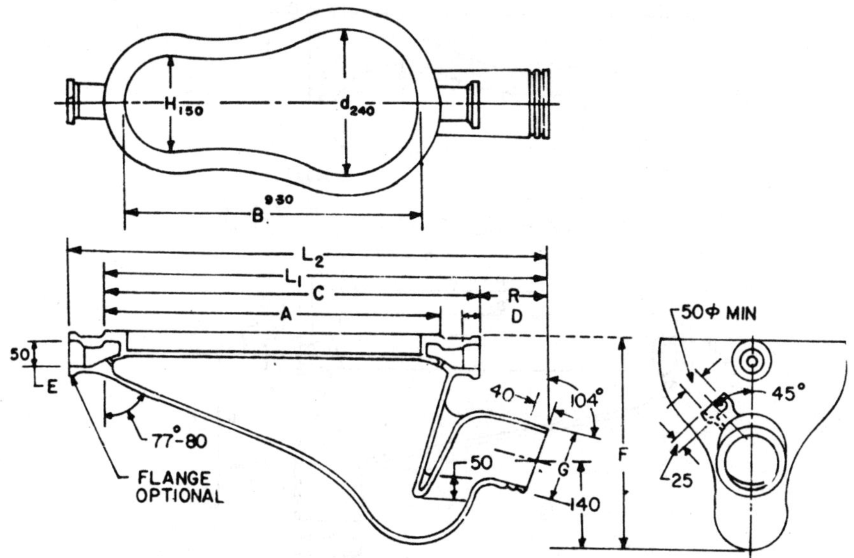

Fig. 18. Long Indian type

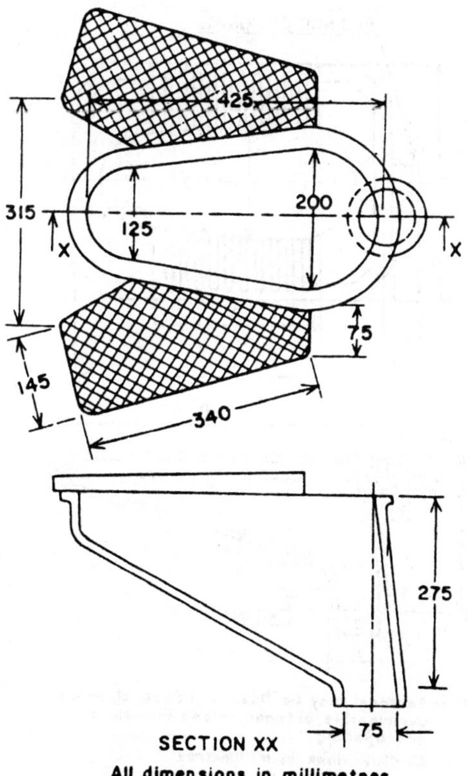

Fig. 19. Squatting plate

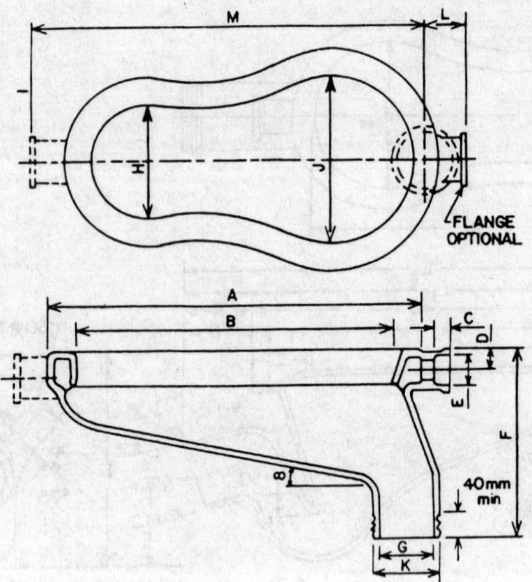

Fig. 20. Indian W.C. Washdown type.

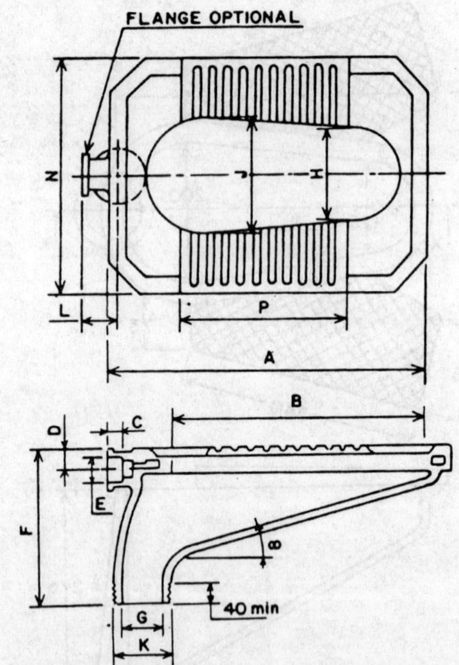

Fig. 21. Orissa pan

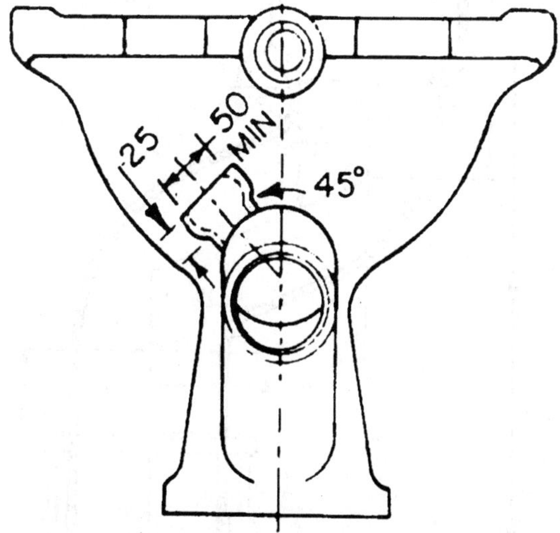

Fig. 22. Antisyphonage Vent hom

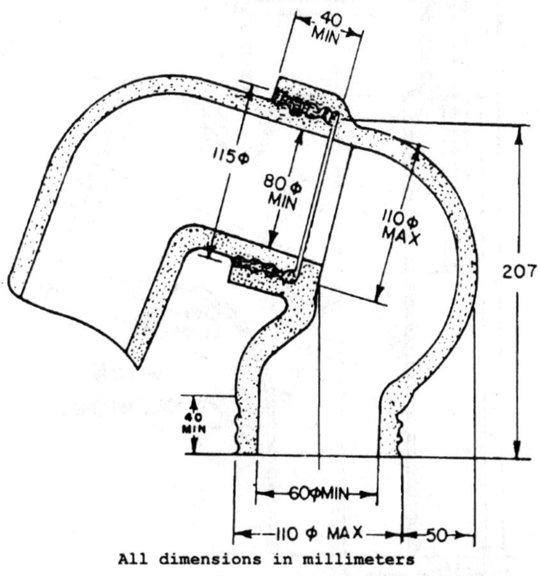

Fig. 23. Separate bend for integrated squatting pan

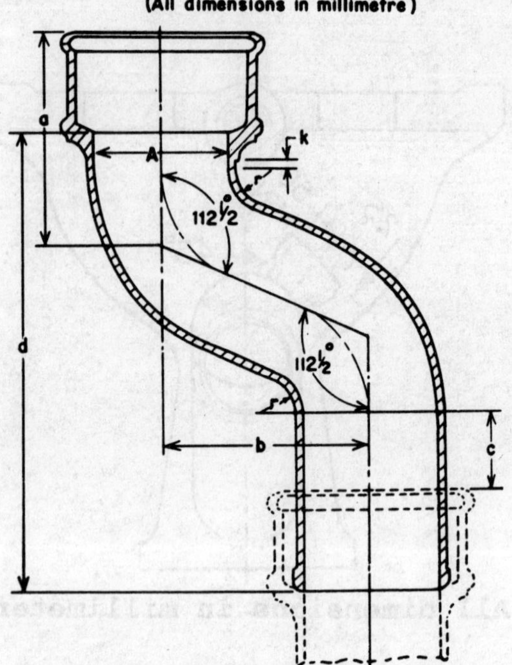

Fig. 24. Offset in pipe

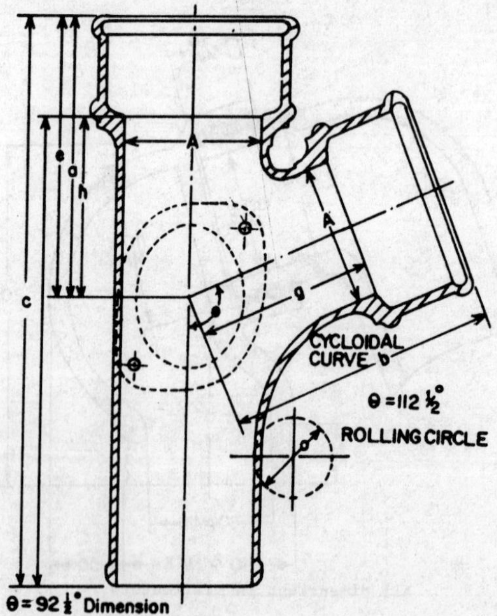

Fig. 25. Equal Branch with inspection door

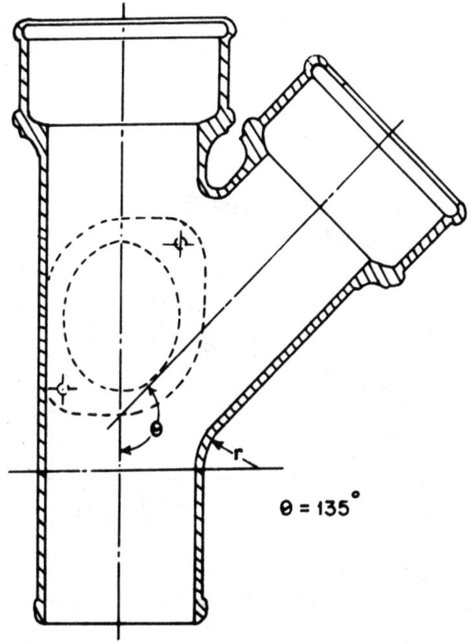

Fig. 26. Unequal branch Y with inspection door

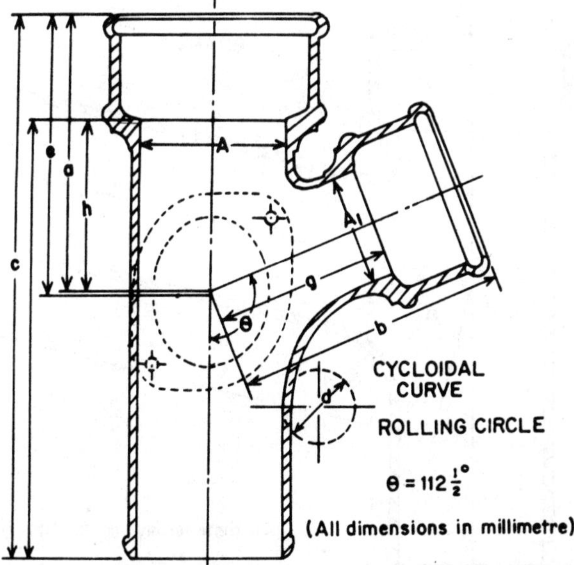

Fig. 27. Unequal branch with inspection door

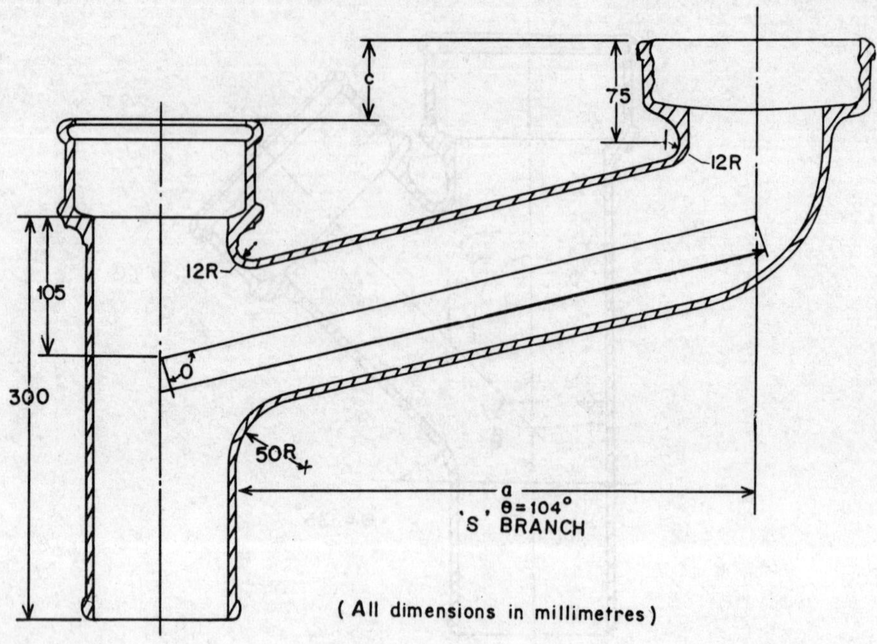

Samitary S & P branches

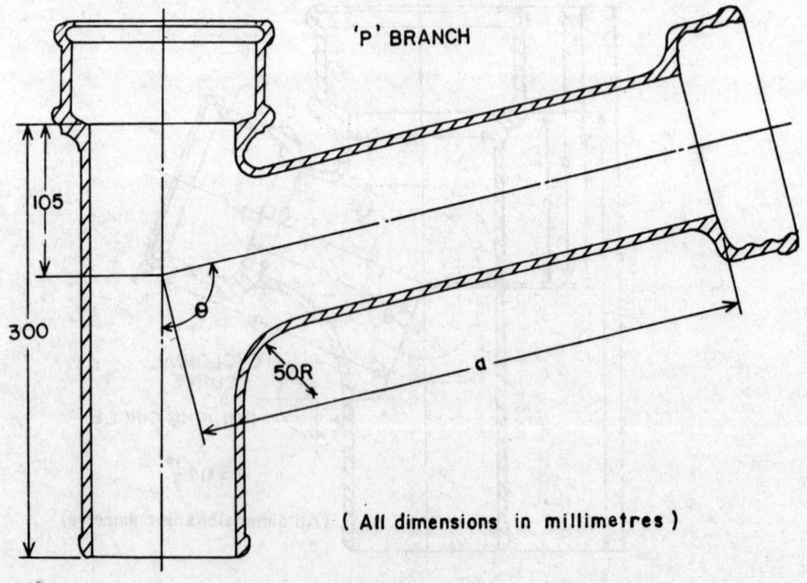

P. Branch

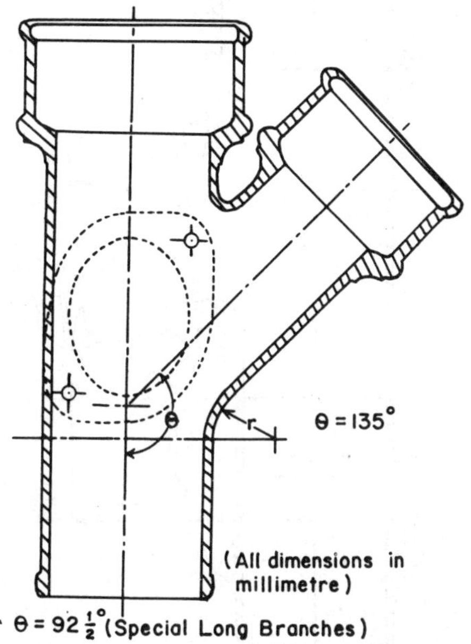

Fig. 28. Long Y branch with inspection door

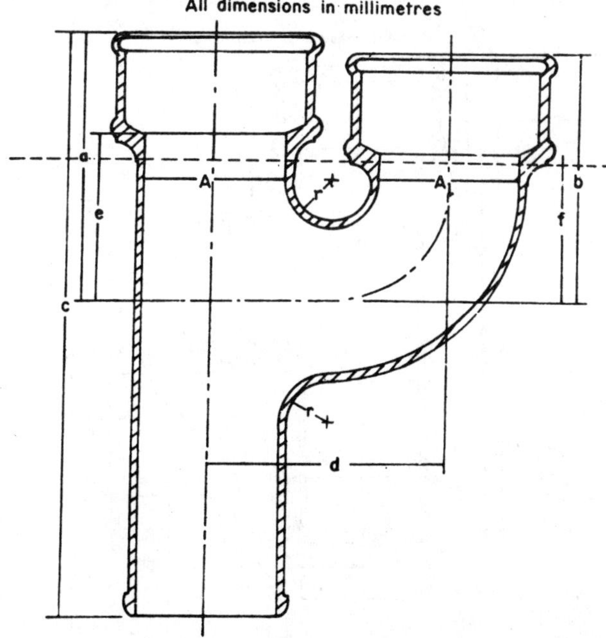

Fig. 29. Parallel Junction

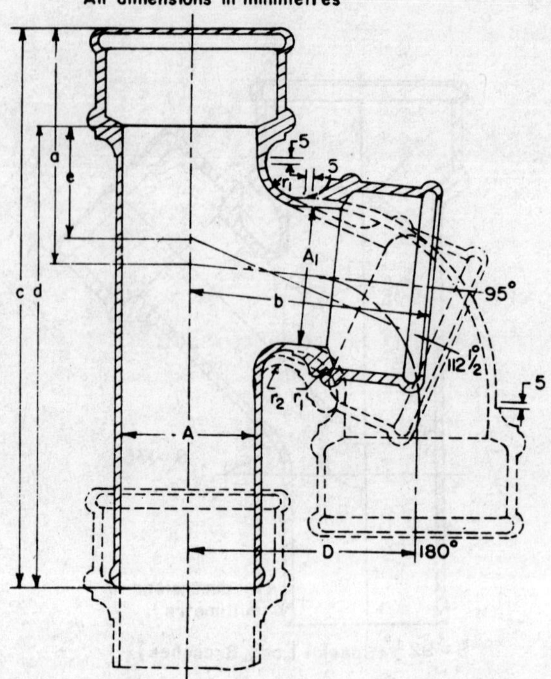

Fig. 30. Invert branch S or P Socket type

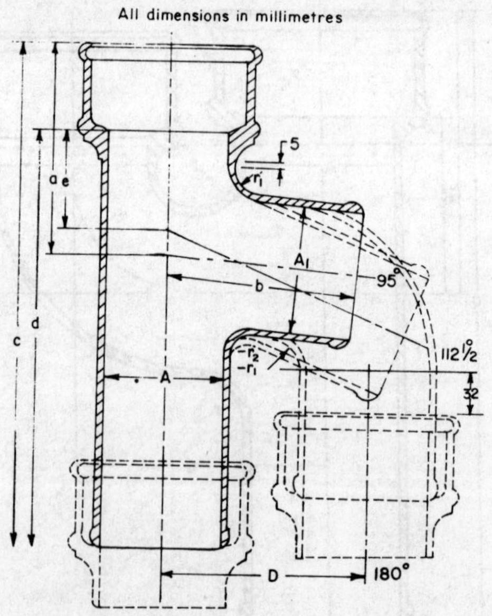

Fig. 31. Invert branch S or spigot type

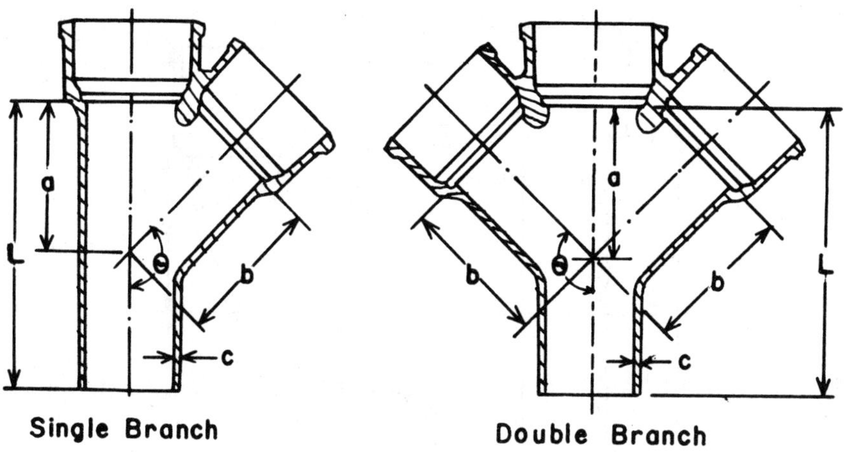

Fig. 32. Equal branch with or without access door

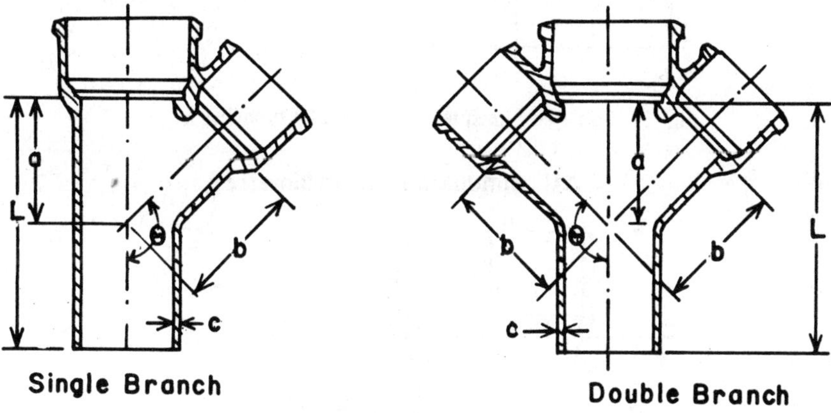

Fig. 33. Unequal branch with or without access door

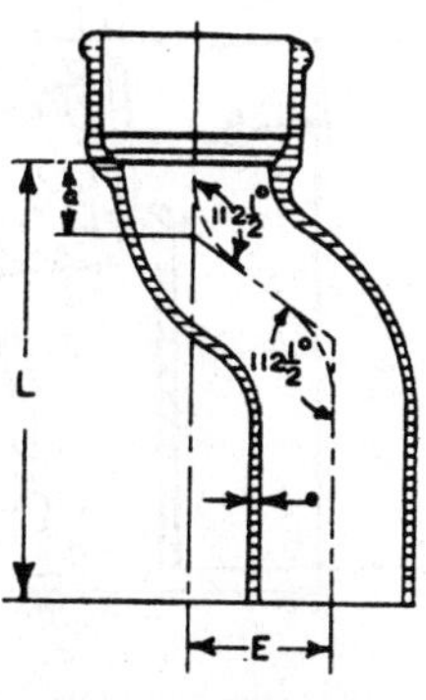

Fig. 34. Offset

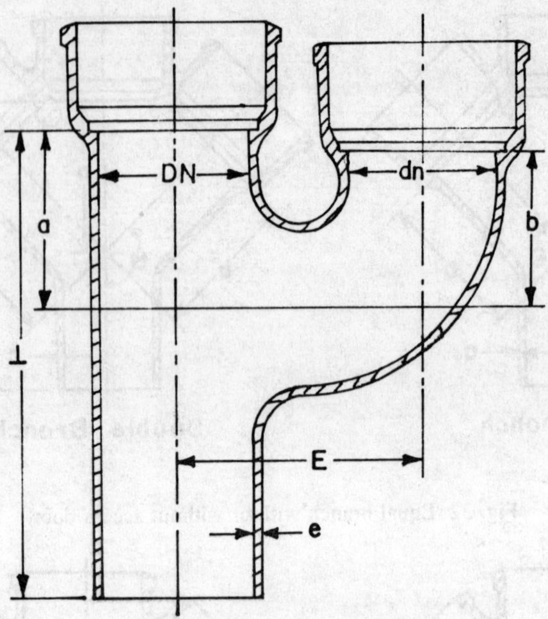

Fig. 35. Equal and unequal single parallel branches

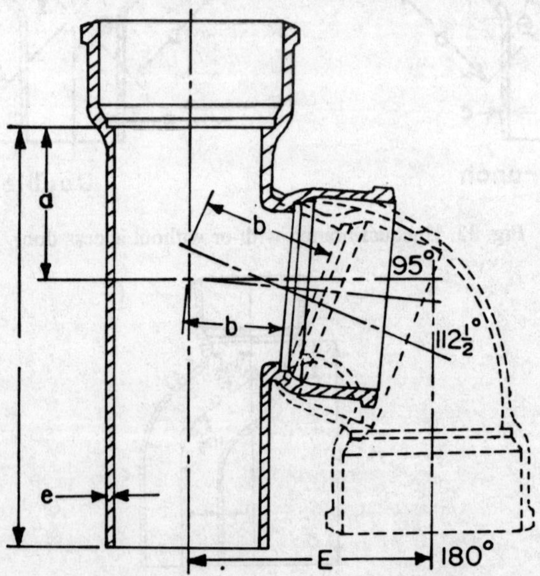

Fig. 36. Inverted branch Socket type

Vitreous China

This is made from the same clays as earthen-ware but feldspar is added. This gives strength and vitrified body impervious to water. Since it is vitrified it does not rely on glaze for its sanitary properties and it is glazed to give smooth glossy finish to allow ease of cleaning.

Even if glaze is damaged fitting is impervious to water. During firing vitreous china tends to distort more than fire clay or earthen ware.

Therefore, larger sanitary appliances such as sinks, urinals and hospital equipment is not manufactured in vitreous china.

Weight for weight vitreous china is strongest.

Fire-clay

Fire clay can be fired at very high temperatures resulting in articles which are heavy and strong with minimum distortion. Fire clay is used in the large sanitary appliances such as sinks etc. Fire clay is heavy in weight and has buff coloured porous body protected by hard glaze.

New person is likely to be bewildered by various nomenclatures like squatting pan, long pan, ordinary type WC, the low level flushing system, etc. The sketches (Fig. 16-36) of the same are given for information. Most of these materials are covered under the Bureau of Indian Standards (Standards No. IS 2556) for which the detailed reference may have to be made. The sketches are given only for guidance.

In the Indian market many types of sanitary appliances are available. The competition amongst manufacturers is fierce and the layman is likely to be taken in by looks and by sales talk.

Sanitary appliance costs quite a lot, hence it is necessary to know important points when selecting a fitting out of bewildering number available.

Sanitary ware has to be checked for blemishes and defects. The blemishes are as follows:

Blister	A raised portion protruding not more than 1 millimetre from surface and not greater than 3 mm at maximum.
Bubble	Raised portion as a sand speck not more than 1 mm.
Dull finish	Fine cracks in glaze.
Crazing	Dull slightly mat or semi glazed finish exhibiting numerous pin holes or non-glossy appearance.
Dunt	A hair line fracture.
Exposed body	Unglazed portion 1.5 mm or more.
Fire Check	A fine shallow crack not covered with glaze. May not be detrimental when not on visible surface.
Pinhole	A hole less than 1.5 mm.
Polishing marks	A spot where minor blemish has been found.
Speck	An area of contrasting colour less than 1 mm. Speck less than 0.25 mm does not constitute a defect unless sufficient in number.

12. VITREOUS SANITARY APPLIANCES

Blemishes and Defects Permitted in Various Sanitary Appliances

Sl. No.	*Location*	*Blemish or Defect*	*Maximum Permitted*
(1)	(2)	(3)	(4)
(i)	General	Warpage:	
		(i) Water closet	6 mm max.
		(ii) Squatting pans	[see IS:2556 (part III) 1973 for details]
		(iii) Other fixtures	Not more than 1 mm per 100 mm; total warpage not more than 6 mm.
		(iv) Foot rest.	Not to exceed +2 percent on all planes.
		Spots, blisters and pinholes.	A total of not over six, no grouping; except that for coloured appliances blister and pinhole limited to two each.
(ii)	Flushing surface and face of rim	Bubbles and specks	Not over two in one pottery square; a total of not over four.
		Polishing marks	One only, None permitted for coloured appliances.
		Spots, blisters and pinholes	A total of not over six no grouping; except that for coloured appliances no blisters are permitted and pinholes are limited to a total of two.
(iii)	Visible surfaces, specks other than above	Bubbles and specks	Not over three in one pottery square; a total of not over ten.

Blemishes and Defects Permitted in Wash Basins and Laboratory Sinks

Sl.No.	*Location*	*Blemish or Defect*	*Maximum Permitted*
(1)	(2)	(3)	(4)
		Warpage:	
(i)	General	Wash basins	Warpage of slab out of horizontal plane not to exceed 6 mm on all sizes (Warpage of backs of washbasins which are

			attached to the wall not to exceed 3 mm.
		Laboratory sinks	Warpage not to exceed ±3 per cent on all planes.
		Spots, blisters and pinholes	A total of not over four; no grouping except that for coloured appliances no blisters are permitted and pinholes limited to two.
(ii)	Service space, top of slab, (inside of bowl, front of fasica)	Bubbles and specks	A total of not over four; no grouping.
		Polishing marks	One only; none permited for coloured fixtures. One only on
		Spots, blisters and pin holes.	back or on either side; a total of not over three.
(iii)	Face of internal back and sides.	Bubbles and specks	A total of not over four; no grouping.

Blemishes and Defects Permitted in Flushing Cisterns

Sl.No.	*Location*	*Blemish or Defect*	*Maximum Permitted*
(1)	(2)	(3)	(4)
(i)	General	Warpage	Warpage of that back portion in case of cisterns not to exceed 5 mm and for bottom portion in case of the couple cistern not to exceed 3 mm.
		Discolouration	None on visible surfaces.
		Wavy finish	Not more than 100 sq cm on sides only; none on cover.
		Spots, blisters and pinholes	A total of not over six, no grouping, a total of not over three on covers. For coloured appliances blister and pinholes limited to two each.
(ii)	Visible surface	Bubbles and speeks	Not over two in one pottery square; a total of not over six, a total of not over three on covers.
		Polishing marks.	One only; none on cover; none permitted for coloured appliances.

The sanitary ware should remain clear and clean during its life and should have resistance to staining and burning.

To check resistance to staining, the following chemicals could be used:

1. 0.5% of methylene blue.
2. 10% acqueous solution of sodium hypochloride.
3. 3% acqueous solution of hydrogen peroxide.
4. Amyl acetate.
5. Carbon tetra chloride.
6. 13 gm of iodine in 1 litre of ethyl alcohol.

One spot of more than 10 mm size is placed on glazed the stain surface and allowed to dry. It should be possible to remove with wet clean cloth.

If a lighted cigarette is placed on surface and kept for 15 minutes. The stain should go away with wet cloth only.

All W.C. Bowls Shall Satisfy the Flushing Test

1. Six pieces of usual toilet paper or polythene sheets of (0.05 mm) approximately 150 × 115 mm size crumpled should get totally flushed out in 3 times atleast out of 4 times.
2. The whole of interior 40 mm below flushing rim is smudged with colour passing through 1.18 mm sieve should get totally removed.

   In case of urinals when properly installed, there should be no liquid left at the bottom of pan after flushing.

13. NOISE IN THE SANITATION SYSTEM

In a single storeyed building or a building belonging to a single owner, the noise of a household is taken to be a solace in as much as a person feels that he is in the company of human being. However, in a multi-storeyed building with large number of people staying together, transmission of noise becomes very difficult to eradicate and at the same time the nuisance caused by the noise can be very irritating. Water supply and sanitation system generate noise. Piping noise generated in one portion of the building is easily conveyed to other parts of the building and many times these noises even seem to be magnified by the piping system. Therefore it is important to install the component parts of the piping system, with due regard to the places where the noise develop and where silence or stilness is required.

Fixtures and Equipment which Make Noise

When a water closet is flushed it creates a noise, which is quite substantial. The noise created by a wash down closet is substantially higher than a noise created by flushing in a syphonic closet. Many times the noise is generated by the particular arrangements of the jets in the water bowl. When flush valves are employed, a noisy flush indicates that adjustment has to be made on a flush valve. Many times the supply of water to the flushing cistern creates substantial noise. The float in the tank, many times, rubs against the side of the tank causing noise.

Syphon closets are definitely less noisy when compared to a wash down closet. However cost of the syphon closet is much higher. In the case of flushing cistern, a silencing pipe could be utilised to the limit amount of noise created by inrush of water. However, whenever, such silencing pipe is provided, a small hole to ensure air entering it has to be provided at a top of such silencing pipe, to ensure that the back siphonage does not take place. If jet of the water closet making a noise, it is much better to choose that W.C. which does not have the problem rather than employ a W.C. design, which makes the noise, as this noise can not be stopped at any stage.

A vibrating loose washer in a sink, lavatory or a bath tub, tap, can create a chatter in the pipe system. The noise generated by the vibration is loud enough and generally transmitted through the larger portion of the piping system. The fault is easily rectifiable one. (The solution is to secure the washer in place). Where the spindle of the tap is bent, a squeel noise will develop, when the faucet is open to a certain degree. It occurs, when the flow of water reaches sufficient velocity to cause the spindle vibrate against the side of the faucet shank. This is more noticeable in hot water taps, where the heat of the water aggrevates the occurrence. The solution, here is to replace the stem or the spindle of the tap or if necessary change the tap itself. Where a gate valve is open or partially open, some times a loose fitting wedge of the gate vibrates and thus transmit noise. Solution is only to specify good quality valve. In the existing system, it is rather difficult to locate the noisy valve, therefore, it becomes necessary to shut off parts of the piping system, until the section where the noise originates is located. Once thc faulty valve is discovered, it has to be replaced.

A globe valve can also create a noise, when a loose washer vibrates, just like a tap. The faulty valve has to be located and the washer tightened. The water supply piping, sometimes, is connected to a pump and in the case of small pumps, every time the pump starts a considerable vibration takes place. Flexible connections laid at the inlet and the outlet connection of the pump will prevent the pump vibration being transmitted to the piping.

Water hammer is the most common cause of piping noise. The basic cause is a quick closing valve and the faucets. Water hammer arrestor should be placed where the water shock waves are likely to originate. Other method commonly used is to go in for screw type spindles which cannot be closed quickly.

Excessive water pressure is the cause of noise in the piping system. It is more apparent in a small diameter piping, when the result is noise generated by high velocity flow, when a tap is turned on. The water hammer when tap is closed are also exaggerated when water flows with high velocity.

Undersize Pipe

A system that is undersize or contains sections of undersize piping will react in a manner which is similar to a system containing excessive pressure. The only positive solution in this regard, is to design a piping system which is adequate and not undersized. The undersizing can also take place because the pipe is corroded or otherwise choked. It is advisible to replace the sections of the piping and at the same time utilise a larger diameter piping, which is more suitable to the needs of the building.

Improper Piping Supports

Improper pipe supports are many times responsible for a noisy piping system. This includes supports for the main pipe runs as well as supports used for the vertical piping risers or horizontal branch piping. The piping supports should not only support a pipe but also provide for expansion and the movement of the piping. Where long runs or horizontal piping are involved, it is better to use roller supports, on which the piping rests. The roller support will prevent a pipe from rubbing against or moving the hangers. The piping should be so placed that they should not, in case of slight vibration, rattle against each other. If, funds permit pipes in hanger should rest on vibration pads.

14. IMPORTANT POINTS IN THE INSTALLATION OF SANITARY SYSTEM

Any system or service is as good as it is installed and the care taken in its installation. In the case of sanitary fittings, the errors in the installations in various pipings and fittings which are apart from being unsightly are dangerous to the structures and can become health hazards to the inmates.

First point to be considered while installing any services is of time. The question to be resolved is when should the water supply and sanitary lines be laid and when the fitmets are to be fixed.

Basically pipe laying is a rough work. It involves making chases, holes, cuts etc. in masonry. Where pipes are laid in ducts etc., then piping can be raised when masonry work is in progress. This process of laying in pipe is called roughing in when pipes are laid and jointed except for taps and sanitary fittings. While masonry is in hand, the mason can make chases and cuts properly in a workman like manner. However, this requires excellent co-ordination between plumbing trade and masonary trade which is many times impossible to attain.

In India, the structural work is completed and then the plumber trade starts. Now comes the question when pipes should be laid before plastering is done or after plastering is done.

The sanitary installations are normally done after the plaster work of the building is over. This is done by cutting chases in plaster or otherwise. One comment always heard is that this gives rise to unsightly patches, while repairing a broken plaster if care is taken it is possible to merge old and new but it is just not feasible to carry out plastering, etc. behind the pipes. The clearance behind piping are very small and a proper plaster is not feasible. If however proper clearance can be given to the piping it is better to do the piping before plastering is done. Proper clearance for G.I. piping is 15 mm and for C.I. piping is 40 mm. This clearance also ensures that in case of leakage in piping entire wall does not get damp. The way installation is normally to be done should be such that minimum damage to plaster results. Marking by chalk or paint the actual dimensions and route of piping and fittings minimum damage results yet in practice this is not done and the patches of plaster much more than necessary are broken. Where a sanitary pipe is to be embedded in the wall, it should be so done that the movements (thermal, shrinkage, etc.) of the building can be accommodated and for crossing a wall a pipe within a pipe is always better than embedding the pipe in the masonry.

Flush Cistern

Flush cistern, whether of high level or low level are supported on cantilever brackets which are firmly embedded in the wall. The brackets should be perfectly levelled in order that the water level inside is correct and therefore ball valve functioning would be without a problem. Tendency of the workman to make up for the difference in the levels of the brackets by shims and pieces should be deprecated. A flush cistern fixed to the wall through a screw which is in addition to the brackets is to be preferred as flushing cistern is subjected to the tugs of pull chain and it is very heavy. A high level cistern is intended to operate with minimum height of 125 cms and a low level cistern with a maximum height of 30 cm between the top of the pan and the underside of cistern.

The overflow pipe from the cistern should be brought down to within 15 cms of floor level otherwise the water dripping from overflow can be of a great nuisance in addition to the spoiling of masonry.

Cistern and the overflow should bc mosquito proof which means any opening should not be more than 1.6 mm whether in flushing or filling mode.

The chain pull should be strong and should be capable of sustaining 10 kg of sudden pull or a dead load of 50 kg without any deformation.

The flush pipe can be of lead (which is costly) or G.I. pipe bent to shape, UPVC pipe, tin pipe (which are cheapest but have very little life), and chromium plated G.I. Pipes.

In the manual flushing cisterns, (1) Bell type and (2) Siphon type cisterns are marketed. The former are noisy and maintenance prone but are cheaper. If possible siphon type cistern are to be preferred.

Flush Values

Flush valves which deliver a fixed quantity of water have become popular. But against the principle that for any sanitary fitting, the flush water should have an air-gap of 25 mm atleast is not observed here and there is a likelihood of contamination of water supply in case of over flooding of sanitary fitment due to any cause, even back siphonage may occur.

Installation of Mirror

A viewing mirror is always provided in the bathrooms. The silvering on the rear side of the mirror is required to be protected from dampness. For this purpose, mirror should be mounted on 6 mm thick plain asbestos sheet ground.

Where the mirrors are of very large dimensions inaccuracies in screwing for fixing the mirror may cause the mirror to crack. Therefore, a 3 mm thick felt should be introduced between the asbestos sheet and the mirror so as to take up the inaccuracies of screwing.

Jointing of Cast Iron Pipes

Cast Iron pipes, either centrifugally cast or in sand moulds, are mostly utilised for vertical stacks and horizontal branches.

The ventilating pipe or the shaft is to be carried above the outer covering of the roof by atleast 60 cms. and the pipes are required to be secured to the wall by stay and clamps. Normally, no leakage takes place through mainbody of a pipe. Leakages always are associated with joints. Better supervised and carefully done joint should not give any problem of leakage at all.

While joining the Cast Iron pipe, the interior of the socket and the exterior of the spigots should be thoroughly cleaned and dried. The spigot end is then inserted into the socket right upto the back of the socket and then carefully centred by 2 or 3 laps of spun yarn well caulked by yarning chisels. No shorter length of the yarn should be introduced and no piece of yarn should therefore be shorter than the circumference of the pipe. Thereafter the lead is poured in. While pouring the lead, each joint should be filled in one pouring which would mean that pouring ladle should be according to the diameter of the pipe to be leaded. While melting the lead it should not be overheated and any scum which appears on the surface of the lead should be skimmed off from time to time. The lead for the purpose of the joint has to be pure lead and one easy test is that the series of pigs of the lead when kept on back of a chair should get bent by itself substantially.

When the lead has run into the joint it has to be caulked by removing extra lead outside the socket and then by using the inside and outside caulking chisels and by using hammer of 2 or 3 kg weight.

Before installation it would be always better to check whether the pipes are leakproof. This can be done by filling it with water. Any crack or sponginess would make it visible by leakage of water.

All pipes and fittings should ring clearly with a metallic ring when struck with a light hand hammer. The cast iron pipes should have "Dr. Angus Smith" paint as anti-corrosive paint.

The pipe have to be fitted with holder bat clamps about 4 cm away from wall surface. Where wall pipes have ears then pipes joint should be on a wooden base 4 cm away from wall.

The pipe has to be atleast 40 mm away from the wall so that in case of any leakage the water does not go over to the wall and make it damp.

If the C.I. pipe which has been given Dr. Angus Smith black paint has to be given another coat of paint then aluminium paint should be used as a primer coat over which any other paint could be applied.

Installation of Wash Basin

The wash basin is normally supported on a cantilever brackets. However, there is a tendency on the part of the plumber is to simply rest the wash basin on the cantilever bracket. The basin is not fixed and even can be taken away easily. The basin should have plaster on the rear side touching the wall resting over the top edge of the basin. Apart from closing one of the gaps through which the water leaks it also makes the basin fixed to the wall and cannot be taken out easily. Other, tendency is to discharge basin waste through a flexible pipe on the floor is not at all good. As many times the water overflows and the floor becomes wet and slippery the correct way of installing the wash basin is therefore through bottle trap, connected to a branch and then to a vertical stack.

Installation of European Type W.C.

In this case the seat cover rests on the low level cistern when not in use. Placement of low level cistern should be such that seat cover rests properly and does not fall down by itself.

Other important point to be seen in the installation is that the screws through which W.C. is fixed to the flooring are strong and properly tightened. Rubber seal should be introduced between the flooring and the pan to allow for minor variation in the level of floor and yet maintain a watertight joint between floor and W.C.

Many times a very crude method of putting some concrete on floor in a mound shape and placing pan over it is used instead of putting rag screws in floor. Such unconventional ways are to be deprecated.

There are many types of W.C.s available like wash down, single siphonic and double siphonic. The low level cistern may be an integral part of W.C. or separate.

Installation of Urinals Lipped, Half Stall

Urinals are fixed in position by using proper rag bolts, etc. at a height of 65 cm from standing level to the top of the lip of the urinal. Tendency to use G.I. piping in urinals is to deprecated. G.I. pipe get corroded in no time due to urine. Either lead pipe or C.I. pipe or channel with floor trap should be used.

The Stall Urinals are to be laid over a fine sand cushion of 251 mm thickness to cater for small variations in thickness or floor.

Installation of Squatting Pan (Indian Style)

Large amount of headaches which occur due to leakage in the building are on account of squatting pans which require depression in the floor to be made to accommodate the pan and the trap. In the course of time, due to the defects in the floor or in the pan or in the joint between the trap and the pan there is a leakage. The correct way to overcome this defect would be to provide water proof layer between the depression and the structural members. This can be done either by water proof plaster by way of bituminous layers, stone, etc. The movement of structure would many times make these water proof layers to crack. Installations by a lead sheet of 3 mm thickness bent to shape is the correct solution. However, considering the high cost of lead, other methods of plastering, bitumen, stonework can be adopted instead. It may be better to provide for 40 mm warning pipe at the lowest point of depression through which leakage water is allowed to escape. Apart from giving a warning that there is some leakage which requires attention, it does not allow heavy build up of water inside the depression.

15. DRAINAGE AND SANITATION OF BASEMENTS

Where sewer lines are deep enough no technical problem exists. It is important to keep in mind that sewer lines may get choked and water may back-flow into basement. The non-return valves if installed cannot be relied to be fool-proof.

It is desirable not to have any sanitary fittings in the basement. If however fittings have to be provided, then the outflow should be taken to a tank and lifted by pump to be dropped into sewer lines.

Even when there are no sanitary appliances in basement, a small sump and pump should be provided to cater for any small amount of water.

Installation of Water Supply Pipes

Pipe network is to be so designed to avoid air locks and noise.

All pipe work should be so planned so as to be available for inspection, replacement and repair. Piping *should not* be buried in solid walls or floors. Wherever it is unavoidable it should be seen that no joints are buried. Wherever pipes are laid in ducts and chases, these should be roomy enough to allow tools for repairs.

G.I. pipe network should be tested to a hydraulic pressure of 10 kg/cm^2 or at least twice, the working pressure expected. The test pressure should be maintained for atleast half an hour.

Internal G.I. pipe network is to be fixed by standard holder bat clamps and should fit tightly. They should be near all fittings and should be spaced at regular intervals for vertical and horizontal straight lengths as follows:

Diameter of pipe (in mm)	*Horizontal*	*Vertical*
15	2	2.5
20	2.5	3
25	2.5	3
40	3	3.5
50	3	3.5
80	3.5	5

Wherever the GI pipes are laid under the ground they should be painted with bitumen and laid with sand all round. This precaution is also necessary in case of pipes which are embedded into the walls and the masonry which should be painted with anticorrosive bitumastic paint and taped. The pipe should not come into contact with lime mortar or lime concrete as G.I. pipe is affected by time. Even in cement mortar, there is some quantity of free lime which causes corrosion in G.I. pipe.

G.I. pipes are fixed with proper design of hold bat clamp to ensure that the minor leakage does not splash on wall. There is a tendency to fix G.I. pipes with locally made U clamps nails bent to shape etc. This is wrong. A proper holder bat clamp keeps the pipe away from wall, it is held securely so that it does not vibrate with changes of pressure.

Placement of Fittings

In the case of sanitary fittings, there is nothing more irritating than a wash-hand basin placed for too below or a shower-head made for too high. These instruments which are for personal cleanliness and also for use are to be utilised by human beings.

However, the human beings come in all types of forms—some are short, some are long and even in the residential houses the fitting are to be utilised by male members of the family, the female members of the family and the children. In most of the cases, some sort of a via media has to be found out so that a person does not get inconvenienced while using.

The dimensions of human beings are categorised in the Authropometric Data which deals with average persons or about 50% of the people using it. Under the American conditions, average height is 1.77 metres which would be fair enough if one designs for the people who are normally tall as in Punjab and Haryana but to adopt the same standard in the south where the general height is less would be incorrect. Therefore, the anthropometric data which is given should be utilised for the purposes of having an average figure. It should be compared with the family likely to reside. The average data for an adult of either sex would be as given below:

16. WATER SUPPLY SANITARY INSTALLATIONS— SOME DO'S AND SOME DONT'S

The water supply and sanitary waste disposal is of fairly recent origin even in developed countries. These two services give maximum benefit to the user, if it is well constructed and well maintained. It, however, gives maximum nuisance if ill designed and badly executed. Due to the leaking water supply and sanitary waste, the damage caused to the structural fabric of the building is enormous and matters have worsened to such an extent now that in India people usually locate these installations by patches of leakage. The leaky installations are also health hazards.

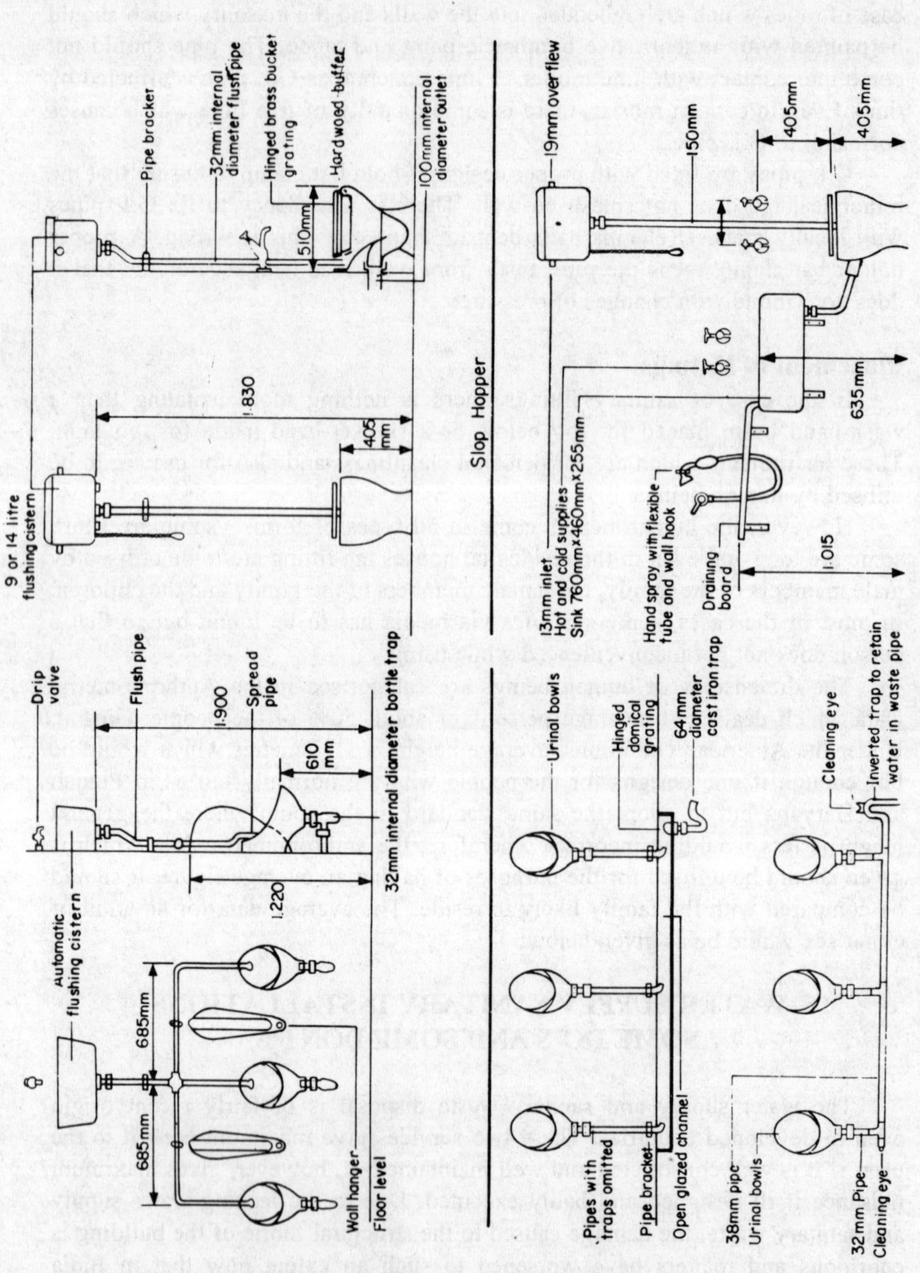

Fig. 37. Recommended heights for fixing various sanitary fittings.

Standing Height Standards

2440	Residential Ceiling.
2135	Office Doors.
2030	Residential Doors, Min Ceiling, Handeliers, Min Door height.
1980	Shower Head (Max)
1905	Highest Head Top
1880	Clothes Line (Max)
1830	No See Over
	Hat Hooks (Max)
	Highest Shelf (Men)
1780	Top of Mirror
1730	Highest Shelf (Women)
1600	Catwalk Head Clear (Min)
1575	Avg. Adult Eye Level
1475	Thermostats
1395	See Over
1370	Grab Bars
	Phone Dial Height
1320	Highest File
1270	Door Push
	Shower Valves
1220	Wall Switch Plate
	Deal Plate
1145	Push Bar on Doors
1120	Bar (Hi)
1065	Counters, Doorknob (Max)
	Safety Handrails, Bars
1015	Entrance Lock (Max)
	Iron Board (Hi)
915	Handrails, Iron Board (Hi)
	Counters, Doorknob (Min)
840	Panic bars
790	Lavatory Rim
760	Letter Slot, Rails on Steps
760	Iron Board (Lo)
455	Wall outlets
405	Highest Step
305	Rung Spacing
205	Bar Rails
190	Stair Riser (opt)
150	Toe Space (Max)
75	Toe Clear
25	Threshold (Max)

Recommended heights of some sanitary fittings are given in Fig 37.

Most plumbing fixtures like W.C.s, urinals, sinks, washbasins, taps pipes are made in factories (they are not made at site). Much of the trouble faced later can be avoided if care is taken to obtain these items from reputed manufacturers instead of obtaining a cheaper variety of doubtful manufacture. If materials of good manufacture are used then plumbing problems do not usually arise on account of fault in the components used. In almost all the cases, it is the faulty installation and faulty maintenance which causes the trouble. A plumber skill includes an everwidening knowledge of different types of metals and fittings. As this range expands, there is a greater risk of error. Plumbing has become a specialised job. However, it is most unsupervised job. There is a tendency on the part of the workment specially, the plumber to do a job with shortcuts in labour as plumbing jobs are strenuous and time consuming. The plumbing, in most of the cases is covered finally by tiles, flooring concrete. As the bulk of the job is hidden, it is difficult to find out the quality of the work. As most of the sanitary system is a non pressure system it takes quite a lot of time to leakage to appear. However, when the leakage appears, it is too late.

Water Supply

In India major piping is of galvanised iron. However plastic pipes, either of UPVC or otherwise are making in roads. The galvanised iron pipes are jointed either by threading or by welding. The pipe installation is a close system and therefore if trash and debrise gets into the pipe fixtures, it is very difficult to get it out. Care also has to be taken to prevent animals like rat, mouse cockroach and such other crawling creatures from entering into the piping system. The support of the piping system is also critical for both the successful operation of the system and the safety of the structure. All G.I. pipes are to be tested to 50 kg. per square cm of water pressure and the pipe network is to be tested to a pressure of 10 kg. per square cm maintained without a drop of pressure before being put into operations.

In the case of galvanised iron pipes they are available in 3 grades and are normally branded by the distinguishing paints. In India the heavy quality pipes are branded red, the medium quality branded blue and the light type yellow. Although all these pipes are tested to 50 kg per square cm, yet the light type of pipes can not be rethreaded many times. In the case of jointing of pipe, which is done by cutting threads and using sockets, it has to be seen that the threads have been done properly. The plumbers while lead, which is used for making joints is to be utilised. However, most of the plumbers have a tendency to prepare joints with yarn only. The valves, which are utilised, whether ball valves, globe valves, gate valves or water taps, have to be of a tested category. The each stop tap, with all the components, should be tested to an internal hydraulic pressure of 20 kg. per square cm and the pressure maintained for atleast 2 minutes during which it shall not sweat or leak. The globe valves and the gate valves also must be able to withstand 20 kg per square cms pressure during testing. Ball valves are available in 2 types. High pressure ball valves are used on mains having a pressure of 1.75 kg. per square cm. or more and they should remain closed at a test pressure of 10.5 kg per square cm. Low pressure ball valves are utilised on mains having a pressure less than 1.75 kg per square cm. and should remain closed at a pressure of 3.5 kg per square cm.

Sanitary Installations—Sanitary Stacks

In India, there are two types of cast iron pipes, available. One is sand cast iron pipe conforming to IS 1759 and another is spun cast iron pipe conforming to IS 3989. The pipe should be checked for its weight. According to the Indian standard codes for sand cast iron pipe of 1.8 metre length the weights are 75 mm, 16.52 kg excluding ears for 100 mm dia, 21.67 kg excluding ears. For spun pipe of IS 3989 for 1.74 metre length 75 mm dia 12.2 kg 100 mm dia 18.4 kg. Tolerances upto 10% can be allowed. However, there is a tendency on the part of the unscrupulous contractors to use rain water grade CI pipes which are very much lighter. The jointing of the pipe is a very very important matter and there is a tendency to put more of yarn and less of lead. This has to be checked.

The China sanitary fittings are classified by the manufacturers into the first grade, commercial grade and off grade. The class of the fittings is written by the good companies, on the fitting or on the wrapping paper and they also mark commercial fittings very boldly that this is commercial. The commercial quality fittings have defects which may not be initially apparent yet later performance of these fittings is poor. Off grade fittings should be avoided at all cost. Testing of the system is a very very important matter. The HCI pipe should be tested for leak proofness and it should be done before the appliances are connected. The static water head should be about 4.5 metre and the system should be capable of withstanding air pressure equal to 65 mm water gauge without showing signs of leakage for 3 minutes. The hydraulic performance of the fittings and the cistern should be seen. The check list for this purpose can be as follows:

1. Pipes—Check for size and strength of materials of proper quality.
2. Valves—Check for conformity to specifications for fittings pressure.
3. Check jointing.
4. Check hydraulics and for leakage.
5. Check that all piping installation is approachable for maintenance.
6. Sanitary fixtures conform to dimensions makes standard of finish.
7. H.C.I. pipe fittings check for weight standard of finish and for anticorrosive paint.
8. Water supply pipe specials check for weights, standards.
9. Lead connection pipes, plasitc connection pipes.
10. Flushing cistern type, material.
11. Brackets for sanitary fitments—materials type of fixing detail.
12. Clamps for pipes, size shape and materials.

13. Quality and quantity of lead in lead point.
14. Quality of jointing of G.I. pipe.
15. Quality of jointing of asbestos pipe.
16. Water tanks, size, fittings, whether mosquito proof, whether lid fits properly, scour pipe, overflow pipes.
17. Manhole covers, gratings weights sizes, make finish.
18. Testing of system.
19. General line and levels of installations.

17. SANITARY PIPING—TROUBLES AND CAUSES

The piping meant for soil and waste water differs from water supply piping in the main objective which is transport of solid matter along with the water flow. In the case of water piping, water is always clear and problems of self cleansing velocity are not felt as acutely as they are felt in the sanitary piping.

The solids which are carried with the waste and soil water get deposited when the velocity of water falls below the self cleansing velocity. The self cleansing velocity depends upon the roughness of the pipe, the weight of the solid carried out and also turbulance of water if any. Velocity of water flow will lessen when there is reduction in the slope of hydraulic gradient. Even beaver dams may get build up in course of time on account of rags, hair, straws which are carried along with the waste and soil water.

Therefore in any sanitary piping network following things are necessary.

(1) Self cleansing velocity to be ensured.
(2) Easy access.
(3) Cleaning of piping network is done at regular intervals in order to remove any deposits which might have occurred.

Normally in sanitary network pipes of 100 to 150 mm dia are utilised and for waste water network, pipes below 100 mm dia are utilised. These pipes are usually of cast iron. The internal surface of pipe is rough although in course of time a slimy deposit takes place and the bore diameter gets reduced by it to a very small extent yet internally pipe is smoother than its original surface.

The Usual Defects in the Pipe Lines are:

(1) Less slope
(2) No provision for clean out.
(3) Incorrect and improper jointing.
(4) Pipes not periodically cleaned.
(5) Non-testing of pipes and pipe joints.
(6) Incorrect supervision.
(7) Use of pipes like thin galvanised iron or tinned pipes which get corroded in a short time.
(8) Pipes not in line and level.

The piping network is not to be designed in such a fashion that:

(1) From flat slope result

(2) Numerous pipe joints result

(3) No thought is given to the various pipes network clashing with each other.

(4) No provision for cleaning of network of pipe exists.

The piping network to be provided should be:

(1) With proper slope.

(2) With minimum of bends and offsets.

(3) Whenever bends are provided, they are of larger radius instead of smaller radius.

(4) Provide clean out at bends and in long horizontal lengths.

(5) Concealing pipes inside masonry and underneath floor is avoided.

(6) Proper rounting of piping is done so that in case the flooring or the masonry is to be ripped open, minimum damage results from such operations.

For attaining self cleansing velocity, the horizontal pipe network should be provided with slopes not less than 1:48 in case of 100 mm diameter H.C.I. pipe and not less than 1:36 in case of 75 mm diameter pipes. Pipes of diameter less than 75 mm should not be used as waste pipe.

18. SEPTIC TANK

In case of a building, the sanitary network should be jointed to the proper disposal system which in certain cases could be municipal sewer mains. Wherever, municipal sewer mains do not exist sewerage is disposed by passing it through the septic tank or an open sewerage pond which reduces to an acceptable unit toxic effect of sewerage. Process of detoxification is either through anaerobic or aerobic bacteria. Anaerobic bacteria function in the absence of oxygen, where as aerobic bacteria require sunlight and also oxygen. Both these bacterias are capable of breaking down the organic matter, in the sewerage, which can be toxic and harmful into matter fit enough for jointing to any natural stream or the water table. The anaerobic and the aeorbic bacterias require certain time frame for their functioning. The example of anaeorbic action is in the septic tank and that aerobic action is best in a river flow. These two systems are discussed separately.

A septic tank is a chamber in which the raw sewage is collected and allowed to decompose by itself through process of anaerobic bacteria. The process of decomposition reduces the biological oxygen demand and renders toxic organic matter ineffective. The sewerage may carry bacterias of various water borne diseases, these bacterias by and large die during the prolonged time interval during which the sewerage remains in the septic tank. The very name septic would indicate that the system is toxic and has to be carefully operated so that it does not become a health hazard. A septic tank system will serve satisfactorily only if it is properly designed, installed and adequately maintained.

The septic tank has to be so located that it does not endanger the water supply system, that the pollution does not take place due to effluent from septic tank. This precaution is all the more necessary when the water supply to the house hold is through a tubewell. The septic tank should be so arranged that no cross connection between the tube well and septic tank takes place polluting the water supply.

For septic tank, basically, time during which the anaerobic bacteria work is the main design factor. From septic tank if not properly designed septic effluent may overflow to the ground surface. These overflows not only create extensive problems of bad smell but can certainly be health hazard on account of bacterias of water borne diseases which might be contained in the sewerage. The ponded effluent also becomes a breeding ground for mosquitoes and other insects.

The septic tank does not change the inorganic matter like stones, glass plastics etc. It is capable of reducing, only the organic matter into disposal state. The soap solution whch is from inorganic matter is trouble-some for the efficient functioning of bacteria which break the matter into a safe effluent. Therefore if a large quantity soap solution is introduced into the septic tank, anaerobic bacteria get killed and the functioning of the septic tank is impaired. Normal use of bleaches, detergents, soaps and cleansing agents in a house hold does not interfere much with the operation of septic tank. However if there are industrial type of working of soaps and detergents like in a hospital etc., it may not be advisible to release the waste water from these laundries into the septic tank. It would be advisable to have soakage pits as laundry waste may not contain organic matter.

The septic tank gets filled up with detritus and other non biodegradable matter in course of time and it requires to be cleaned periodically of the sludge and removing the scum for proper functioning. The frequency of cleaning depends on the size of the septic tank and the adequacy of the capacity. In any case the frequency of cleaning should not be more than 1 year. However the correct criteria for undertaking cleaning operations is when the bottom of the scum, which normally floats on the top of the sludge is within 75 mm of the bottom of the outlet of the tank. The scum if it gets discharged to the outlet is a potential hazard. The sludge which is a non-biodegradable accumulates at the bottom. It is allowed to accumulate in large quantity, then the capacity of the active portion of the tank is reduced and the sewage escaping without adequate treatment increases. The sludge is required to be removed periodically, atleast once a year. Where a large amount fo non-biodegradable matter is expected, then it may be better to introduce cleaning screen before a sewerage is allowed to get in the septic tank.

There are no chemicals or bacteria which are capable of reducing the sludge and scum so that the periodical cleaning of the septic tank is made unnecessary.

Number of Users	Length Metre	Breadth Metre	Liquid Depth Metres			Liquid Capacity M^3			Sludge to be Removed M^3			Depth of Sludge to be Withdrawn Metres		
			For Cleaning Interval of Months			For Cleaning Interval of Months			For Cleaning Interval of Months			For Cleaning Interval of Months		
			6	12	24	6	12	24	6	12	24	6	12	24
5	1.5	0.75	–	1.0	1.05	–	1.12	1.18	–	0.36	0.72	–	0.32	0.64
10	2.0	0.90	–	1.0	1.40	–	1.80	2.52	–	0.72	1.44	–	0.40	0.80
15	2.0	0.90	–	1.30	2.0	–	2.34	3.60	–	1.08	2.16	–	0.60	1.20
20	2.30	1.10	1.0	1.30	1.80	2.53	3.30	4.55	0.72	1.44	2.88	0.28	0.57	1.14
50	4.0	1.40	1.0	1.30	2.0	5.60	7.28	11.20	1.80	3.60	7.20	0.32	0.64	1.28
												partition position form inlet		
100	8.0	2.8	1.0	1.0	1.04	22.4	22.4	23.3				5.3		
150	10.6	2.7	1.0	1.0	1.15	28.6	28.6	32.9				7.1		
200	12.4	3.1	1.0	1.0	1.15	38.4	38.4	42.2				8.3		
300	14.6	3.9	1.0	1.0	1.15	56.9	56.9	65.5				9.7		

Cleaning of the tank should always be done through a sludge pump. M anual cleaning of the tank is to be avoided on account of likelihood of infection to the worker on account of toxic material gasses etc. The septic tank creates methane gas and therefore it should not be near a fire prone area. Septic tank should be adequately ventilated so that the explosive gases are released in a harmless quantity into the atmosphere.

Obviously the septic tank should be such that they do not get flooded by storm water. Flooding with storm water will introduce lot of mud stone i.e. deteritus into the septic tank. The dilution of sewage water would seriously interfere with the anaerobic process.

The septic tank contains lot of water and the effluents also contain the manure. Therefore vegetation grows luxuriously by the side of the tank. Vegetation from near the tank may introduce cracks in the tank by entry of roots. Hence care has to be taken that strong rooted trees and shrubs do not grow near tank.

Septic tanks do not function when the temperature of the water goes very low which may happen in the Northern India where the winter temperature is near freezing point or less. Under such circumstances, anaerobic action of septic tank is completely impaired. Hot water if poured in the sewer raises the temperature of the septic tank water fairly high so that anaerobic bacteria do not die out.

When in an existing septic tank anaerobic bacteria have died or where the new septic tank is to be put in operation it is required to be seeded. The seeding operation is carried out by taking 2 or 3 buckets of sewage from the septic tank which is already functioning. With this seeding operation the septic tank will start its own becterial reproductional cycle and keep the entire system working.

The septic tank produces many gasses including H_2S thus the reinforced cement concrete is liable to get corroded fairly quickly. This fact should be kept in view whenever septic tanks are thought of. The capacities and sizes of septic tanks are as given on page 161.

Low Cost Non-Conventional Sewage Treatment

The following methods can be called as non-conventional sewage treatment

— Aerobic ponds

— Anaerobic ponds

— Oxidation ponds

There are non-conventional sewage treatment processes which do not require any electrical or mechanical equipment. The level of skill required for maintenance of these ponds is not very high.

An aerobic pond requires huge area of land as its depth is restricted to 0.6 meters maximum. The stablisation takes place due to algal-bacterial inter-play aided by sunlight.

An anaerobic ponds are used basically for treating strong industrial wastes. The depth of pond is from 3 to 4.5 m. These are seldom used for sewage.

An oxidation pond combines the features of aerobic and anaerobic ponds. The range of depth is between 1 to 1.5 meters. In the top 0.5 m or so the aerobic action takes place with algal-bacterial inter-play with sunlight.

The aerobic water lay prevents spreading of odour from the pond bottom.

A comparative study of faculties is as follows:

		Aerobic	*Anaerobic*	*Oxidation*
1.	Depth	0.3 to 0.6 m	3 to 4.5 m	0.6 to 1.4 m
2.	Loading rate in Kg. of BOD/acre/day	45 to 90	225 to 450	9 to 22
3.	Detention time in days	2 to 6	30 to 50	7 to 30
4.	Influent BOD in mg/litre	less than 200	over 500	200–500
5.	Ideal pH range	6.5 to 8	6.6 to 7.6	8.5 to 10
6.	BOD removal efficiency	80 to 95%	50 to 80%	70 to 85%

Because of longer detention period virus removal in the oxidation ponds is about 90%.

Oxidation ponds are often neglected. There are certain pre-cautions to be taken such as—

- The screen chamber, detritus tank provided at inlet should be cleaned and maintained. The grit should be removed daily. After the grit rcmoval thoroughly clean and brush. The grit removal should be buried and not kept open.
- Care should be seen that pond is exposed to sun and there is no shadow causing tree near the pond.
- The pond bottom should be above ground water. If it is not possible, the pond bottom and side slope should be made leak-proof by lining with asphalt or soil cement.
- The oxidation pond should not be in flood prone ara.
- Protection measures should be taken to avoid erosion.
- The oxidation pond may be loaded 5 cm. of depth per day in winter to 13 cm. of depth per day in summer.
- The detention would be 3 to 5 days.

The colour of effluent and odour can give an indication of plant function.

An oxidation pond functioning properly will look green on the liquid surface. When colour is black with floating matter on the surface very rapid fermentation of the bottom sludge and over-loading is there. If the colour is light brown light or greyish pink pond is functioning anaerobically. When colour is deep red it is due to more sulphate in in-coming sewage.

- When anaerobic condition is developed Sodium Nitrate should be added to supplement oxygen and the liquid surface agitated with re-circulation of pond effluent.

– Mosquito breeding may be prevented by removing aquatic welds and cutting vegetation regularly.

19. DOMESTIC SEWAGE TREATMENT

The main characteristic of domestic sewage is its almost complete biodegradability (susceptible to biological purification). Biodegradability depends on the existence of a balanced food supply for the bacteria in the sewage and correct type of bacteria.

In any community there will be a fixed and quantifiable organic matter based on per person of a given country, the standard of living etc. and the sewage purification plant can be made accordingly.

The smallest type of sewage treatment plant i.e., the septic tank has been discussed separately. Apart from septic tanks which use anaerobic type of action, oxidation ditches, oxidation ponds and standard sewage treatment plants which use aerobic type of bacterial action are used. The sewage treatment plants used for very large community concentration and the maintenance requirements of such sewage treatment plant are very complicated and outside the scope of this book. For further details on such plant any good book on sewage treatment plants is to be consulted. In this chapter smaller plants upto 5000—1500 persons capacity are discussed.

In any system of sewage purification plant, it is desirous that the sewage reached the treatment plant in a sufficiently fresh state. Malodorous sewage is toxic to the treatment process and should undergo preliminary aeration or prechlorination before primary settling.

Sewage purification is essentially a biological process involving bacteria, protozoa, rotifers and algae.

In the sewage teh measure is Biological Demand "BOD" and the days at which it is measured is suffixed such a BOD on 5 days of incubation.

In the normal domestic sewage 60-70 gram is the BOD per head per BOD 5 day. However, the BOD concentration varies according to the time of day and the hourly peak may be as high as 10 times the mean.

Stabilisation Ponds

Stabilisation ponds or oxidation ponds are engineered ponds in which the organic waste material is detained for sufficient time to effect its stabilisation. These ponds can function successfully where sunshine is good and the temperatures are not too low. The process of purification is essentially same as in the conventional sewage treatment i.e. aerobic and anaerobic.

In aerobic ponds the waste material is stabilised wholly through the action of aerobic oxidation. This system may depend on mechanical aeration and/or photo synthesis. The oxygen is supplied through photosynthetic oxygenation and surface aeration.

Aerobic ponds treat sewage which has been degritted or otherwise pretreated so that sludge accumulation is reduced. The surface area of the pond is comparatively large to provide for oxygen and to maintain aerobic conditions for the full depth of the pond. The depth is usually 0.90 m. to enable full penetration of sunlight. Aerobic ponds present no chance of odour.

Anaerobic Ponds

The anaerobic ponds treat screened and degritted waste water. These are designed for higher organic load and anaerobic conditions prevail in most of the pond volume. They are 2 to 5 metres in depth and there will be scum on top. The effluent is devoid of dissolved oxygen and have high BOD value.

Most of the ponds are designed to have aerobic conditions at top and anaerobic at Bottom.

Aerobic Ponds

The depth of 0.9 to 1.5 metres and organic loading as below will give sufficient detention time.

Latitude (in degree)	*BOD in kg/hectare/day*
8	325
12	300
16	275
20	250
24	225
28	200
32	175
36	150

Hence in incoming sewage has BOD 5 of 360 mg/l and the desired effluent is of 30 mg/l of BOD 5 and place is near 24 degree latitude and there are 600 persons and 120 litres is the sewage/capita.

Hence $$\text{area} = \frac{6000 \times 120}{225} \times \frac{330}{1000} \times \frac{1}{1000}$$

= 1.05 say 1.1 hectare

If pond has -liquid depth of 1 m, the detention period

$$= \frac{1.1 \times 10000 \times 1}{\dfrac{6000 \times 120}{1000}} = 15.27 \text{ days say 16 days.}$$

The sludge accumulation range from 0.03 to 0.05 m^3 per person per year and pond cleaning interval depends on the rate of sludge accumulation.

Anaerobic lagoons are designed for BOD 5 loadings of 150-200 kg/day and with detention time of 2 to 7 days depending on temperature etc.

The faecal organisms remain alive from a longer period. Hence Effluent may further be kept for 5 to 7 days in maturation ponds.

When new pond is to be brought into operation, it is generally filled to a small depth with dilute sewage and growth of algae is established in the pond within a short time.

The maintenance work in such ponds is of good house keeping and consist of repairs to embankments, weed and grass cutting and periodic desludging.

When the characteristic green colour of the pond changes to grey brown or pink it is sign of over loading and anaerobic conditions which are generally accompanied by mal odour.

20. OXIDATION DITCHES

Aerobic biological treatment consists of making a culture of bacteria which physically and physio-chemically feed on the organic matter in the raw sewage. This culture can be achieved by placing the bacteria in suspension in the sewage and this process is known as activated sludge process.

The activated sludge process is a process in which raw sewage which has been degritted sedimented is brought into contact with activated sludge (where aerobic bacteria exist). This process is operationally simple and less costly when compares with bigger systems using activated sludge systems. The oxidation ditches which are simpler versions of main plants using activated sludge are extended aeration system. However, it is to be remembered that these extended aerobic systems work only when BOD 5 loading is low enough.

Some Indian data on properties of raw sewage are

	PH	*Dissolved solids*	*Total N*	*Choloride*	*BOD 5*
Madras	7.6-6.9	2700-750	90-32	443-152	695-133
Nagpur	7.2	1400	77	120	232
Madurai	7.8	1105	50	296	442

Properties of a typical effluent mg/I

Suspended Solids	25
BOD 5	25
Total N	20
Total P	20

In the oxidation ditch, the raw sewage is stirred for integral mixing with the return sludge and pre-existing liquor. The activated sludge is transferred into the next compartment the clarifier. Clarifier allows the sludge to settle, part of which gets returned to the aeration tank to maintain an adequate concentration of activated sludge. The excess sludge is taken out and excess liquid is discharged.

The typical design details of an extended aeration plant are:

MLSS Mixed liquor suspended solid

1.	Organic loading rate	0.15 kg BOD/kg/MLSS/day
2.	Average MLSS of Circulation tank	400–4500 mg/1
3.	Velocity of circulation	0.3 M/sec
4.	Liquid depth	1.3 Metre
5.	Free board	0.3 Metre
6.	Sludge recirculation	50–100% average flow to maintain the desired MLSS.
7.	Excess sludge produced	2.5 to 7.5 grams/capita/day
8.	Sludge age	30 days
9.	Sludge volume index	50–100

The SVI is defined as the volume in milligram of 1 gram of sludge after settling for 30 minutes.

$$= \frac{\text{ml settled sludge} \times 1000}{\text{mg/1 suspended matter}}$$

10.	Oxygen required	1.5 to 2.0 kg Oxygen/kg BOD applied.
11.	**Rotor**	
	(i) Speed	70-75
	(ii) Depth of immersion	15 to 16 cm
	(iii) Power	1.4 kw/metre length of rotor.
	(iv) Oxygenation capacity	2.8 kg Oxygen/metre length of rotor/hour
	Setting tank	
	(i) Surface loading	30-40 m^3/m^2/day
	(ii) Detention`	1-2 hour
	Sludge	
	(i) Excess sludge	0.05-15 kg dry solid/kg of BOD removed.
	(ii) Area of sludge	0.025
	(iii) Over land required	1 hectare/10 mld

With the above data, it should be possible to work out the time for which rotor is to be run the average desludging time etc.

Normally in the aeration tank the concentration of suspended solid is maintained at 2000 to 3500 mg/I

Aerated Lagoons

Detention period	— 3 to 4 days
Oxygen requirement	— 1.3 to 1.4 kg/kg BOD
Oxygen capacity of surface aerators	— 1.8 - 2.2 kg O^2/KWH
Liquid depth	— 2.5 to 3.0 m
Free board	— 0.6 m
Type of aerator	— Fixed or Floating
Organic loading rate	— 2-4 kg BOD/kg MLSS/day
Organic loading on volume basis	— 8 kg BOD/1000 m^3/day

Averaged mixed	— 100-400 Mg/1
Liquor suspended solids	— 8 to 16 KW/1000 m^3
Facultative	— 1.6 to 3.2/1000 m^3

Operation Troubles

1. *Floating sludge*
   The cause of floating sludge is its decomposition and the solution is to remove sludge completely more frequently.
2. *Content Black and Odourous*
   This is caused by septic sewage. Septicity of sewage may be due to long time of travel.
   Disconnect all septic tank from collection system, remove accumulation of solids. Preparation and chlorination helps to reduce septivity.
3. *Excessive sedimentation*
   Increase Velocity
4. *Fouling*
   Remove sewage solids and plant growth.
5. *Sludge hard to remove*
   High content of grit clay etc.
   Reduce grit content by having a grit chamber.

In the activated sludge process, the sludge bulks in volume and setting may become poor which in turn affects purification. Chlorination of return sludge at 10-20 mg/C may help slightly. The correct method is to take out bulked sewage completely and to newly generate active sludge.

Rising Sludge in Secondary Tanks

This is due to denitrification. The solution lies in removing the settled sludge faster out of the secondary setting tanks. Denitrification can be reduced by reducing aeration.

Detergent Cause Frothing

It can be prevented by spray of water or treated effluent in forthing areas or increasing MLSS.

PART III—MAINTENANCE OF WATER SUPPLY & SANITARY INSTALLATION

1. DAY-TO-DAY CARE OF BATHROOMS & WCs IN HOME

In case of plastic bath tubs daily cleaning the tub with damp cloth with warm water is needed. In hard water areas use a cream cleaner.

Small patches of dirt and scratches can be removed by metal-polish applied on dry surface and rinsed well. For deeper scratches a fine wire wool may be used to even out the scratch before applying metal polish. Certain substances like nail polish remover, paint strippers, cigarettes etc. harm plastics.

Lavatories can be kept clean by daily cleaning with brush. The cloth kept for lavatory cleaning should be separate for obvious reason. The area should be applied with dis-infectant solutions. Once a week, the bowl should be cleaned more thoroughly with "Harpic" or similar agents or leave undiluted bleach over night. In case of a very bad case dilute hydro-chloric acid may be used. After use of hydro-chloric acid, the flush should be operated two or three times in order that all traces of acid are removed.

Bad stains can be removed with cream of tartar and hydrogen peroxide.

Wash basins can be cleaned with bleach, but the over-flow can harbour black slime which can be cleaning with old tooth-brush.

Taps should be cleaned. The chrome plated taps should be cleaned with detergent.

Showers

Unscrew the shower head. Clean the deposits. Re—pierce the shower head holes with a pin.

Mould on the bottom of shower curtain should be cleaned with domestic bleach.

2. LEAK DETECTION

A regular exercise of leak detection can lead to considerable reduction in the wastage of water. Four methods are available for locating leaks—

1. Visual
2. Sounding
3. Waste metering
4. Shutting of mains and recording flows.

All these method can give only an indication of where the leak might be. The final test to expose pipe to find the actual leak.

Visual

Visual observations are a guide. Presence of dampness, green grass when rest of area grass is not there are some of the indicators. Whereas in house the damp patch may surely mean a leaky pipe but on the outside the pipe may be leaking but no dampness will be noticed specially when the water table is nearby.

Sounding

Sounding is done by using a listening stick which is nothing but a light bar of solid metal about 1.5 m long. One end is placed on the service stop cock and the other end which is provided with ear-piece is placed against ear. The sound of leak is a small low drumming or continuous buzz, which is continuous and stops when water is shut off. A good listener may detect a leak (if it is making sound) even 10 meter far off. Small leaks from valves or leaks from plastic pipes are seldom detected by sounding.

Electronic devices exist which are called "leak detectors". These work on the principle of amplifying the leak noise. There are instruments which are more effective in pinpointing the possible position of leak, which employ two probes and it is possible to delay electronically the sound waves received by one probe till it matches another. It is possible by time lag to locate the leak.

Waste Metering

Waste metering is not taken to locate specific leaks but to find out mains which leak. This is done by operation of valves, so that supply to it is from a single main. The control valve has a bye-pass with a meter. The control valve is shutt off in order that the leakage water is passing through the bye-pass. Then one by one each sub-main is cut off and the discharge for every 30 minutes is noted after each cut off. When there is a substantial drop of flow that sub-main is leaking.

Shutting of Mains

Shutting of mains and then subjecting the sub-main to high pressure can also heighten the leakages.

Leakage of water in mains is not so abnormal. This is because of continuous ground movements which affect pipes and pipe joints, corrosion which can not be totally stopped.

Experience in developed countries is that losses of 100-200 litres/hr./km. is normal for new mains, and 150-300 litres/hr./km. for older mains in good condition.

The unaccounted water i.e. water which is stolen, leaked etc. should be kept to the least possible by efficient monitoring of wastages and leakages.

Percentage of total supply	*Typical area*
6 to 9%	Small residential area with good metering.
10 to 13%	Small system with leakage or large system with little leakage.
16 to 17%	Lowest for city
20 to 22%	Achievable in large system with efficient leakage & waste control.
25%	Average maintenance.
26 to 35%	Poor condition.
35 to 55%	System require immediate attention.

Typical one family in-house domestic flow requirements (litres/per minute)

	Fast Flow	*Good Flow*	*Reasonable*	*Just adequate*
Tapin				
Kitchen	20	15	12	7
Bath	20	15	12	10
W.C. Cistern	–	7	6	4
Wash basin	15	10	7	6
Storage	–	10	7	6

3. MAINTENANCE OF SEWER

The principle objective in maintaining sewer line is to keep it clean and unobstructed. A sewer line may get obstructed due to deposit of mud, stones, brick, beaver dams of sticks etc and even roots of trees. Work required in the maintaining of sewer include inspection, cleaning, flushing etc. The maintenance tools required for a small sewer line where man cannot enter and where manholes are not deep are:

1. 150 to 200 metre of sewer cleaning rods. (with drags, Augers etc.)
2. Buckets and shovels, rope.
3. Sewer brushes.
4. Root cutters.
5. Flash light. (Explosion proof).
6. Gas detector.
7. Rubber boots gloves and coat.
8. Steel sewer tapes and heavy wire for dragging.
9. Traffic sign indicators.
10. Lamps.
11. First Aid Kit.

Where sewer lines are big enough and with deep manholes, additional tools are:

1. Power operated drain cleaner.
2. Hydrogen sulphide detector.
3. Carbon monoxide detector.
4. Combustible gas detector.
5. Hose mask with safety harness.
6. Complete First Aid.
7. Safety belts.

The persons employed on cleaning operation have to be provided with soap, towels, oil etc. They should be given innoculation against various deseases and given antitetanus injections from time to time.

Maintenance of G.I. Pipe (Emergency Repairs)

For emergency repair of leaks in a G.I. pipe line, pipe clamps, with rubber padding, have been found to be extermely useful. Pipe clamps of various sizes should be available in stock.

It is many times necessary to insert a fitting into an existing line of pipe, or to replace a pipe which has developed defects or is broken. In case of G.I. pipes, it is very easy, wherein a union joint can be made, which has got reverse threads, on one side and normal threads on the other side. Therefore, after cutting the defective pipe or after finding out where a new fitting or a connection is to be introduced, the pipe can be unscrewed. While introducing a new pipe, a union joint facilitates the pipe piece to be properly tightened up.

In the case of sanitary piping the joints are lead joints and it is rather difficult to insert a new pipe or to make connection. Collar can be utilised in such cases, where on both sides of the collar, a lead joint could be made. However, collar does not give a proper joint and as such another method to insert a new pipe is to melt the lead joints both from above and below, either break the defective pipe. Where a new fitment is needed, then a long socket joint pipe is arranged which has double the ordinary depth, then the fitment is placed into the position, and all joints are caulked. In this fashion, although it introduces one more spigot, yet the entire line is leakproof.

4. Maintenance Survey

Anything is as good as it is maintained. Even the best work ever constructed will get ruined if it is not maintained properly. In case of building civil engineering component some delay in the maintenance operation may be tolerable. However, if any service does not function apart from being nuisance it can lead to hazards which are danger to human life.

In case of water supply and sanitation system periodic surveys are necessary to observe how the system is functioning.

A survey which is carried out should be systematic and it should be possible to frame a clear and satisfactory report. The defects should be noted accurately. Many defects are on the surface which are of minor importance. The skill of person surveying the system is in tracing major defects where presence is indicated by minor surface blemishes.

A proper inspection is a time consuming job and there should be not many occasions when the inspection has to be done again. Normally the inspector should start from the top of the building and work downwards. Proper way to start inspection is to obtain the drawings according to which the services have been initially laid and any subsequent modifiacations indicated separately. The water supply lines, the sanitation stacks and drainage lines should be shown on the drawings by different colours so that a systematic way of checking would be worked out. It will facilitate the survey of pipelines for various services are marked separately with distinctive colour.

Site notes are prepared which are later used to prepare a comprehensive report. Preparation of site notes will depend on the skill and temperament of inspector. However, the method adopted should allow no large margin for errors and ommissions.

The best method to go about would be preparation of check lists. The check list could be sectionalised so that the inspection is carried out without any portion left over and all points are looked into without fail. Check lists should be comprehensive, systematic, simple to follow and not complicated by unnecessary verbage.

The report when framed should have a brief description of site, the age of the installation, the general layout, the usage frequency in general terms.

The report may be in the following format:

1. Report of	:	Name S/O Office Residence
On the work	:	
Carried out on	:	
2. Location	:	
3. Name of owner	:	
Address	:	
Telephones	:	
4. General description of property		
Age	:	
Accommodation	:	Residential Commercial Officc Laboratory Specialities.
5. Water supply		
Rising main	:	Size, Material, Position, Condition
Storage tanks	:	Size, Material position Condition Adequacy Last cleaning done on
Hot water	:	Control, Storage, Material Insulation, Adequacy, Venting, Sanitation
Water heaters	:	Insulation, Adequacy, Venting; Sanitation.
Waste pipes	:	Material, Size, Points, Conditions, Adequacy.
Vent pipes	:	Materials, Size, Joints, Condition
Shafts	:	Materials, Size, Cleanliness Approachability, Wet patches
Tests	:	Smoke, Hydraulic, Pneumatic results
Septic tanks	:	Size, Capacity, Condition outfall, Last Cleaning-Adequacy
Drains	:	Test, Hydraulic, Pneumatic Settlements, Chokage.

Manholes : Covers, Rendering, Channels.
Out fall : Adequacy, back flooding whether choked.
Fresh air inlets : Placement, adequacy whether choked.

5. MAINTENANCE AND REPAIRS TO PLUMBING SYSTEMS

The Plumbing requires proper maintenance and repairs from time to time to ensure that this system will continue to give satisfactorily service. The plumbing system can be separated in two parts; one water supply, second sanitation.

The troubles with these three will be discussed separately.

Water Supply

The plumbing problems which relate to the water supply are connected with taps (faucets) and valves which regulate water supply to the water closets and water supply piping.

Whenever any leakage is observed or a wastage of water is noticed, it is necessary to identify the systems by observing what is happening. It could be that more than oen problem crop up simultaneously. Therefore the problem areas have got to be located, which is not easy, and when the cause is found, a proper system procedure is to be adopted. In the case of leakage from the pipe a twin approach is necessary. A temporary repair in order to prevent the wastage of water, and finally the total repair, which may involve closing down the system, may be got done.

Taps

Most of the problem which relates to the taps are on account of very heavy use and many times abuse to which the taps are subjected to. Sometimes even the original tap is defective one. With a non-standard tap proper repairs or functioning is not feasible. It is therefore necessary, whether bib-cock or stop-cock, or any valve is being specified or being purchased standard and reputed makes of manufacture should be preferred to a cheaper and unknown one.

When a tap does not completely stop water flow there are three possible causes (a) A defective handle prevents washer from being pressed against the seat (b) The washer has deteriorated or broken or the seat is broken or pitted. It should be understood that a steady drip which comes drop by drop can waste as much as 9,000 litres of water every 3 months. A stream, less than a millimetre thick, or a bit higher size leak can waste as much as 1,40,000 litres every 3 months and a 3 mm thick pouring stream can result in as much as 15 lakh litres of wasted water every 3 months. It will thus be seen that leakage from the tap is a very costly proposition and it must be attended to as soon as leakage is observed.

If the tap is of a good quality then the question of its not functioning properly will not arise for a very long time, as a tap has a life of almost 10 years, under the normal use, and therefore in most of the cases, it is the washer, which cost very little, is the main culprit. Where stem has become defective, the handle should be removed and threads inside the handle, and on the stem should be inspected. If one or both are badly worn out the tap is required to be replaced. To correct such a tap temporarily, by putting cotton thread, may work, for some time, yet in the long run, considering the high cost of water it would be cheaper to replace the tap.

Where the washer has deteriorated or broken, it is easy enough to take out the upper part of the tap and take out cartridge which contain the washer. The washer is fixed to the cartridge by a screw. Therefore after removing dirt, take out washer by tackling the screw put in a new washer and refix the screw and cartridge and handle. In most of the cases, it will usually stop the leakage of water and the problem will not recur for atleast 3 to 6 months, depending on the quality of the washer.

The washers which are available are either of leather rubber or nylon. It has been observed that by and large nylon washer, produced by a good company, lasts very much longer when compared to a leather washer, even though the nylon washer is costlier, it is positively cheaper in the long run.

Where the seat of the tap is worn or pitted, it is necessary to replace the tap as re-seating is very difficult. Usually the seat will not get worn out or pitted by the functioning of the tap and thus if this difficulty is observed, it is on account of the original bad manufacture. While purchasing a tap, therefore, it is better, to check up the smoothness of the seat so that the washers also do not get cut due to pitted seat, burrs ridges or any other imperfections.

A good tap should normally run for one lakh operations of turning in and turning off.

Many times top handle is defective and handle rotates without changing the water flow, if the top is loose, it is better to replace the handle. This problem can also arise when the screw threads on the spindle are worn out and does not make it possible for the stem to get a grip on the tap.

If the water leaks around the stem then it is due to either a deteriorated packing around the handle spindle or worn out stream. A deteriorated packing can easily be replaced, but if the spindle is worn out, then it is better to replace the tap. Many times aerator fittings are provided so as to reduce splash. These aerators get clogged. They can be cleaned by a brush and pin.

Now in the market ceramic cartridge taps are available. These are washer-less taps and require technical experience to repair such taps.

W.C. Cistern

In the case of W.C.s, flushing cisterns are provided. Many times these cisterns do not work properly. The problem is either of water flowing continuously or the water not flowing, at all.

Where the water from the flowing cistern flows continuously, it is on account of the fact that the ball valve is improperly adjusted or the ball cock is punctured. A ball valve is expected to shut off water which is incoming when the water reaches a level mark indicated in the flushing cistern. Ball cock has to be, therefore, adjusted. In a flushing cistern, a level is indicated usually on the rear wall of the cistern by a raised line mark at which the ball cock should cut the water supply. The ball cock connected to the ball valve by a rod and by bending the rod it is possible to adjust the level. By bending rod downwards, the ball cock will operate at a lower level of water and if it is bent upwards then its action is delayed. Where the float of the ball cock has developed a leak, it is better to replace the ball. The balls are available in the various types or plastic material and it is easy enough to replace them by unscrewing the old valve ball and screwing in the new valve ball.

Many times the water closet will not flush, which may mean that the bell type or syphone type arrangements is out of alignment. Many times, the bell which induces the syphon jumps out off its sitting is required to be placed back in position. Sometimes, in the case of syphonic type flushing cistern, the chain which connects the push lever to the syphon, is either broken, worn out or it is stuck. This should be replaced.

The water supply piping, sometimes develop leak. Repairing leaks in galvanised pipe requires tools of the plumber and it is better to call a good plumber for the job. If, however, a small leak has sprung out, on account of damage due to the impact or pressure and immediate action is needed, then emergency treatment could be a pipe sleave with a rubber liner. Even an ordinary cycle tube could also be utilised and a pipe clamp fixed over the leak.

Sanitation

In the case of sanitary drain pipe, the chokage due to the accumulation of various dirty matters can occur in the fitment like W.C. pan or it can occur in a stack. Clearing a choked water closet is many times feasible with a force cup which is a very simple device. Force cup is rested on the W.C. hole and pumped up and down. Due to pumping action air pressure inside cup undergoes violent changes. The air pressure changes caused by the cup makes the water, which is stuck up move upwards and downwards and in many cases this is enough to displace the obstructions and permit the drain be brought to its normal operation. While using the force cup, it is necessary that the cup is properly placed over the hole through which the water is drained out. It is also, necessary to, seal off, in the case of Washbasin, over flow channel, as changes in air pressure will be nullified through it.

When the horizontal pipe branch is choked, the chokage is normally removed by removing bolts from the inspections doors and rodding the pipe. For this purpose, the drain cleaning rods or flexible shafts are utilised with various implements like cutters etc. Care has to be taken while using these instruments that the pipe does not break, otherwise while doing one part the other part of the system will get broken thus leading to far more damage than what is necessary.

Similarly when a vertical pipe gets choked, it can be rodded from the top cowl side in case of low rise buildings. When this can not be done, then rodding has to be done through inspection bends. In case of stubborn chokage (this is extremely rare) the pipe can be broken and a new pipe introduced. When chokage takes place at or near heel rest bend then the pipe length between heel rest bend and starting manhole is to be rodded.

In case of cracked or broken ceramic fitments, it is better to replace the fitments as early as possible. Repairs to a ceramic material can not be done satisfactorily even though the possible leakage is very small.

6. MAINTENANCE PROBLEMS OF TRAPS IN THE SANITARY INSTALLATIONS

Trap, whether it is utilised with Water Closets urinals or to take away the waste water from kitchen outlets, bath outlets etc. has to be properly installed in order that no maintenance problems arise.

Even though it is a reiteration, functional requirement of the trap is that it should be self-cleansing and it should be able to pass water freely without mechanical aid. It should have no recesses, cavities, pockets and internal projections (these recesses can not be conducive to the flow of water and internal projections will hold hair lints, bits of cotton and in course of time a beaver dam will get formed and the trap would be choked.) The trap should have smooth inner surface so that every part of it is automatically scoured by the flow of water. The maintenance problems of the traps arise on account of

(a) Defective design,

(b) Less seal and

(c) Defective installations.

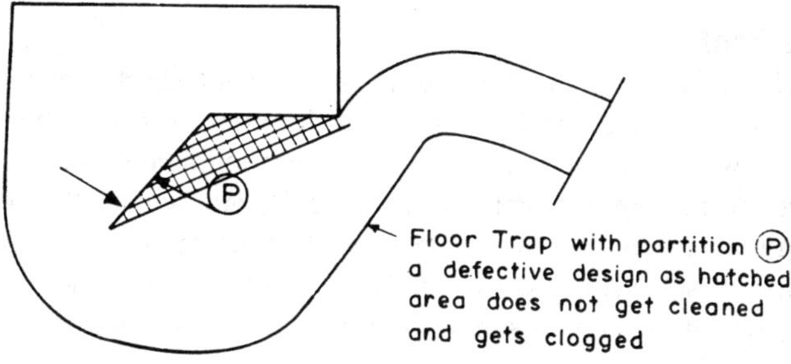

Fig. 38. Floor Trap with partition P, a detective design as hatched area does not get cleaned and gets clogged.

Defective Design

The defects in the design of a trap can be stated as follows:

1. The presence of partition in the trap.
2. The top cover of the trap being loose.

The proper type of trap which is nothing but a pipe bent to a 'U' shape. It consumes more material like cast iron and has a substantial depth due to the casting process and depth of seal needed. In order to reduce cost by way of less metal a partition is introduced which substantially reduce the height.

The partition reduce the cost of trap, substantially, yet the very presence of partition means that there are now pockets or voids in the trap, which do not get cleaned with the flow of water. These traps therefore become muck-holders in course of time and muck which accumulates behind the partitions can not be cleaned. The partition in the trap also means that, now, there are projections where bits of hair, cotton rags can get stuck. Thus the partition trap is neither self-cleansing nor it satisfies the basic requirement of the trap is neither self-cleansing nor it satisfies the basic requirement of the trap being without recesses, cavities and internal projections. Such type of trap even though it is cheaper, it is functionally poor and liable to get choked oftener.

The top cover of the trap is, as per good engineering practice, to be screwed on, or made an integral part of the trap. Many times the covers are found to be loose, which create a tendency on the part of the user to put lot of undesirable material inside the trap, like ends of vegetables, the floor dust etc. Where as the trap has a wider mouth inlet of more than 100 mm it is brought down to an outlet of 75 mm. Addition of vegetable ends etc. into the trap simply means that the horizontal line between the trap and to the pipe gets choked, at very frequent intervals and has to be cleaned. Which is difficult, time consuming and also costly. In addition all sanitary lines both horizontal and vertical harbour insects. It is, therefore, absolutely necessary that the top cover should be screwed on or positioned so that the user will not be able to unscrew it out and throw the waste inside. If the cover is tight and has only 10 mm round holes, cockroaches and other insects cannot come out from inside trap.

Less Water Seal

Water seal of a trap is the minimum distance between the weir of the trap and the normal water level inside many times. In order to reduce the cost of the trap, by using less metal, the traps of less seal are deliberately provided. In the two pipe system, minimum water seal is to be 38 mm and in the single stack system 50 mm. Traps with less seal are therefore of no use, what-so-ever, as they are prone to self-syphonage or induced syphonage and they are nothing but simple pieces of pipes with some being introduced, serving no purpose.

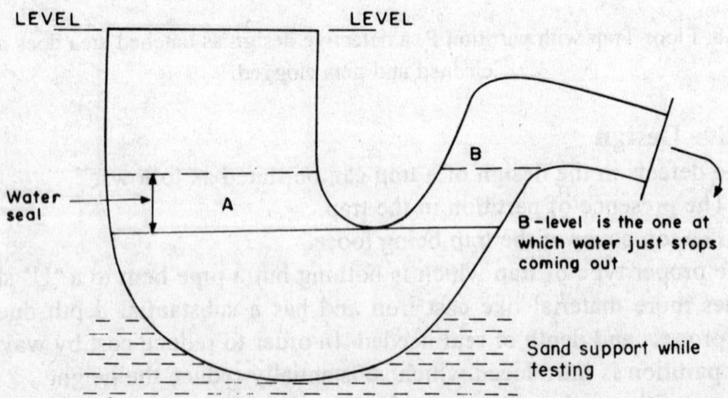

Fig. 39. Water seal in a floor trap B-level is the one at which water just stops coming out

The seal of the trap can be very easily checked by the following method. The trap is placed with its mouth, horizontally. Then water is poured till it comes to the level of the first bend as shown in the sketch. A level and the depth from the bottom of the trap to this water level is measured. Water is then continued to be poured till it flows out from the outlet B level. Once the water flows out measurement is again taken and the difference between A level and B level is the water seal.

Defective Installation

Defective installation of the trap is by far the main cause of leakage and it is mostly the floor trap which is badly installed. The floor installations of trap can be summarised as follows:

1. Installations where the trap is seated deep from the floor level.
2. Installations where one or more pipe empties into the floor trap.
3. Installations where the trap is over flooded.

The level of the trap is determined by the level of connection of the horizontal piping. The present practice is to locate the trap below the floor and seat it into a mass of concrete mix with a fervent hope that this mass of concrete, it will stop a leakage. However, trap is, normally, made of cast iron and concrete is in small quantities of uneven and many time bad mix. Even if concrete is of good mix the trap and concrete will nto form a tight joint and small quantity of leakage will take place. Thus to depend upon a piece of concrete as a stopper of water leakage is wrong. Right from the floor level down to the trap. Therefore, a water tight pipe connection which could be mild steel sleeve with a lead joint to the cast iron could be provided.

Where one or more pipe empties into the floor trap, many times the horizontal pipe from the other fitments does not reach the trap at all. In many cases, the flow of the horizontal pipe, (from the fitment) over shoots the trap. Therefore, as far as possible such arrangements, where one or more pipe empties into the floor trap should be avoided. If it becomes inevitable to use such an arrangement then custom built inlet which take cares of the incoming pipe, and its joints to the CI pipe with proper lead jointing should be utilised.

7. COMMON REPAIRS AND ADJUSTMENTS OF SANITARY INSTALLATIONS

— W.C. flush manually operated
— Tap
— Automatic flush cistern
— Flush valve
— Cleaning a chokage
— Use of acids

Proper maintenance and quick repairs are the keyword for prolonging life of any system and plumbing is not anything different.

Plumbing troubles can be categorised as:

— Troubles in water supply.

— Troubles in sanitation.

The system can be handled for rectification of minor problems by user and a plumber which is many times hard to get quickly can be called for major jobs only.

The Taps

A well manufactured water tap (Bid-cock) is expected to last about 1,00,000 operation of opening and closing before it can be thrown out. This represents almost 10 years of use in a normal house hold.

A good tap of 15 mm size should give a flow rate of 20.5 litres per minute. In a layman's terms with a good tap an ordinary water bucket should get filled in about a minute. Many times taps are seen which when opened do not give a stream of water but a spray. This may be due to poor design of tap or it could be due to very high pressure in the pipe line. (The exit pressure should be about 0.018 N/mm^2). A good 15 mm tap should not give a stream of water exceeding 50 mm dia at a distance of 30 cm from the tap.

A good tap should be able to withstand a water pressure of 20 kg/cm^2 for atleast 2 minutes without leaking or sweating.

The tap (Bib-cock, faucets) and globe valves are very similar and their repair is quite simple once their design is understood.

Dripping Tap

When a tap does not completely stop water flow there are three possible causes.

(a) A defective handle or stem prevents the water from being brought up against seat.

(b) The washer has deteriorated or broken.

(c) The seat against which washer pressure is worn and pitted.

A defective handle has to be replaced. The washer can also be replaced easily. If the seat is worn or pitted replacement of the tap is the answer.

With the new tap design in the market even user can dismantle and repair a tap easily as they are of cartridge design.

When Tap Vibrates and is Noisy When Water is Running

There are four possible causes:

1. Washer is loose
2. Stem is worn and wobbles
3. Deterioration of packing
4. Tap base is loose.

8. IMPORTANCE OF CLEANOUTS

Problems connected with the new plumbing lines begin almost immediately after a building is put to use. The pipes get choked, they go out of alignment, joints of pipe become loose due to temperature, movements which are daily and seasonal and also due to shrinkage movements of the building. Problem may also arise on account of settlement of structures.

Of this the choking of pipes may be dealt with first. A pipe getting choked may be on the following accounts:

1. Choking objects are seen into the pipeline such as rubber, plastic or cotton balls, sticks, rags etc. This may be due to mischeif mongers or may be brought in by birds for nest building.
2. Accumulation of hair and other matter like kitchen waste, vegetable ends etc.
3. Deposits of grease, fat and other substances.
4. Construction garbage or garbage during maintenance operation.

The chokage may be partial or complete. Partial chokage creates disturbance in the flow characteristics of flow in pipe and this will in turn create problems in the venting system. When the venting is unbalanced the traps may get self siphoned creating problems. Compelete chokage would change the behaviour of some parts of the system and may turn it into a pressure system for which a sanitary pipe joint is not designed. Malodour; and spill of sewage would result which is dangerous to health.

Hence all pipe network whether horizontal or vertical should be kept free from choking and for this purpose they will have to be cleaned by rodding from time to time.

The sanitary network has traps and fitments on one end hence rodding from this end is precluded. The other end ends in a manhole and vertical stacks can not be cleaned from manhole.

The pipe fitments like branch etc. can be had with or without inspection doors and the use of these inspection doors to rodding of pipe is limited. Many times these inspection doors come at odd points at points which are inaccessible or acessible with difficulty.

In case of lowrise building the vertical stacks can be cleaned by removing top cowl. This is not feasible in case of very tall structures. It is also not feasible when vertical stack has horizontal offsets.

Sticks, stones, rubber balls, rage toys get stuck up in the vertical stack. These might have been thrown inadvertently or deliberately by mischief makers or they might have pushed into water closet and flushed. Such objects may get lodged in between floors and present a problem which is difficult to solve.

Various Methods of Cleaning

Vertical Line

To dislodge the object a steel snake of sufficient length is inserted from the roof terminal and the object is worked loose in order that it falls down the stack. At the bottom of the stack it is easier to remove the object.

Branch Lines

Branch lines are those lines from various fitments to the vertical stack. These are mostly nearly horizontal. The line ends in a special which has an inspection door. However, the other end normally is a fitment or a floor trap from where access is not feasible. The main culprits in chokages are cigarette butts, tea leaves, vegetables, rags, or just accumulation of soap fat grease. With the inspection door cleaning is feasible but it can not be vigorous. The branch piping is many times below floor. Such pipes have mild slope requiring cleaning at frequent intervals. Cleaning through the vertical stack inspection doors is inconvenient. For access from the side of fitments cleanout plugs are necessary. The cleanout plug is fixed in a cleanout piping so arranged that the plug is flush on the wall. The piping is cleaned by a steel snake.

Base of Stack

The base of stack is quite important from cleaning angle because all objects dropped in the vertical stack get generally trapped at the base. Where ground floor fitments are connected directly to the manhole, the water head upto first floor level which would be about 2.5 to 3 metres, which would be sufficient to prevent minor chokages. Cleaning from manhole side is also easier provided the horizontal length is not long. A long sweeping curve made out of two 135 bends is better inplace of a sharp 90 bend.

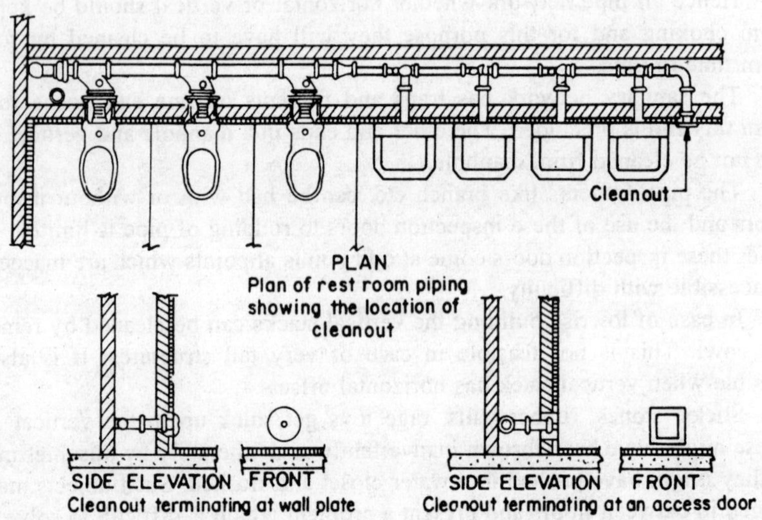

Fig. 40. How a cleanout may be installed on piping located above the floor slab.

If the length of pipe from heel rest bend to first manhole is short one say 1 to 2 metres, it will be easier to clean base of stack by vigorous rodding. Objects which get stuck can be drawn out by an auger fitted at the end of a drain cleaning rod.

Where a vertical stack has an offset in the vertical length this place is likely to suffer more from chokage. Such an offset should be provided with a special having an inspection door.

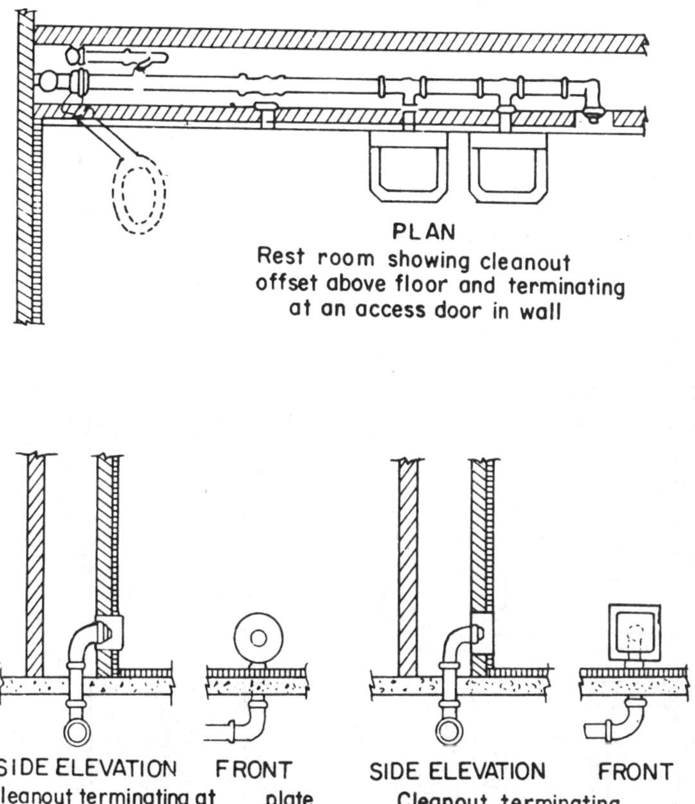

Fig. 41. How a cleanout may be installed on piping located below the floor slab.

Fixture Traps

Fixture like urinals, washbasins have a trap which is called a bottle trap. The bottle trap is cleaned easily by opening it which incidentally gives access for cleaning. A urinal is likely to get choked oftener than a washbasin.

Where horizontal piping has bends or is longer than 3-4 metres length then it is better to provide a cleanout.

9. NON-ACCESSIBILITY—A MAJOR PROBLEM

To the occupant as well as to the visitor cleanliness and sanitation in the building create great impact. Bad impression results due to unclean building, damp patches leaking, broken sanitary fittings, dripping water taps and the like. In case of leakages short circuiting of Electricity is possible with dangerous results.

Apart from impressions created, leakages cause corrosion in reinforced cement concrete structures, steel structures. Even ordinary dust can be deadly

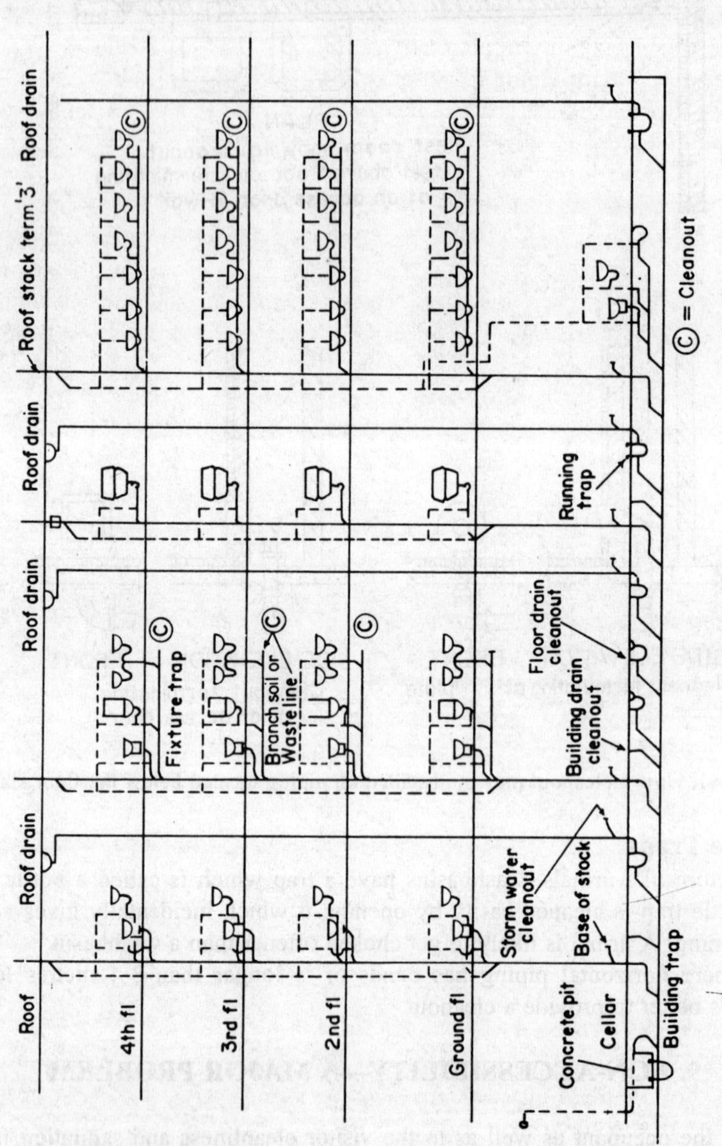

Fig. 42 A typical plumbing riser diagram to show the use of various cleanouts.

destructive when it combines with moisture. Hence it is absolutely important that building and service are clean and piping whether of sanitation or of water supply are sound and without any leakage.

For any service piping repairs from time to time become necessary whether due to normal wear and tear or chokages or due to accident. For any repairs to be carried out accessibility in plumbing can result from:

1. Embedding of piping in masonry and/or in flooring.
2. Insufficient space for maintenance in shafts in nitches, above false ceiling etc.

Flow in sanitary pipes is not a uniform flow as use itself is intermittent and the flow has a surge characteristics. When a flow is less, velocity is less and deposition of solids take place. Even with a self cleansing velocity design of piping it is almost impossible to avoid straw or small pieces of lint in the waste and soil pipe. Therefore, it becomes essential that the pipe network is cleaned at regular intervals and solids are not allowed to get builf up resulting in chokage.

In any sanitary network following are must:

1. Self cleansing velocity is to be ensured in order that the deposition of solids is avoided to the best extent.
2. Cleansing of pipe net work is done at regular intervals in order to remove any deposits which might have occurred.
3. Painting of piping to avoid damages due to corrosion.
4. Easy access for doing above.

Inspite of a sincere maintenance engineer the sanitary system may leak. The reasons for which are to be traced in the design of system which renders its maintenance extremely difficult if not impossible.

Common defects in this connection are:

(a) The pipe network is laid at slopes flatter than what is needed to ensure self cleansing velocity.
(b) Piping network is so designed that numerous pipe joints result. A joint in a pipe is a potential leakage point. Hence more joints means more possiblity of leakage.
(c) Pipes are so laid that they clash with each other resulting in some pipes being laid with no slope at all or even with reverse slope.
(d) Pipe joints are to be done in site in awkward and cramped situations. Such joints can never be made in a workman like fashion and as such are prone to leakage.
(e) In accessible piping under floors, embedded in masonry.
(f) Defective pipes inadvertently used.
(g) Use of inappropriate materials.
(h) No cleanouts provided for periodical cleaning.

Sometimes all vertical piping is taken through vertical shafts called sanitary shafts. Many problems which are connected with such piping are due to inadequate size of shaft and inappropriate placement of pipes and specials.

The building byelaws normally stipulate that "Every bathroom or water closet shall be so situated that at least one of its walls shall open to external air with the size of openings (Windows, Ventilator, Louvers) not less than 0.3 m and not directly over any room other than another water closet washing place, bath or terrace." (Extract. from Bombay Municipal Corporation Byelaw) Where shafts are provided the byelaw provides:

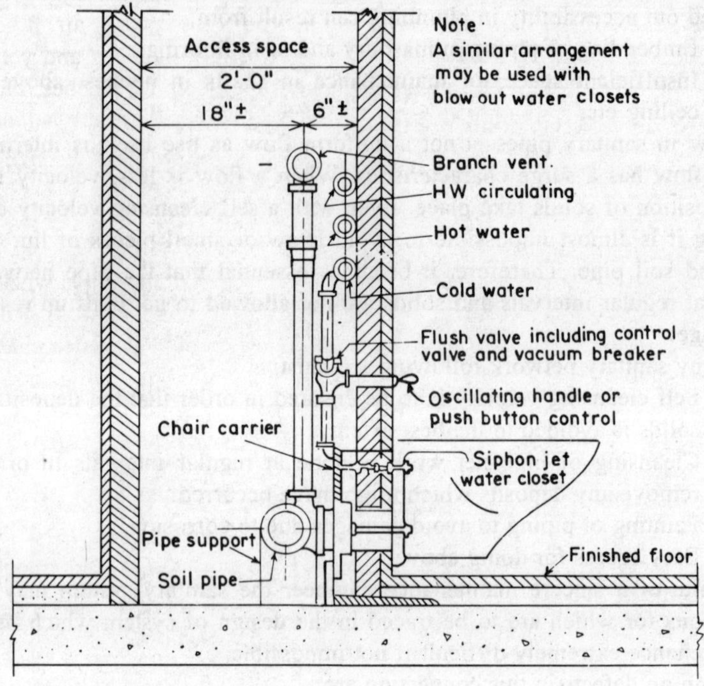

Fig. 43. Access space for a single battery of fixtures.

For ventilating the spaces for water closets and bathroom if not opening on the front side, rear side or interior open spaces shall open to the ventilation shaft the size of which shall not be less than the values given below:

	Height of building (metre)	*Size of Ventilation Shaft (Sq. metre)*	*Minimum size of shaft (metre)*
up to	12	2.8	1.2
	18	4.0	1.6
	24	5.4	1.8
	30	8.0	2.4
above	30	9.0	3.0

For above 30 m high buildings mechanical ventilation system is to be installed besides provision of minimum ventilation shaft.

As a thumbrule it can be stated the ventilation shaft should have a horizontal area of at least 1 sq ft. for each W. Closet or urinal adjacent thereto.

Cat ladders or U clamps are provided for plumber to climb. It may be that in a multistorey building even a cat will not climb through such devices. Apart from getting tired through climbing with all plumbers tools, it may have to be kept in mind that these shaft smell foul and are deficient in fresh air. It will not be possible for a man to hang on precariously to these devices and yet carry out repairs in a workman like manner. Operations of pipe wrenches, cleaning tools require proper foot hold which is not feasible with these cat ladders and U clamps. It is absolutely needed that inspection and maintenance platforms are provided without obstructing the ventilation needs.

Embedded Pipe Lines

Architects and engineers have fascination for embedding pipes whether of sanitary, water supply or drainage network. What is forgotten that all structures undergo thermal strains in addition to the shrinkage creep and settlement strain. These are of both short duration and long duration. The pipes being more rigid than masonry cannot adjust to these changes and joints open up with resultant leakage. Repairs to an embedded pipe is costly cumbersome and many times the leakage patch would be miles away from actual leakage point.

Galvanised iron pipes get corroded with lime which is available even in cement mortar. Life of such embedded pipe is very short. (3 to 8 years).

A proper systematic way of taking pipe lines in shafts and trenches is shown in Fig. 44 to 48.

10. TESTING THE PIPE NETWORK

Any new plumbing work, or any existing system which has been modified, should be inspected to see whether any cross connection or dangerous connections have been made to the original work. The sanitary and the water supply systems are expected to be the leak proof. The tests to be carried after completion or after major repairs the water supply lines and the sanitary lines is detailed below.

Testing Sanitary System

In the case of sanitary system portions which are prone to leakage are the pipes and the joints. The sanitary pipes are normally of cast iron which may be either sand cast type or spun cast type. In the case of piping test can be carried out before the fitments are fitted. Normally all the outlet point where the fitments are fitted are tightly closed either by plugging or by simply putting the cover. Then each section is filled in with static head of water. In the case of sand cast iron pipes the static water is expected to be of the order of 0.4 kg. per square cm. and in the case of spun cast iron about 0.7 kg. per square cm. (In the layman terms it would amount to so much metres head of water. In the case of sand cast iron 4 metres and spun cast iron pipe, 7 metre of head of water).

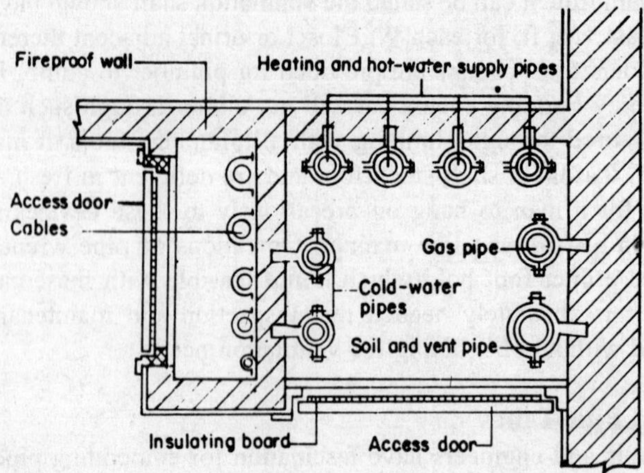

Fig. 44. Built out vertical duct for large buildings with separate duct for electric cables.

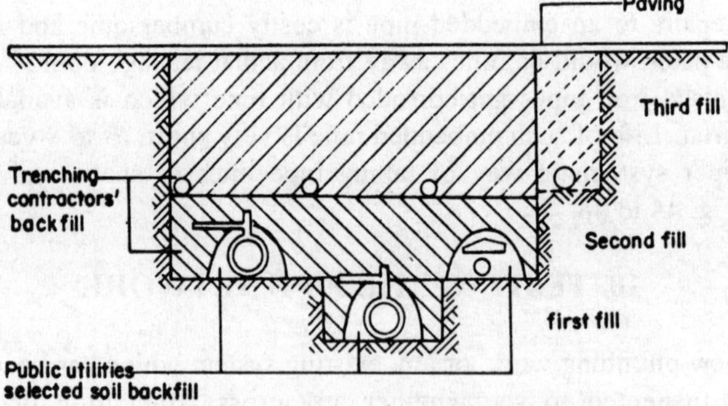

Fig. 45. Horizontal trench for various services and how back fill is to be done.

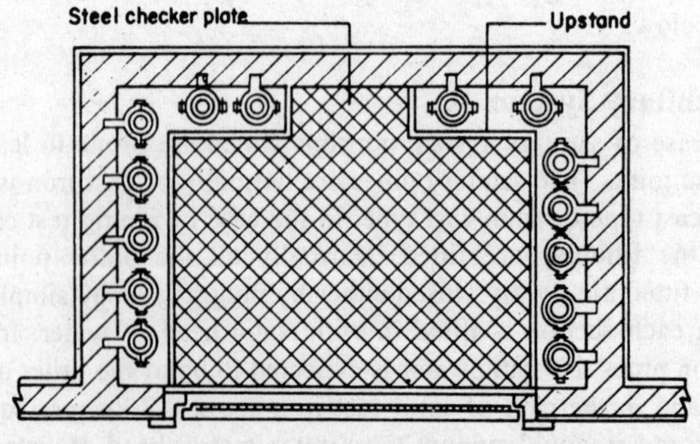

Fig. 46. Walk in vertical duct.

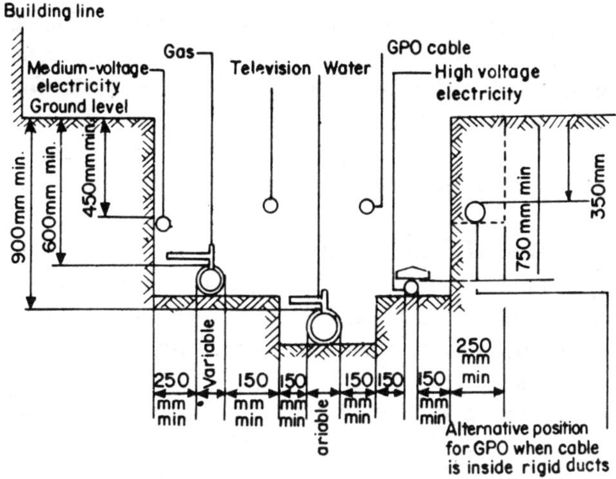

Fig. 47. Cross section of trench showing position of services.

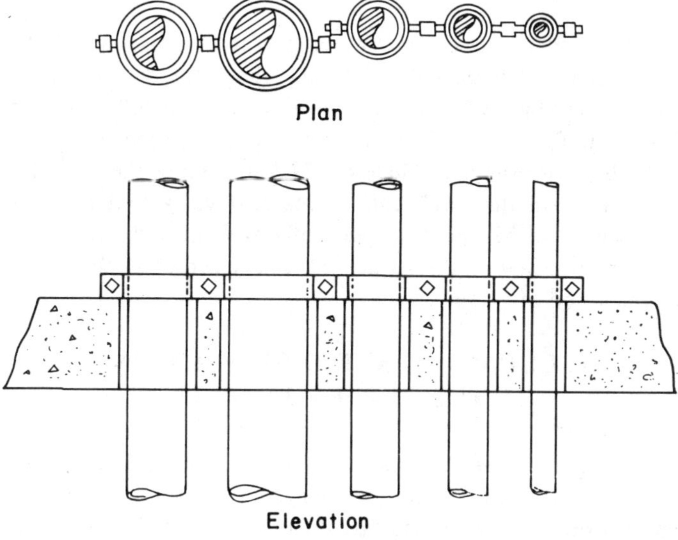

Fig. 48. Support Clamp for services in a vertical building duct

The water shall not indicate any leakage for a period of 5 minutes. In the case of sanitary system when all the fitments have also been fitted, an air test could be carried out. The air test consists of introducing air in the system which will generate pressure equivalent to 25 mm of water can be easily checked by noting down the changes in the level of the water in the traps and it should be possible to maintain this head for a period of 3 minutes without any loss.

In the case of testing of water supply system all taps should be closed and the system should be tested under a water pressure. Generally water network is tested to a pressure of 10 kg/cm^2. When the pipes are to be filled with the water, whether for water supply or for sanitary, it should be slowly and carefully charged with water, allowing of air bubbles to escape. If air is allowed to remain within the system, the readings will be wrong.

Periodical Cleaning of Water Mains

Cleaning requires a flow of 1.5 to 2 m/sec. to remove silt from 80 to 100 mm dia. main and higher scouring velocities are required for larger mains. Flushing with fire hydrants or wash-out is principally adopted for removal of dirty water after repairs.

Air scouring can be used to generate high velocities without using as much water.

The injection of filtered compressed air will force slugs of water along the pipes which will cause more disturbance of deposits on the pipe wall as slug of water forms and collapses. This can be used for pipes upto 200 mm dia. and for length upto 1000 m. It's effectiveness lies on the skill of operator to form slugs.

Foam swabs can be used for removing soft or loose material such as organic matter iron and manganese deposits, sand, silt & small stones. The swabs are of poly-urethance foam. When swab comes out full then it means its hardness is suitable for the job. The swab should have a diameter 25 to 75 mm larger than the bore of pipe and a length of 1.5 to 2 times the bore. For mains of 80 mm to 100 mm the swab can be inserted via a hydrant. For bigger diameter mains have to be opened. Speed of travel of swab will be regulated by controlling the out-flow at discharge end. The speed of swab will be half to three-fourth the speed of water.

11. CLEANING AND DISINFECTION OF THE SUPPLY SYSTEM

Before putting in to use all water mains, communication pipes, service and distribution pipes used for water for domestic purposes are to be thoroughly and efficiently disinfected, and also this disinfection is required to be carried out after every major repairs. The disinfection of lines and tanks has to be carried out at regular intervals of time to avoid pollution due to moss, lichens etc. In addition water supply lines which are buried get polluted due to small holes created by corrosion etc. and at socket junction. Normally overhead tanks require cleaning and disinfection at 6 monthly interval and small tanks which are more approachable at 3 monthly interval. The tanks, water distribution pipe network is to be disinfected as follows:

The tank and the pipes are first filled with water and then thoroughly flushed out. Then the storage tank is again filled with water and disinfecting chemical (normally containing chlorine) is added, gradually, while on the tanks are being filled so as to ensure thorough mixing. The dosage of the chlorine is 50 mg/litre (proportion will be 150 gms of bleaching powder to 1 kilo litre of water). The powder of the bleaching is to be mixed with water to a creamy-consistency, before being added to the water in the storage tank. Wherever, a proprietary brand of chemical is utilised the makers recommendations will be followed. When the storage tank is full the supply should be stopped and the taps on the distribution network is opened successively, working progressively, away from the storage tank. Each tap is closed when the water discharges begins to smell of chlorine. This is an indication that the entire pipe has been totally chlorinated and there is extra chlorine which is available finally. Under normal circumstance a strength of 10 mg/litre is recommended for contact period of 12-24 hours. In an emergency for a contact period of one hour 120-240 mg/litre consistancy should be used. High chlorine content can cause corrosion which is to be guarded.

The storage tank is to be then topped up with the water and more disinfecting chemical is added. The storage tank and the pipe will remain charged with this type of chlorinated water for atleast 3 hours and finally the entire chlorinated water is thoroughly flushed out, before any water is utilised for domestic purposes.

Solid Waste—Enemy of Sanitary System

Any maintenance engineer, plumber will tell many tales of choked pipes, havocs due to leakage—all caused by vegetable pieces, pieces of bones, bidi ends, waste cloth etc. In case of hospitals it is a common experience to find medicine bottles, lint, gauze, cotton, injection syringes etc in pipelines.

Why do these objects go into pipe lines. Simple answer is lack of facilities for solid waste disposal.

Whereas in a single storeyed or two storeyed houses, the inmates are expected to throw garbage into municipal dump bins. In case of multistoreyed structure, the problem is that the inmates would not come down with garbage pail and dump it into dustbin. Even sweepers would try to dump all dust into a W.C. and flush it. He feels that the problem is over. The only thing is that the problem remains out of sight.

Solid waste is a term generally used to describe non-liquid waste material. It is a conglomeration of various heterogenous material. Commonly it is known as rubbish trash, refuse, garbage and it is a mixture of vegetable and organic matter, glass, metal, stones, pipe, textiles wood shavings, grass etc. The bio-degradability would very according to organic content.

Domestic waste is due to various domestic activities like cooking, cleaning, discards broken pieces of glass.

Offices, hospitals, etc. have in addition medicine syringes, rubber, electrical globe discards, papers, carbons pins, etc.

Solid waste has following approximate composition in India.

	Bombay	Madras
Moisture	50-60%	20%
Veg., fruit etc.	35%	30%
Ash, dust, sand etc.	37%	45%
Paper	9%	12%
Grass, leaves, coal, wood etc.	15%	10%
Glass ceramic metal	Rest	Rest

From a residential premises about 350-500 gms/head/day solid waste results. Thus a family of 5 would contribute about 2 kg of waste. The density of garbage is 30 kg/m^3.

If even a small position of garbage find way into sanitation pipes of 75 mm-100 mm dia chokage is very quick. Area of 100 m dia pipe is 78.5 cm^2 and one day garbage is 57 cubic centimetre. Thus it can choke 75% of pipe in a day. Hence dumping of rubbish in pipe line is to be discouraged.

This can be done by providing strainers on nahani trap, floor trap basins, sinks etc. which can not be unscrewed. However, this alone will not solve problem.

Portable containers have to be provided where garbage would originate like in kitchen, W.C.s etc.

The normal capacities of such are:

Plastic Buckets with lid	:	10 litres 30 litres
G.I. bins with lid	:	70 litres 200 litres

Use of plastic sacks which are disposable should be encouraged.

In case of larger institution a closed glazed tile space should be provided with proper drain and exhaust where garbage could be kept.

In public premises, these bins have to be made vandal proof by chaining etc.

12. HOUSE-KEEPING IN WATER SANITARY INSTALLATION

Any installation or nature of water supply and sanitation, if it is allowed to go to seed on account of it not being kept spic and span, is of little use. As these services are of basic importance for the purposes of personal cleaning, if these sources are not very clean, the basic purpose is defeated..

No person would like to wash his hands under the tap which, by itself, is smeared with mud and he would also not like to look into a mirror which is cracked and otherwise disfigured. In the case of sanitary engineering mal-odours would be prevalent when the system is not looked after everyday as the organic matter putrefy over time and create odours. As a general rule, it could be stated that the lavatories; water points should be cleaned as frequently as possible.

Any cleaning has to have an objective and a detailed description of the work to be carried out. In the case of toillets, the following could be the objective:

The lavatory in an office, a commercial complex represent the true attitude of the management towards hygiene. If the lavatories present a poor condition with leaky fittings, dirty sanitary ware and watery floors, use of such poorly maintained toilets becomes difficult if not possible.

The penalty of ill-maintenance of these areas is enormous, bad smell spoiling the atmosphere and in turn affecting working efficiency. Leakage of water would induce corrosion in RCC and steel. Corrosion reduces the life of fittings. Cleaning of toilets specially meant for general public use is a time consuming job and it is best done when there are no users. To service a toilet during rush hours would mean hurried work and inconvenience to users. The staff for the cleaning of toilets should be bifurcated into gangs which are responsible for proper maintenance and servicing of public toilet rooms and persons responsible for care of private toilets. Normally no separate personnel should be employed for care of private toilet, Employees assigned to clean the offices in which the private toilets are located should be responsible for the care and maintenance of private toilet.

The job of toilet cleaning and servicing should include:

(1) Sweeping, mopping and scrubbing of floors.
(2) Cleaning the urinal stalls along with partitions, water closets, urinals, wash basins.
(3) Cleaning tile walls, mirrors, shelves, receptacles.
(4) Cleaning work inside which can be reached while standing on floor.
(5) Emptying waste receptacles.
(6) Servicing toilet paper holders, soap dispensers, W.C. seat dispenser, paper towels.
(7) Dusting windows, door ledges partitions, grills and similar items.
(8) Polishing metal work.

The staff should also be responsible for reporting improper functioning of any fittings, sanitary ware, leakages, burnt out lights, etc.

Items	Frequency
Check soap Towels Tissues Damp wipe-Porcelain Chrome Empty Waste receptacle Spot waste receptacle Spot mop floor	1 × day

Cleaning:

Items	Frequency
Commodes Urinals Wash basins	2 × day

Damp wipe spot wash

Item	Frequency
Partitions Receptacles Dispensary Ledges and sills	2 × day
Walls Doors	1 × day
Wash wall	1 × 4 months
Wash light fixture	1 × year
Wash and rinse floor	1 × day

APPENDICES

1. LENGTH

TABLE 1 : Basic Units of Length

British Units		Metric Units	
12 inches	= 1 foot	10 *millimetres mm*	= 1 *centimetre (cm)*
3 feet	= 1 yard	10 *centimetres*	= 1 decimetre
220 yards	= 1 furlong	10 decimetres	= 1 *metre*
8 *furlongs*	= *one mile*		(1 m = 100 cm = 1000 mm)
		10 *metre*	= 1 dekametre
		10 dekametres	= 1 hectometre
		10 hectometre	= 1 *kilometre*
			(1 km = 1000 m)

Conversion Factors

1 inch	= 25.4 millimetres (exact)
1 foot	= 30.48 centimetres (exact)
1 yard	= 0.914 4 metre (exact)
1 mile	= 1.609 344 kilometres (exact)
1 centimetre	= 0.393 701 inch
1 metre	= 1.093 61 yards
1 kilometre	= 0.621 37 mile

2. CAPACITY

TABLE 2 : Basic Units of Measure

British Units		Metric Units	
4 gills	= 1 pint	10 *millimetres*	= 1 *centilitre* (cl)
2 pints	= 1 quart	10 centilitres	= 1 decilitre
4 quarts	= 1 gallon (Imp)	10 decilitres	= 1 *litres*
			(1 litre = 1000 ml)
		10 *litres*	= 1 dekalitre
		10 dekalitres	= 1 hectolitre
		10 hectolitre	= 1 *kilolitre*

Conversion Factors

1 pint	= 0.568 24 litre
1 quart	= 1.136 49 litres
1 gallon (Imp)	= 4.545 96 litres
1 litre	= 1.759 80 pints
1 litre	= 0.879 90 quart
1 litre	= 0.2199 76 gallon (Imp)

NOTE —In addition to Imperial gallon, gallon as recognized in the United States is also used in India. The conversion factors for gallons (US) to litres and gallons (Imp) are:

1 gallon (US) = 3.785 33 litres
= 0.832 68 gallon (Imp)

3. WEIGHT

TABLE 3
Basic Units of Waight

British Units		Metric Units		Indian Units	
16 drams	= 1 ounce	10 *milligrams* (mg)	= 1 centigram	80 tolas	= 1 seer
16 ounces	= 1 pound	10 centigrams	= 1 decigram	40 seers	= 1 maund
28 pounds	= 1 quarter	10 decigrams	= 1*gram* (1 g = 1000 mg)		
4 quarters	= 1 hundred weight	10 *grams*	= 1 dekagram		
20 hundred weights	= 1 ton	10 dekagram	= 1 hectogram		
		10 hectograms	= 1 *kilogram* (1 kg = 1000 g)		
		10 *kilograms*	= 1 myriogram		
		10 myriograms	= 1 quintal		
		10 quintals	= 1 *metric tonne* (1 tonne = 1000 kg)		

Conversion Factors

1 gram	= 0.035 274 0 ounce	= 0.085 735 tola	
1 kilogram	= 2.20 4 62 pounds	= 1.07 169 seers	
1 metric tonne	= 0.98420 ton	= 26.792 3 maunds	
1 ounce	= 28.349 5 grams	1 tola	= 11.663 8 grams
1pound	= 0.453 592 4 kilogram	1 seer	= 0.933 10 kilogram
1 ton	= 1.016 05 metric tonnes	1 maund	= 0.3732 42 quintal
9 pounds	= 350 tolas (exact)		

4. AREA

TABLE 4
Basic Units of Area

British Units		Metric Units	
144 square inches	= 1 square foot	100 *square millimetres* (sq mm)	= 1 *square centimetre* (sq. cm)
9 square feet	= 1 square yard	100 *square centimetres*	= 1 square decimetre
4840 square yards	= 1 acre	100 square decimetres	= 1 *square metre* (1 sq m = 10,000 sq mm)
640 *acres*	= 1 *square mile*		
		100 *square metres*	= 1 are or 1 square dekametre
		100 ares	= 1 *hectare* or 1 square hectometre (1 ha = 10000 sq. m)
		100 hectares	= 1 square kilometre

Conversion Factors

1 square inch	= 6.45 16 square centimetres (exact)
1 square foot	= 9.290 3 square decimetres
1 square yard	= 0.836 13 square metre
1 acre	= 0.404 686 hectare
1 square mile	= 2.589 99 square kilometres
1 square centimetre	= 0.155 000 square inch
1 square metre	= 1.195 99 square yards
1 hectare	= 2.471 05 acres
1 square kilometre	= 0.386 101 square mile

TABLE 5
Gallons (Imp) to litres

Gallons (Imp)→ ↓	0	1	2	3	4	5	6	7	8	9
0	0	4.546	9.092	13.638	18.184	22.730	27.276	31.822	36.368	40.914
10	45.460	50.006	54.552	59.097	63.643	68.189	72.735	77.281	81.827	86.373
20	90.919	95.465	100.011	104.557	109.103	113.649	118.195	122.741	127.287	131.833
30	136.379	140.925	145.471	150.017	154.563	159.109	163.655	168.201	172.746	177.292
40	181.038	186.384	190.930	195.476	200.022	204.568	209.114	213.660	218.206	222.752
50	227.298	231.844	236.390	240.936	245.482	250.028	254.574	259.120	263.666	268.212
60	272.758	277.304	281.850	286.395	290.941	295.487	300.033	304.579	309.125	313.671
70	318.217	322.763	327.309	331.855	336.401	340.947	345.039	345.493	354.585	359.131
80	363.677	368.223	372.769	377.315	381.861	386.407	390.953	395.499	400.044	404.590
90	409.136	413.682	418.228	422.774	427.320	431.866	436.412	440.958	445.504	450.050
100	454.596	459.142	463.688	468.234	472.780	477.326	481.872	486.418	490.964	495.510

Illustrative Example—To find the litre equivalent of say 67 gallons, turn to the row corresponding to 60 gallons and column corresponding to 7 gallons. The intersection of the row and column gives the figure 304.579, which is the litre equivalent of 67 gallons.

Pressure

1 meter of water head	= 1.422 lb/in^2
1 Kgf/cm^2	= 14.223 lb/in^2
1 N/mm^2	= 145.038 lb/in^2
1 N/mm^2	= 10.197 kgf/cm^2
1 Kgf/cm^2	= 10 meters of water
1 bar	= 10.197 meters of head of water
1 m^3/s	= 35.31 ft^3/s
1 m^3/s	= 19.00 mgd.
1 litre/s	= 13.20 gpm = 0.019 mgd.
1 m^3/s	= 86.4 Ml/d

BUREAU OF INDIAN STANDARDS—STANDARDS FOR SANITARY APPLIANCES AND WATER FITTING

S.No.	IS Standard No.	Title
1	651	Specifications for salt glazed stoneware pipes and fittings.
2	771 Part 2	Specification for glazed fire-clay sanitary appliances General requirements.
3	771 Part 2	Specification for glazed fire-clay sanitary appliances-Specific requirements of kitchen and Laboratory Sinks.
4	771 Part 3	Specification for glazed fire-clay sanitary appliances—Specific requirements for urinals Section I Stall Urinals.
5	771 Part 3	Specifications for glazed fire clay sanitary appliances—Specific requirements for Urinals Section II Slab Urinals.
6	771 Part 3	Specifications for glazed fire-clay sanitary appliances—Specific requirements for Urinals Section III Stall Urinals.
7	771 Part 5	Specifications for glazed fire clay sanitary appliances—Specific requirements for shower trays.
8	771 Part 6	Specifications for glazed fire-clay sanitary appliances—Specific requirements for bed pan sinks.
9	771 Part 7	Specifications for glazed fire-clay sanitary appliances—Specific requirements of slop sinks.
10	772	Specifications for general requirements of enamelled castiron sanitary appliances.
11	773	Specification for enamelled castiron water closets railway coaching stock type.
12	774	Specification for flushing cisterns for water closets and urinals (other than plastic cisterns).
13	775	Specifications for cast iron brackets and supports for wash basins and sinks.
14	778	Specifications for copper alloy gate, globe and check valve for water works purposes.
15	779	Specifications for water meters (domestic type).
16	780	Specifications for sluice valves for water works purposes (50 to 300 mm size)
17	781	Specifications for cost copper alloy screw down bib taps and stop valves for water services.
18	782	Specifications for canlking lead.
19	1700	Specifications for drinking fountains.
20	1701	Specifications for mixing valves for ablutionery and domestic purposes.
21	1702	Specifications for copper alloy float valves (Horizontal plunger type) for water supply fittings.
22	1711	Specifications for self closing taps water supply purposes.
23	1726 Part 1	Specifications for self closing taps for water supply purposes.
24	1726 Part 2	Specifications for cast iron mainhole covers and

		frames—Specific requirements for HD double circular type.
25	1726 Part 3	Specifications for cost iron mainhole covers and frames—Specific requirements for H double triangular type.
26	1726 Part 4	Specifications for cast iron mainhole covers and frames—Specific requirements for HD circular type.
27	1726 Part 5	Specifications for cost iron mainhole covers and frames—Specific requirement for HD rectangular type.
28	1726 Part 6 Sec. 1	Specifications for cast iron mainhole covers and frames—Specific requirements for LD rectangular type—Single seal.
29	1726 Part 6 Sec. 2	Specifications for cast iron mainhole covers and frames.
30	1726 Part 6 Sec. 2	Specifications for LD rectangular type-Double seal.
31	1726 Part 6 Sec. 1	Specifications for cast iron mainhole covers and frames—Specific requirements for LD square type-single seal.
32	1726 Part 6 Sec. 2	Specifications for cast iron mainhole covers and frames—Specific requirements for LD square type—Double seal.
33	1726 Part 8	Specifications for cast iron mainhole covers and frames—Specific requirements for HD square type
34	1795	Specifications for pillar taps for water supply purposes
35	2104	Specifications for water meter boxes.
36	2326	Specifications for automatic flushing cistern for urinals.
37	2373	Specifications for water meters (Bulk type)
38	2401	Code of practice for selection, installation and maintenance of domestic water meters.
39	2548 Part 1	Specifications for plastic seats and covers for water closet—Thermo—plastic seats and covers.
40	2548 Part 2	Specifications for plastic seats and covers for water closet—Thermo—plastic seats and covers.
41	2556 Part 1	Specifications for vitreous sanitary appliances (Vitreous China)—General requirements.
42	2556 Part 2	Specifications for vitreous sanitary appliances (Vitreous China)—specific requirements of wash down water closet.
43	2556 Part 3	Specifications for vitreous sanitary appliances (Vitreous China)—Specific requirements of squatting pan.
44	2556 Part 4	Specifications for vitreous sanitary appliances (Vitreous China)—specific requirements of wash basins.
45	2556 Part 5	Specifications for vitreous sanitary appliances (Vitreous China)—Specific requirements of laboratory sinks.
46	2556 Part 6 Sec. 1	Specifications for vitreous sanitary appliances (Vitreous China)—Specific requirements of urinals—Bowl type.
47	2556 Part 6 Sec. 2	Specifications for vitreous sanitary appliances (Vitreous China)—Specific requirements of urinals—Half stall urinals.
48	2556 Part 6 Sec. 3	Specifications for vitreous sanitary appliances (Vitreous China)—Specific requirements of urinals—squatting plate.

49	2556 Part 6 Sec. 4	Specifications for vitreous sanitary appliances (Vitreous China)—Specific requirements of urinals—Partition slabs.
50	2556 Part 6 Sec. 5	Specifications for vitreous sanitary appliances (Vitreous China)—Specific requirements of urinals—Waster fitting.
51	2556 Part 6 Sec. 6	Specifications for vitreous sanitary appliances (Vitreous China)—Specific requirements of urinals—water spreaders for half stall urinals.
52	2556 Part 7	Specifications for Vitreous China—Specific requirements of half round channels.
53	2556 Part 8	Specifications for Vitreous China—Specific requirements of syphonic wash down water closets.
54	2556 Part 9	Specifications for Vitreous China—Specific requirements of dibets.
55	2556 Part 10	Specifications for Vitreous China—Specific requirements of foot rests.
56	2556 Part 11	Specifications for Vitreous China—Specific requirements of shower rose.
57	2556 Part 12	Specifications for Vitreous China—Specific requirements of floor traps.
58	2556 Part 13	Specifications for Vitreous China—Specific requirements of traps for squatting pans.
59	2556 Part 14	Specifications for Vitreous China—Specific requirements of integrated squatting pan.
60	2556 Part 15	Specifications for Vitreous China—Specific requirements of universal water closets.
61	2685	Code of practice for selection, installation and maintenance of slince valve.
62	2693	Specifications for ferrules for water services.
63	2906	Specifications for sluice valves for water works purposes.
64	2963	Specifications for copper alloy waste fittings for wash basins and sinks.
65	3004	Specifications for plug cocks for water supply purposes.
66	3006	Specifications for chemically resistant glazed stoneware pipes and fittings.
67	3042	Specifications for single faced sluice gates (200 to 1200 size).
68	3311	Specifications for waste plugs and its accessories for sinks and wash basins.
69	3489	Specifications for enamelled steel bath tubs.
70	3450	Specifications for surface boxes.
71	4038	Specifications for foot valves for water supply purposes.
72	4346	Specifications for washers for use with fittings for water services.
73	5219 Part 1	Specifications for cast copper alloy traps—P and S traps.
74	5312	Specifications for swing check type reflux (non-return) valves—Single door pattern.
75	5434	Specifications for non—ferrous alloy bottle traps for marine use.
76	5455	Specifications for cast iron steps for manholes.
77	5869	Specifications for pillar taps for marine use.
78	5917	Specifications for Vitreous (Vitreous China) wash basins

		for marine use.
79	5961	Specifications for cast iron grating for drainage purposes.
80	6249	Specifications for flush valves and fittings for marine use.
81	6251	Specifications for shower fittings for marine use.
82	6411	Specifications for gel-coated glass fibre reinforced polyster resin bath tubs.
83	6784	Method for performance testing of water meters.
84	7231	Specifications for plastic flushing cisterns for water closets and urinals.
85	8718	Specifications for vitreous enamelled kitchen sinks.
86	8727	Specifications for vitreous enamelled steel wash basins.
87	8931	Specifications for copper alloy fancy bib-taps and stop valves for water-services.
88	8934	Specifications for cast copper alloy fancy pillar taps for water services.
89	9076	Specifications for vitreous integrated squatting pans for marine use.
90	9338	Specifications for cast iron-screw down stop valves and stop and check valves for water works purposes.
91	9739	Specifications for pressure reducing valves for domestic water supply systems.
92	9758	Specifications for flush valves for water closet and urinals.
93	9762	Specifications for polythene floats for ball valves.
94	9763	Specifications for plastic bib and stop valves (rising spindle) for cold water services.
95	10500	Specifications for water for drinking purposes.
96	11246	Specifications for glass fibre reinforced polyester resins (GRP) squatting pans.
97	12234	Specifications for plastic equilibrium float valves for cold water services.
98	12701	Specifications for rotational moulded polythene water storage tanks.